D1416615

This is the first detailed study of the interaction between drama and politics in the reign of Henry VIII. The subject is addressed both in general terms and through a series of case-studies of individual early Tudor plays.

Through its innovative use of dramatic texts as historical source material, the book provides new and illuminating insights into the political and cultural history of the Henrician period, and into the perceived character of the King himself. It focuses on the troubled religious and political history of the reign, the culture of the Court, and the personality and governmental style of its head. In doing so the book argues for a reassessment of the reign, which places the King once more at the centre of affairs, and acknowledges the determining effect which this egotistical, charismatic, but above all pragmatic monarch exercised on the artistic culture, as much as on the politics, of the Court. The book also demonstrates the close and specific links between the drama and the politics of the reign, through a close study of a number of key works, links which have hitherto been viewed only as general or peripheral.

PLAYS OF PERSUASION

PLAYS OF PERSUASION

Drama and politics at the Court of Henry VIII

GREG WALKER

*Fixed-term lecturer in English,
University of Queensland*

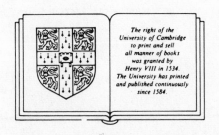

The right of the
University of Cambridge
to print and sell
all manner of books
was granted by
Henry VIII in 1534.
The University has printed
and published continuously
since 1584.

CAMBRIDGE UNIVERSITY PRESS

Cambridge
New York   Port Chester
Melbourne   Sydney

Published by the Press Syndicate of the University of Cambridge
The Pitt Building, Trumpington Street, Cambridge CB2 1RP
40 West 20th Street, New York, NY 10011, USA
10 Stamford Road, Oakleigh, Melbourne 3166, Australia

© Cambridge University Press 1991

First published 1991

Printed in Great Britain by Redwood Press Limited, Melksham, Wiltshire

British Library cataloguing in publication data
Walker, Greg
Plays of persuasion: drama and politics at the court of
Henry VIII.
1. Drama in English, 1400–1558. Special subjects.
Politics. Critical studies
I. Title
822.209358

Library of Congress cataloguing in publication data
Walker, Greg.
Plays of persuasion: drama and politics at the court of
Henry VIII / Greg Walker.
p.   cm.
Includes index.
ISBN 0 521 37436 7 (hardback)
1. English drama – Early modern and Elizabethan, 1500–1600 – History
and criticism.   2. Henry VIII, King of England, 1491–1547, in
fiction, drama, poetry, etc.   3. Great Britain – Court and courtiers –
History – 16th century.   4. Politics and literature – England –
History – 16th century.   5. Henry VIII, King of England, 1491–1547 –
Art patronage.   6. Great Britain – Politics and
government – 1509–1547.   7. Political plays, Engish – History and
criticism.   8. Kings and rulers in literature.   9. Persuasion
(Rhetoric)   I. Title.
PR649.P6W35   1991
822'.209358 – dc20   90–39989 CIP

ISBN 0 521 37436 7

For George

CONTENTS

ABBREVIATIONS

B.I.H.R.	*Bulletin of the Institute of Historical Research*
B.L.	British Library
C.S.P.Sp.	G. A. Bergenroth, *et al.*, eds., *Calendar of State Papers Spanish*
C.S.P.V.	R. Brown, *et al.*, eds., *Calendar of State Papers, Venetian*
E.E.T.S.	Early English Text Society
E.H.R.	*English Historical Review*
Hall	Edward Hall, *The Union of the Two Noble and Illustrious Houses of Lancaster and York*, ed., H. Ellis (London, 1809)
L.P.	J. S. Brewer, *et al.*, eds., *Letters and Papers, Foreign and Domestic, of The Reign of Henry VIII*
M.E.Th.	*Medieval English Theatre*
P.M.L.A.	*Publications of the Modern Language Association of America*
P.R.O.	Public Record Office
R.E.E.D.	*Records of Early English Drama*
R.Q.	*Renaissance Quarterly*

ACKNOWLEDGMENTS

No academic study is solely the work of its nominal author. Every scholar gains immeasurable assistance from the advice and suggestions of colleagues and fellow researchers, and from the pleasurable and stimulating experience of reading work already published in the field. This has certainly been true in my case, and I could not have completed this book without the assistance of numerous fellow scholars, organizations and individuals. I am indebted to each of them for the time and trouble which they have invested in helping this project to fruition.

In particular I should like to record my gratitude to C. S. L. Davies, for help and encouragement, both with this project and with my earlier work. I am also very grateful to Professor Sir Geoffrey Elton, whose support and advice at key stages in the completion of this study were invaluable. His subsequent kindness in reading the text in draft form, and making comments upon it, both general and particular, which he returned with typical despatch and good humour were greatly appreciated.

I am also grateful for the chance to discuss Tudor literature and history with a number of scholars working in the field, most notably Dr John Guy, Professor V. J. Scattergood, Professor Alistair Fox and Mr Peter Gwyn. The latter was kind enough to read two of the chapters printed below in their earliest incarnations. I am also grateful to Mr Gwyn for the chance to discuss with him, on a number of occasions, his own work on Cardinal Wolsey, and to read and cite material from his biography of Wolsey, *The King's Cardinal* (London, 1990), in advance of publication. I am similarly grateful for the help and advice given by Dr Steven Gunn, who read and commented upon a draft of Chapter 2 of this study, and discussed Tudor politics and literature with me at length on many occasions.

For the majority of the time during which the research for this book was conducted (and, indeed, for a number of years before that) I was based at the University of Southampton. I should like to thank all my former colleagues in the Departments of History and English for their support and friendship over the years. I should especially like to thank Mrs Jill Whale, formerly of the History Departmental office, for her patient and friendly assistance in matters both great and small, and my colleagues and friends, both Cavalier and otherwise, for making my stay at Southampton so enjoyable. In particular I should like to record my thanks to Tony Kushner, Nicholas Kingwell, Brian Golding, John Oldfield, Tessa Webber, John J. McGavin and Kevin Sharpe. The last two named, through both their inspirational teaching and their subsequent advice and encourage-ment with my research, have done more than most to stimulate my love for literature and history and my desire for an academic career.

Since leaving Southampton in 1989, I have been working in the Depart-ment of English at the University of Queensland, and I should like to thank my new colleagues there, in particular Dr Elizabeth Moores, for their friendship and generosity with their time, which have made the transition to a new post and a new continent so pleasurable.

In financial terms I am greatly indebted to the President and Fellows of the British Academy for the award of a Post-doctoral Research Fellowship, held between 1986 and 1989. Without this grant I, like many academics of my generation, would almost certainly not have been able to pursue my career even thus far. I am also grateful to the University of Queensland for the award of a Special Project Grant, which has enabled me to bring the work published here to its conclusion.

Some of the material printed in Chapter 4 of this study also appears in 'Cardinal Wolsey and the satirists: the case of *Godly Queen Hester* re-opened', in S. J. Gunn and P. G. Lindley, eds., *Cardinal Wolsey: Church, State and Art* (Cambridge, 1991). Many thanks are due to the editors for permission to reproduce that material here.

My greatest personal debt is to my wife, Sharon, for her love, patience, and encouragement at all times. Her contribution to this study, and to my life in general, is incalculable.

As always, my greatest academic debt is to Dr G. W. Bernard, who, through his friendship and encouragement, and still more by the example of his own teaching and research, has inspired me to undertake and complete this study, and to aim, more generally, for the highest standards of academic integrity which he has set. In dedicating this volume to him I hope that I can at least acknowledge, if not repay, some small measure of that debt which I owe him. If this study has strengths, the credit will be due in large part to Dr Bernard and to those other scholars acknowledged here. If it does not, the fault is entirely mine.

INTRODUCTION

This is primarily a study of the role of Court drama in the political history of the reign of Henry VIII. It is not a study of early Tudor drama which employs political history as its point of entry into the literature. This may appear to be a difference simply of critical emphasis rather than of methodology, but it nonetheless determines the nature of the chapters which follow. These examine Henrician drama chiefly with regard to its political implications rather than any of its many other linguistic, dramaturgical, philosophical or moral significances.

First in general terms and then through a series of case studies of individual plays, this study explores the interaction of drama and politics in the reign of the second Tudor king. It is designed to address a number of inter-related questions. Most obviously, what do we mean by the term 'political drama'? In the broadest sense all drama and all literature can be said to be political in as much as it concerns human relationships and social conditions. But so undiscriminating a definition conceals the important distinctions between types of drama which will be considered below. If, however, we are to adopt a more specific definition, what prescriptive criteria should we employ? What of those plays which, like John Heywood's *Play of Love*, are not primarily concerned with political issues, yet contain passing allusions to political events or eminent individuals? Or, conversely, what of those plays which, like the Wakefield *Second Shepherds' Play*, underpin religious drama with references to contemporary social conditions?[1] Are these plays political? Or do they simply contain political material? And, if such a distinction has any validity, where are we to draw the line between the two categories?

As what follows will demonstrate, there are considerable benefits in employing a relatively tight definition of what constitutes a political play, restricting the term to only those texts which seem actually to concentrate

---

[1] For a possible allusion to Cardinal Wolsey in *The Play of Love*, see R. J. Schoeck, 'Satire of Wolsey in Heywood's *Play of Love*', *Notes and Queries*, 196 (1951), pp. 112–15. The play itself may be found in J. S. Farmer, ed., *The Dramatic Works of John Heywood* (London, 1905). For the Wakefield play, see M. Rose, ed., *The Wakefield Mystery Plays* (London, 1961).

on political issues and themes rather than those which refer to them only incidentally. This sharper focus enables one to ask more specific questions about the nature and function of political drama in the period. What sort of issues seem to have interested the writers of such plays, for example? And what might this tell us about the interests of their audiences? Indeed, what sort of audiences would these plays have reached, and what did the playwrights hope to achieve by using the dramatic form to raise political issues before such gatherings? The broad thesis of this study is that the political plays considered below were persuasive documents, designed to plead particular cases and sway minds. But, if this assumption is correct, who was seeking to persuade whom, and about what? And what does the existence of so politically engaged a form of drama tell us more generally about the nature and forms of political activity in the Henrician Court?

It may well be that a number of these questions cannot be conclusively answered, and that, where answers do suggest themselves, they simply raise further questions of their own. But it is nonetheless important to begin to ask such questions of this dramatic material. For it constitutes a valuable historical source largely neglected by students of the period.

Too often political analysis of early drama has contented itself with a short journey into the *cul-de-sac* named 'Topical Allusion'. In this respect the editors of play-texts have largely set the agenda for future commentary. During their research they identify a number of passages within a text which seem to refer to historical events or individuals. These they use to date the play, or to suggest a location for its first performance(s). But nothing further is done. References to such allusions are generally relegated to a separate portion of the critical introduction to the text (usually labelled 'Date') and left there. Their significance is taken to be merely antiquarian; their identification a necessary, if rather uninteresting, part of the editorial groundwork, which ought to be swiftly despatched in order that one might move on to those more exciting sections labelled 'Themes', 'Sources' and 'Language'.

But 'topicality' ought not to be treated in the same way one might examine a writer's use of proverbs, dialect or rhyme-scheme. This study rests upon the contention that to say that a play contains topical material ought to be only the first stage of the analytical process, not the last. For the plays considered below were 'topical' in the same sense that any historical document is topical. They did not simply allude to or reflect current political issues; they actively involved themselves in those issues and sought to influence their outcome through that involvement. They are political plays not merely because they touched upon political acts, but because they were themselves political acts, written to explore and determine questions of considerable import to their authors; to persuade, cajole and convince their audiences, and thus to achieve political ends. Their topicality is fundamental to their creation. It lies in the fact that they are the products of their historical moment. They sought to address specific issues in a specific context. To dismiss this as mere 'topicality' and to isolate it as a separate concern, divorced from theme, language or structure, would be to dismiss the contemporary relevance of the plays entirely. In attempting to bring the drama and the politics of the Henrician era together once more, this study will suggest the centrality of 'topicality' to the structure and function of these plays.

Recent years have witnessed something of a rebirth of historical, or neo-historical, treatments of literature. Most notably, work on the cultural history of the Elizabethan and early Stuart periods has led to valuable inquiry into the areas where literature and political history meet.[2] But the literature, and particularly the drama, of the first half of the sixteenth century has largely been neglected in this respect. The period was covered by David Bevington's pioneering study, *Tudor Drama and Politics: A Critical Approach to Topical Meaning*, to which a good deal of what follows, although it frequently reaches different conclusions, is indebted.[3] But the wide scope of Bevington's project, covering all drama from 1485 to 1603, meant, as he acknowledged himself, that he was able to offer only tentative suggestions concerning many of the individual works concerned, concentrating instead upon broader questions and 'overall patterns' and, in doing so, opening up areas of inquiry for future scholars to pursue. With only a small number of creditable exceptions, however, Bevington's suggestions have not been followed up by scholars of early Tudor drama.[4] This is unfortunate, as both historical and literary study of the Henrician

---

[2] See, for example, D. Norbrook, *Poetry and Politics in the English Renaissance* (London, 1984); K. M. Sharpe, *Criticism and Compliment: The Politics of Literature in the England of Charles I* (Cambridge, 1987); R. M. Smuts, *Court Culture and the Origins of a Royalist Tradition in Early Stuart England* (Philadelphia, 1987); M. Butler, *Theatre and Crisis, 1632–42* (Cambridge, 1984) and a number of the essays in Kevin Sharpe and Steven N. Zwicker, eds., *The Politics of Discourse: The Literature and History of Seventeenth Century England* (Berkeley, 1987) and Heather Dubrow and Richard Strier, eds., *The Historical Renaissance: New Essays on Tudor and Stuart Literature and Culture* (Chicago, 1988).

[3] D. M. Bevington, *Tudor Drama and Politics, A Critical Approach to Topical Meaning* (Harvard, 1968).

[4] In the field of Henrician drama only Ian Lancashire's fine edition of the plays *Youth* and *Hick Scorner* (I. Lancashire, ed., *Two Tudor Interludes* (Manchester, 1980)) has so far taken up the challenge of individual texts with any conviction. The first two volumes of *The Revels History of Drama in English* (London, 1983 and 1980) and G. Wickham's, *Early English Stages* (3 vols., London, 1959–81) also contain valuable work but, again, their broad scope prevents the sort of sustained detailed analysis attempted below. Most recently the period has been covered by Alistair Fox's *Politics and Literature in the Reigns of Henry VII and Henry VIII* (Oxford, 1989), which contains one chapter on the drama of the reigns. Although this study appeared too late to be given full consideration in the following chapters, I have referred to it where appropriate in the footnotes.

period can benefit from the sharing of sources, experiences and approaches.

There are evident gaps in the historian's knowledge of the political culture of the period which a study of the work of its dramatists can help to fill. Indeed, the failure to notice that these dramatists *were* engaged in political activity provides in itself one of the most obvious of those gaps. Conversely, a detailed knowledge of the political and religious contexts in which plays such as John Bale's *King Johan* or John Heywood's *Play of the Weather* were written can only be of benefit to scholars of drama. Such developments should in their turn suggest new ways of looking at the play-texts concerned, not as artifacts of interest only in and of themselves, but as part of a wider system of political and social discourse and activity. They might then be studied, not only for what they drew from that system, but also for what they contributed to it.

What follows is not a comprehensive study of all forms of dramatic activity practised in the Henrician era. A work which would do justice to so wide a range of material would have to be many times the length of the current text. As has been suggested, this study concentrates upon those dramatic texts written between 1509 and 1547 which contain specifically political material and engage directly, not simply with general social or economic issues, but with contemporary political debates. In practice this limits the plays under consideration, not only in terms of content, but also of form. For those texts which emerge as 'plays of politics' also prove to be those written, almost exclusively, in the form of interludes for perform-ance in the environs of the royal Court (here defined, not narrowly as the physical confines of the royal palaces, but more broadly as the social circle in which moved the King, his courtiers and advisers) or of noble house-holds. There, in the ambit of the political elite, debates were conducted which were to shape the future of the Tudor political and religious polity. And there too, as what follows will suggest, most of the political drama of the period (even much of that frequently described as 'popular' rather than as elite) was patronized, produced and performed.[5]

Inevitably the limitations placed upon the type of drama considered involves a degree of artificial exclusivity. We shall not, for example, be concerned here with the numerous disguisings, mummings or costumed jousts which were also presented at Court at this time and which fre-quently carried distinctly political overtones. Such activities have already been the subject of much fruitful research which it is unnecessary to

---

[5] For the suggestion that even a play such as *The World and the Child* (*Mundus et Infans*), usually considered popular in its auspices, was in fact the product of a noble household, see Ian Lancashire, 'The Auspices of *The World and the Child*', *Renaissance and Reformation*, 12 (1976), pp. 96–105.

duplicate here.[6] Moreover, a study of such activity would involve a rather different methodology from that employed here. In eschewing the comprehensive survey approach, this book will concentrate upon detailed close readings of complete (or near-complete) play-texts. No such texts survive – if indeed they ever existed – for those other quasi-dramatic Court entertainments. Thus one might offer only the most provisional accounts of their structure and content. In contrast, by concentrating upon texts sufficiently complete to allow one to trace in some detail their development of political ideas and their pursuit of rhetorical strategies, it should be possible to transcend the generalized account and provide a more specific analysis of the political implications of Henrician Court drama.

Throughout the following chapters I shall attempt, in so far as it is possible for a political historian to do so, to mediate between historical and literary approaches, whilst stressing the political and historical implications of the material under consideration. But within this general strategy the emphasis will vary from chapter to chapter. At times, as in the studies of the anonymous *Hick Scorner* or John Skelton's *Magnyfycence*, the major result of this historical approach will be an improved appreciation of the dramatic text, in that placing a text more firmly in its contemporary context will bring new aspects of it to light. At others the political history of the period will receive the greater illumination. Thus in the chapters on Heywood's *Play of the Weather* and the anonymous *Enterlude of Godly Queene Hester* study of the plays reveals new aspects to contemporary debates about the future of the Church in England and suggests the existence of opinions, arguments and even interest-groups largely unnoticed by historical accounts of the period. In each case the net result should be a more detailed and more penetrating reading of the plays as political documents than has hitherto been possible.

[6] See, for example, S. Anglo, ed., *Spectacle, Pageantry and Early Tudor Policy* (Oxford, 1969); G. Kipling, *The Triumph of Honour* (Leiden, 1977).

Chapter 1

POLITICAL DRAMA IN THE REIGN OF HENRY VIII: AN INTERPRETATION

To study the interaction of drama and politics in the reign of Henry VIII is to study a period of considerable significance in both spheres of activity. The political and religious events of the 1520s and 1530s; the royal 'divorce(s)'; the break with Rome; the sessions of the Reformation Parliament and the religious innovations and reactions of the late 1530s and 1540s have all received detailed scholarly analysis, and will continue to do so as we still have much to learn about each. The drama of the period, although less well known, is no less vibrant.

The years between 1509 and 1547 saw the continuation, and in some cases the growth, of a wide range of dramatic and quasi-dramatic activities.[1] There were the magnificent Corpus Christi play cycles performed in York, Chester, Wakefield and many other provincial towns and cities. There were also the moral plays designed for open-air performance, generally by touring companies, of which the fifteenth-century *Castle of Perseverance* is perhaps the most obvious extant example, and shorter moral and religious plays put on on an occasional basis by members of the religious orders, townsfolk or professional players.[2] Again, there were the folk plays, whose content may now be approached only through eighteenth-century texts, but which must have formed an important part of agrarian festive culture throughout the realm at this time. Still more specific and localized were the quasi-dramatic revelries, Mayings and disguisings which frequently find a place in the accounts of late medieval and Tudor dramatic activity. At the universities and Inns of Court, in schools and religious houses, and very probably in the vast majority of

[1] For a sense of the diversity of dramatic activities in this period, see, for example, *The Revels History of Drama in English*, vols. I and II (London, 1983 and 1980); G. Wickham, *Early English Stages* (3 vols., London, 1959–81); E. K. Chambers, *The Medieval Stage* (2 vols., London, 1903); A. W. Reed. *Early Tudor Drama* (London, 1926); R. Axton, *European Drama of the Early Middle Ages* (London, 1974); D. Bevington, *From Mankind to Marlowe: Growth of Structure in the Popular Drama of Tudor England* (Harvard, 1962); T. W. Craik, *The Tudor Interlude* (London, 1967).

[2] Note, for example, the elaborate production of the play of 'the holy martyr St George' at Bassingborne in Cambridgeshire, o 20 July 1511, for evidence of how substantial even local dramatic productions might be. Chambers, *Medieval Stage*, II, p. 338.

noble and greater gentry houses, such Christmas and Eastertide activities, and those associated with the various incarnations of the Boy Bishop or Lord of Misrule, would have contained a more or less formal element of dramatic action. Personae would be adopted for the duration of the celebrations; appropriate costumes would be worn, ritualized actions performed and set words spoken. Thus drama reached into every corner of the realm and involved a wide cross-section of the population, whether as patrons, performers or spectators.

What it is important to note, however, is that, where it existed, drama was not simply a recreational diversion. The Henrician period, unlike our own, was one in which drama 'mattered'. It mattered not only to the commonalty and those who made their livings by entertaining them, but also to the sophisticated, the rich and the powerful. It mattered to the civic authorities who saw in the Corpus Christi cycles both an expression of urban honour, pride and magnificence and a potent ritual of communal and spiritual reaffirmation.[3] It mattered to those clerics who crafted religious and moral drama as a vehicle for spiritual instruction. And, most significantly for our present concerns, it mattered to influential lay men and women who saw in the writing, the patronage or the commissioning of plays the opportunity, not only for diversion, but also for self-expression, advancement and the persuasion of others.

The records are far from comprehensive. But what evidence exists suggests a remarkable degree of noble and ministerial involvement with drama and with acting companies. In this as in much else, the Crown set a conspicuous example. Henry VIII himself employed two companies, in addition to the Gentlemen and Children of the Chapel Royal who also acted. These companies, the Old and New King's Players travelled extensively between their appearances at Court. Each of Henry's queens also had their own actors, as did his illegitimate son, Henry Fitzroy, and the other royal children.[4] In addition, virtually every noble family seems to have sponsored an acting troupe at some point during the period. And such troupes would have performed, not only at the various residences of their patron, but also, as they toured the country under the protection of his

---

[3] M. E. James, 'Ritual, Drama and the Social Body in the Late Medieval English Town', in *Society, Politics and Culture: Studies in Early Modern England* (Cambridge, 1986), pp. 16–47; M. Stevens, *Four Middle English Mystery Cycles* (Princeton, 1987) *passim*; David Mills, 'Religious Drama and Civic Ceremonial', in *The Revels History of Drama in English*, I, pp. 152–206.

[4] I. Lancashire, ed., *Dramatic Texts and Records of Britain: A Chronological Topography to 1558* (Cambridge, 1984), pp. 373–4; 378–9; 385; 387–92; 397–8. For the development of the royal dramatic establishment, see, W. R. Streitberger, 'The Development of Henry VIII's Revels Establishment', *Medieval English Theatre*, 7:2 (1985), pp. 83–100 and 'William Cornish and the Players of the Chapel', *Medieval English Theatre*, 8:1 (1986), pp. 3–20.

name and recommendation, at other noble seats, monastic houses and civic halls.

Notably it was not only those noblemen influential at the political centre, such as Charles Brandon, Duke of Suffolk; Thomas Grey, Marquess of Dorset or Thomas Howard, third Duke of Norfolk, who patronized actors.[5] Such men may have been expected to contribute to the cultural magnificence of the Court. But the great shire magnates, such as George Talbot, fourth Earl of Shrewsbury and John de Vere, fifteenth Earl of Oxford, whose provincial seats acted as courts in miniature for their localities, also retained troupes.[6] Similarly even quite modest, less politically influential noblemen, such as George Brooke, Lord Cobham; Henry, Lord Daubeney and Edward, Lord Grey of Powis, had their own companies.[7] A number of non-noble courtiers and administrators, such as Sir Edward Belknap and Sir Edward Guildford also thought it worthwhile to give their support to troupes.[8] And when even shrewd politicians such as Thomas Cromwell can be found sponsoring actors and encouraging playwrights,[9] it strongly suggests that there was more to patronizing drama than simply self-indulgence or social posturing.

DRAMA AS A DIDACTIC MEDIUM

The assumption that literature in general and plays and players in particular existed in an apolitical sphere of activity, divorced from the immediate concerns of the political elite, would be inaccurate whichever period was considered. But it is a particularly misleading description of sixteenth-century attitudes. In the early modern era literature in almost all its forms was seen as a branch of rhetoric; as essentially a persuasive rather than a meditative exercise. And this inevitably brought it into contact with public and thus with political issues. This fact is nowhere more obviously demonstrated than in the case of English drama in the period before the construction of purpose-built, commercially run, playhouses.

The noblemen and civil servants who retained actors and writers in this period were, by and large, not foolish. Nor were they motivated by charity

---

[5] Lancashire, *Dramatic Texts*, pp. 376–7; 386–7; 394. Brandon's company seems to have been active from at least 1520 and probably earlier, and is known to have toured East Anglia and the South of England in the following twenty years (see Chapter 2, below). Dorset's players are recorded as performing at Thetford in 1529–30, and Norfolk's troupe seems to have played throughout East Anglia, London and the South East between 1529 and 1544.

[6] Ibid., pp. 406 and 407. That the Earls of Shrewsbury supported players in 1495–6 is evident from the records cited by Lancashire. But it is likely that they maintained their patronage throughout the reign of Henry VIII.

[7] Lord Cobham's company appeared at Court in 1538–9, ibid., pp. 377; 380; 386.

[8] Ibid., pp. 375 and 387.

[9] Ibid., p. 380. See Chapter 6 below.

or liberality alone. As what follows will suggest, they appreciated the didactic and persuasive potency of the dramatic medium and employed it for their own ends. Whilst it might have been acceptable to employ, for part of the year at least, minstrels, jugglers or bearwards with only the hope of some entertaining diversion and a sense that they were maintaining a household fitting to their status as recompense, patrons seem generally to have expected something more in return for lending their name and financial backing to an acting troupe.

In a world in which no generally accepted model of political lobbying existed, influence over an acting company and access to an elite audience through drama gave one a voice with considerable political potential. More subtle and flexible than a formal oration, more immediate and effective than a printed tract and probably more congenial to the listener than a sermon, a play possessed a number of advantages over the other forms of intellectual and political exchange generally employed. Thus it is perhaps hardly surprising to discover that drama was employed didactically, not only for spiritual, but also for political and social ends, in an elite society in which didacticism was widely admired and encouraged.

As Erasmus declared, political and moral persuasion, even indoctrination, were ends important enough to warrant the employment of all the diverse media at the persuader's disposal. If a prince (the supreme object of all secular advice) was to be educated to recognize the value of virtuous conduct, he must constantly be surrounded by encouragements and inducements to virtue. His teachers (or, if he was of age, his ministers) should ensure that every channel of communication, almost every object upon which his eyes fell, or to which his ears were turned, should be employed to reflect and bestow wise counsels,[10]

now by a fable, now by example, now by maxims, now by a proverb. They should be engraved upon rings, painted in pictures, appended to wreaths of honour.

Thus every feature of the environment, every cultural practice, should be utilized as a vehicle for persuasion. And this was not simply idealizing; the projection of a scholarly Utopia. In the harsh reality of the north of England the theory was given a concrete form in the household of Henry Algernon Percy, fifth Earl of Northumberland. There, the Earl's son and heir, Lord Henry Percy, was raised to manhood with the object of a virtuous life held forever before him – literally held before him. For upon his chamber ceiling was inscribed an admonitory dialogue in verse, between hedonistic Youth and sober Manhood, whilst in the garret, over the

[10] D. Erasmus, *The Education of a Christian Prince*, ed. and trans., L. K. Born (New York, 1936), p. 145.

bath, was written a similar dialogue, between the personified faculties Sensuality and Intellect.[11]

There in the stucco and plaster of Leconfield Castle, Northumberland turned the very fabric of his daily existence into a medium for virtuous education. Clearly he felt that any opportunity for didacticism and moral instruction was to be grasped and employed. And he did not limit his attentions to his domestic architecture. More interesting in the present context are the uses which he made of drama.

Like the majority of his peers, Northumberland retained the services of actors. He had the members of his chapel perform Nativity and Resurrection plays before his assembled affinity on the appropriate days in the liturgical calendar. And he also kept a separate troupe of 'Interluders' whom he seems to have employed to perform, *inter alia*, the play *Youth*; a didactic morality of spiritual and personal development, again probably written for the instruction of the young Lord Henry by another member of the household.[12] In *Youth* the Percy family, its servants, retainers and friends, would have seen dramatized the follies and vices to which the untutored young were particularly prone, and witnessed a practical demonstration of the value of humility and charity in the Christian life. All of which would have provided an object lesson in obedient behaviour for the Earl's potentially wayward son.

Northumberland clearly saw the value of drama for the pursuit of those virtuous goals advocated by Erasmus. It provided a further vehicle and, moreover, a uniquely effective one, for the transmission of good counsel. And what Northumberland might employ for general moral effect might equally, of course, be set towards more particular and less exalted ends.

The very form of the interlude, a play performed between or immediately after the courses at a banquet,[13] made it an ideal vehicle for the dissemination of opinions, advice or information to an elite (and therefore

---

[11] I. Lancashire, ed., *Two Tudor Interludes* (Manchester, 1980), pp. 28–9. See also, M. E. James, 'A Tudor Magnate and the Tudor State: Henry Fifth Earl of Northumberland', in *Society, Politics and Culture*, pp. 48–90, esp. pp. 83–90.

[12] Ibid., pp. 18–22; 26–8. As Lancashire shows, the play, which is the major source for the interlude of *Hick Scorner* examined in the following chapter, can be dated on internal evidence to the period August 1513–May 1514.

[13] The precise etymology and significance of the word 'interlude' are vexed issues. The term might suggest a play ('*Ludus*') between ('*inter*') the courses of a meal or, more loosely, one played 'between' different actors or speakers. The anglicized spelling 'enterlude' might, alternatively, indicate that the term derives from the fact that the actors 'entered' the acting space with their play. The very loosest definitions assume that the word means no more than 'play'. In what follows the more specific usage, describing a performance in an aristocratic or civic Great Hall during or after a meal will be employed. For a helpful discussion of the history of the term, see N. Davis, 'The Meaning of the Word "Interlude": A Discussion', *Medieval English Theatre*, 6:1 (1984), pp. 5–15. See also Chambers, *Medieval Stage*, II, pp. 181–3.

influential) audience. To take the case even at its simplest level, the advantages of being able to expound upon a theme at some length to guests who were perforce kept relatively silent and attentive, are obvious. Short of pointedly leaving the hall before the conclusion of the meal, the spectators could do little other than absorb the ideas presented.[14] And dramatic presentation had other advantages over the sermon or oration which made it a particularly potent didactic tool in such circumstances.

As the protestant polemicist Richard Morison suggested to his employer, Thomas Cromwell, the strong visual element in drama made it an effective medium for addressing a poorly educated audience.[15]

Into the common people thynges sooner enter by the eies, then by the eares: remembryng more better that they see than that they heere.

Hence he argued for the suppression of the 'Papist' Corpus Christi cycles and their replacement by protestant plays demonstrating rather the 'abhomynation and wickednes' of the Bishop of Rome, 'monkes, ffreers, nonnes, and suche like'.

The potency of the visual over the verbal for a contemporary audience was also attested by Stephen Gardiner, bishop of Winchester, a man of quite different religious preferences to Morison. Taking the Great Seal as his model, he suggested, in a letter to the Captain of Portsmouth, Edward Vaughan, that, although the written inscription might be incomprehensible to many, the symbols accompanying it retained a compelling social force.[16]

He that cannot read the scripture written about the Kinges great seale, either because he can not rede at al, or because the wax doth not expresse it, yet he can rede Sainct Georg on horsback on the one side, and the kinge sitting in his majestie on the other side, and readeth so much written in those images as, if he be an honest man, he wil put of his cap.

What was true, in Morison and Gardiner's conception, of the

14 The only possible evidence of a guest actually leaving the hall during a dramatic performance is John Payne Collier's story, now widely disregarded as an invention, of Henry VIII 'departing to his chamber' before the end of a production of Henry Medwall's *Of the Finding of Truth*, during 1513, on the grounds that the play was too long for his taste. J. P. Collier, *The History of English Dramatic Poetry to the Time of Shakespeare: And Annals of the Stage to the Restoration* (3 vols., London, 1879), I, p. 69.

15 B.L. Cotton MSS Faustina C 11 ff. 15v–18v; Royal 18 A1. See S. Anglo, 'An Early Tudor Programme for Plays and other Demonstrations Against the Pope', *Journal of the Warburg and Courtauld Institutes*, 20 (1957), pp. 176–9; G. R. Elton, *Policy and Police: The Enforcement of the Reformation in the Age of Thomas Cromwell* (Cambridge, 1972), pp. 185–6.

16 Gardiner to Vaughan, 3 May 1547, J. A. Muller, ed., *The Letters of Stephen Gardiner* (Cambridge, 1933), p. 274.

commons, clearly had a wider currency. The 'quick pictures' of a dramatic performance provided, not only 'poor men's books', a simple message for the uneducated spectator, but also considerable immediate impact for an elite audience.[17] By giving an iconographic dimension to verbal expression, drama provided a powerful vehicle, not only for the transmission, but also for the recollection of ideas, as surviving accounts of responses to dramatic imagery suggest. Witnessing a dramatic performance was often one of the most memorable experiences in an individual's life. When prompted to speak about Christ, an aged resident of Cartmel in Lancashire, for example, could recall nothing which he had been told by priest or preacher, but mentioned having seen,[18]

that man you spake of once in a play at Kendal, called Corpus Christi play, where there was a man on a tree and blood ran down.

As late as 1639 'R.' Willis, a man higher up the social scale than the anonymous Lancastrian, recalled a childhood visit to a performance of an interlude, *The Cradle of Security*, in Gloucester during the 1560s or 1570s. 'This sight tooke such impression in me', he subsequently recalled, 'that when I came towards man's estate, it was as fresh in my memory as if I had seen it newly acted'.[19] And it was not simply the spectacle which impressed him. For, as his recollections make clear, he was evidently more than

---

[17] Note the stress upon the physical, observable, presentation of spiritual truths in, for example, the York and Chester Corpus Christi cycles. Frequently the audience is asked to judge the veracity of the message expounded on the strength of their own observation. Hence characters repeatedly refer to what the audience has seen, does see or will see. See, David Mills, 'The Behold and See Convention in Medieval Drama', *Medieval English Theatre*, 7:1 (1985), pp. 4–12. For the importance of the visual and active 'sign' in the didactic programme of the Chester Cycle, see J. J. McGavin, 'Sign and Transition: The *Purification* Play in Chester', *Leeds Studies in English*, II (1980), pp. 90–104. For a late medieval assertion of the superiority of the 'quick' books of the Miracle plays to the 'dead' (because unmoving) books of religious painting, see C. Davidson, *A Middle English Treatise on the Playing of Miracles* (Washington, 1981), p. 40. The hostile author puts into the mouth of a defender of such plays the argument that 'sithen it is leveful to han the myraclis of God peyntid, why is [it] not as wel leveful to han the myraclis of God pleyed? Sythen men mowen bettere reden the wille of God and his mervelous werkis in the pleying of hem than in the peyntynge, and better thei ben holden in mennus mynde and oftere rehersid by the playinge of hem than by the peyntynge, for this is a deed bok, the tother a qu[i]ck.' Against this view, the author suggests (p. 45) that, although plays provide the more affective medium, they lead their audiences rather to sin than to virtue. For, whereas unadorned paintings might suggest spiritual truths, 'myraclis pleyinge . . . ben made more to deliten men bodily than to ben bokis to lewid men. And therfore, yif thei ben quike bookis, thei ben quike bookis to schrewidenesse more than godenesse.' See also below, pp. 191–3.

[18] P. Williams, *The Tudor Regime* (Oxford, 1979), p. 290. I. D'israeli, *Curiosities of Literature* (London, 1843), p. 539.

[19] R. Willis, *Mount Tabor, or Private Exercises of a Penitent Sinner* (London, 1639), S.T.C. 25752, pp. 110–14.

capable of interpreting the play (perhaps with some parental help) in a quite subtle fashion, concluding that the central character, a prince,

did personate in the morall, the wicked[ness?] of the world; the three ladies, Pride, Covetousness and Luxury, [and] the two old men, the end of the world, and the Last Judgement.

The dramatic form had, then, considerable potential as a didactic medium. Dramatic delivery not only gave an emotive force to words, but accompanied them with a visual dimension which contemporary audiences, attuned to the iconography of heraldic devices, royal pageantry and, perhaps most tellingly, religious images and the symbolic gestures of the Mass, were used to associating with the revelation of important truths. Drama performed in the great hall, during or after a banquet, also, as we have seen, enjoyed a captive elite audience, enjoined by the rules of courtesy and etiquette to behave with a degree at least of attention and decorum.

Where there was close co-operation between patron, author and actors, drama in performance could also, despite appearances to the contrary, be one of the most 'controllable' of artistic media. Unlike the poet or author of a prose tract or printed dialogue, who had to release his work into the reader's domain with only the occasional marginal gloss as an aid to interpretation, the playwright, where he was able to collaborate with his actors, was able to lead his audience quite deliberately towards the kinds of responses he desired. Whereas the reader of a written work, secluded with the text, is able to interpret it in any way which seems plausible, detecting in it ironies, allusions and implications far from the author's original intention, the dramatic audience is limited in its interpretive freedom by the very act of performance.[20] The actors might, through gesture, tone of voice, the use of particular costumes, or any of the other extra-linguistic accompaniments to their speeches, enforce an interpretation upon all but the most prejudiced onlooker. Thus the playwright intent upon making political or moral statements in his work might, through the careful schooling of his actors in the nuances of delivery, careful costuming, the use of properties or even direct impersonation of known individuals, foreground his intentions in the minds of his audience.

Where the playwright could supervise his work in production, then, the scope for disseminating propaganda, or more subtle forms of political

[20] In an age of public reading, in which the literate, or the more-literate, would commonly read aloud to their less-adept companions, the reader gained even greater power over the text, being able, not only to create his or her own interpretations, but to impose them upon the listening group. Hence Henry VIII's concern that the public reading of that most sensitive of texts; the vernacular Bible, was restricted to those individuals felt to be politically and socially responsible. See below, pp. 217–19.

persuasion, through his work was actually far greater than in purely textual literary forms. And in the following chapters our concern will be with plays which, I will suggest, were originally performed in precisely those circumstances.

There has been considerable criticism, not all of it unjustified, of attempts to link the dramatic texts of the Renaissance period with specific social and political events, occasions and personalities.[21] And in the era of the public commercial theatre, where multiple performances and revivals were prompted as much by commercial concerns as by questions of specific audiences or patronage, attempts to tie performances to particular state and patrician celebrations are certainly problematic. But in the pre-theatrical era, when all elite drama (and much of the supposedly popular repertory) was tied to noble and civic patronage, the vast majority of dramatic productions were more certainly designed for predetermined locations and, broadly speaking, known audiences. This generalization applies not only to the interludes designed for performance in royal or noble halls, but also to the Corpus Christi cycles and many of those plays designed for touring. In the case of the cycle plays, the dates of performances, the stations at which the plays would be performed and the composition of the patrician element in the audience were all well established in civic tradition and thus well known to the plays' creators, and the local authorities took pains to regulate the texts in order that material thought inappropriate to the occasion was not included. Similarly the touring plays were equally well-tailored to suit a known type of audience, as the interest-arousing banns which preceded performances suggest. The disparaging remarks about prominent East Anglian personalities to be found in *Mankind* further suggest that even 'popular' plays were designed for a particular kind of audience whose tastes and sense of humour the author thought he knew.[22]

A number of the courtly plays may subsequently have been absorbed into the repertoire of touring companies and their original, specific, connotations consequently lost. But this does not mean that, in their original incarnations, the plays were not characterized by particular contemporary allusions and political arguments. Such plays may have been revived or (re)printed at later dates, but then new and equally specific circumstances

---

21 For an overview of the debate to 1968, see Bevington, *Tudor Drama and Politics*, pp. 1–26. For its *reductio ad absurdum*, see R. Levin, *New Readings vs Old Plays* (Chicago, 1979), pp. 146–93. For a stimulating account of one aspect of the problem in its contemporary manifestation, see Leah S. Marcus, *Puzzling Shakespeare: Local Reading and its Discontents* (Berkeley, 1988).

22 For the references in *Mankind*, see Mark Eccles, ed., *The Macro Plays*, E.E.T.S., 262 (Oxford, 1969), pp. 154–84, lines 504–21.

would govern the decision to do so. Like all artifacts existing through time, plays accrete new significances and shed old ones as circumstances change. When *The Enterlude of Godly Queene Hester*, which as what follows will suggest was a highly political play written in the late 1520s, was printed in 1561, its printers, William Pickering and Thomas Hacket, attempted to market it as a mirror for godly women. The quarto edition was prefaced with the additional injunction

> Com nere vertuous matrons & women kind
> Here may ye learne of Hesters duty
> In all comlines of vertue you shall finde
> How to behave your selves in humilitie.

What had begun life as a political drama was resurrected (presumably for commercial reasons, although here again there may have been a hidden political agenda) and pressed into service as an unlikely contribution to the burgeoning genre of 'handbook' advice literature.[23]

COURT DRAMA AS PROPAGANDA

To appreciate how the didactic potential of drama was realized by its patrons, not simply to the moral and educative ends envisaged by Erasmus and practiced by the Earl of Northumberland, but to further specific political intentions, we need only consider those plays known to have been performed in or around the Henrician Court during the 1510s and 1520s at moments of heightened political and diplomatic activity. This period represents, or seems to represent, something of a golden age for court drama, if the surviving documentary evidence is to be relied upon. For, with the coming of the 1530s, a combination of a number of factors – chiefly the deaths of a number of the key members of the incipient royal 'Revels Department' and what seems to have been a general decision to turn to more vociferous forms of expression in troubled times – brought about a marked reduction in courtly dramatic activity.

The performance of plays in the royal Court had a venerable history. King Arthur in the fourteenth-century romance, *Sir Gawain and the Green Knight*, refers quite familiarly to the 'laykyng of enterludez' as an appropriate activity for Christmas at Court.[24] But whether such plays were, from the first, used for propagandist ends, or whether what started as pure entertainment was subsequently exploited for political purposes is

---

[23] W. W. Greg, ed., *A New Enterlude of Godly Queene Hester* (Louvain, 1904), p. 1.
[24] *Gawain*, line 472, in M. Andrew and R. Waldron, eds., *The Poems of the Pearl Manuscript* (London, 1978), p. 225.

unclear.[25] Certainly, by the reign of Henry VIII, one can detect clear evidence of drama being employed at Court for both generally moralistic and specifically political ends.

In 1515 the Children of the Chapel Royal, led by their Master, William Cornish, performed the interlude *Troilus and Pandar* before the King, in conjunction with the presentation of a pageant castle, a disguising and dance and a fight at the barriers.[26] Neither this, nor their subsequent appearance, in 1519, in a play written by Cornish involving personifications of Winter, Summer, Sun, Moon, Rain and Lust, is known to have carried a specifically political burden.[27] But both the Children's company and their adult counterparts were employed in propagandist roles at other times, as circumstances dictated.

Among courtly patrons Cardinal Wolsey seems to have been particularly alert to the opportunities which drama presented, not only to display to foreign guests the magnificent hospitality of his royal master and to suggest the sophistication of his Court, but also to make more particular points in furtherance of his diplomatic negotiations. In December 1521 Wolsey entertained the Imperial ambassadors, with whom he and Henry VIII were currently negotiating the details of their intended 'Great Enterprise' for the invasion of France, with 'many sumptuous and gorgious disguisynges, enterludes and bankettes made in the same season'.[28] That

---

[25] During the Christmas festivities of 1427–8, for example, the Court of the infant Henry VI was entertained with 'diverses jeuues et entreludes' performed by 'Jakke Travail et ses compaignons' and the 'autres jeweis de Abyndon' (E. K. Chambers, *Medieval Stage*, II, pp. 256–7). There is, however, no way of determining the content, or even the precise form, of these performances. More is known about the series of 'Mummings' written by John Lydgate for Henry's Court during the same decade. These productions, consisting of a dumb-show accompanied by explanatory verses delivered by a narrator, are perhaps more akin to later court pageants than to the Interlude as defined here. They nonetheless give some indication of the nature of dramatic performances at Court in the early fifteenth century. The themes of these shows seem to have been generally apolitical and comic in tone. In 1430, for example, the King and his entourage, taking Christmas at Hertford Castle, were entertained by a petition from a group of 'rude upplandishe people compleynyng of hir wyves' and then by a counterpetition from the wives against the husbands. What topical references can be found in the pieces seems to have been of a broadly propagandist kind. Thus, during Christmas 1427–8, a dumb-show of Bacchus, Juno and Ceres presented the young King with olive bows symbolic of the concord between his realms of England and France. In 1529, as Henry prepared to travel to Rheims for his coronation as King of France, Lydgate presented a mumming of King Clovis, depicting 'howe th'ampull and the floure de lys came first to the kynges of Fraunce by myrakle at Reynes' (D. Pearsall, *John Lydgate* (London, 1970), pp. 184–8).

[26] See the account book of Richard Gibson, Henry VIII's Yeoman Tailor of the Great Wardrobe (himself a former interluder), usefully reprinted in H. N. Hillebrand, *The Child Actors* (Urbana, Illinois, 1926), p. 324.

[27] Ibid., p. 57. The same may have been true of the performance in May 1527 before the continental ambassadors by the Gentlemen and Children of the Chapel of a debate with songs, concerning which was most necessary for a prince, Love or Riches, Hall, pp. 722–3.

[28] Hall, p. 628.

these were the occasion for political propaganda is not stated, but the likelihood is that they were. Certainly the same witness's rather fuller account of a play performed before the visiting Emperor Charles V and his entourage on Sunday 15 June 1522 would suggest as much. This later 'disguising or play', probably again the work of William Cornish, took as its subject,[29]

a proud horse which would not be tamed nor brideled, but amitie sent prudence and policie which tamed him and force and puyssaunce brideled him.

This was no simple beast fable, but a continuation of diplomacy by other means. For Edward Hall at least, the political message behind the fable was clear.

This horse was meant by the frenche Kyng, and amitie by the King of England and themperor and the other prisoners were their counsail and power.

In producing such a play at that moment, Wolsey made the most of the opportunity created by the banquet to reinforce his diplomatic efforts to convince the Emperor of English good-will and Henry's continued commitment to the Great Enterprise. The play added a further voice to those others which were already assuring the Imperialists of English good intentions. The play should not, however, be dismissed as simply a piece of partisan self-congratulation of the crudest kind. It must be noted that at precisely the time that the play was vaunting Anglo-Imperial amity, both King and Cardinal were arousing the suspicions of some of Charles' advisers on this issue. For the previous two months reports had been reaching the Emperor from his ambassador in Venice, Alonso Sanchez, and especially from Juan Manuel, the Imperial representative in Rome, suggesting that English commitment to the enterprise against France was at best lukewarm.[30] Thus the directness and, to modern ears at least, the banality of the allegory served a useful purpose in helping to dispel suggestions of English diplomatic ambivalence or duplicity. The play's very naivety was itself a useful device.

By 10 November 1527, the next date for which substantial records of a play performed at Court survive, the focus of English foreign policy had shifted markedly. No longer was the intention to invade France with Imperial support. Henry's mind was now concentrated upon the need to secure a 'divorce' from Katherine of Aragon. And for this he needed a Papal dispensation. But the Pope, Clement VII, was currently held captive

[29] Ibid., p. 641. For an account of the play from the Imperial side, see *C.S.P.Sp.* II, 437. See also S. Anglo, *Spectacle, Pageantry and Early Tudor Policy* (Oxford, 1969), pp. 203–4 and 'William Cornish in a Play, Pageants, Prison and Politics', *Review of English Studies*, N.S. X (1959), pp. 357–60.

[30] See, for example, *C.S.P.Sp.* II, 393, 395, 396, 403, 408, 414, 428, 440. For possible grounds for such (mistaken) doubts, see *L.P.* III (ii) 2126–8, 2180.

by Imperial troops following the sack of Rome earlier in the year. And
Charles V had a vested interest in preventing the humiliation of his aunt,
Queen Katherine, in any divorce settlement. Hence the diplomatic priorities, from the English point of view, were, as far as was practicable, first to
free the Pope from Imperial influence and second to exert as much pressure
as possible on him themselves in order to bring about a favourable judgement on the divorce question. In order to counter Imperial influence in
Italy Henry was forced to rely upon French support, trusting that a desire
to secure English help against his Spanish enemy would prove sufficient to
ensure the co-operation of Francis I. It is against this diplomatic background that one finds Wolsey and Henry treating the French ambassadors
to a lavish entertainment reflecting their mutual ambitions.

Before pageant fountains resplendent with allegorical trappings proclaiming Anglo-French unity, a densely plotted drama was played out by
the boys of St Paul's Grammar School, led by their Master, John Ritwise.[31]

When the kyng and quene were set, ther was playd before them by children in the
Latin tongue in maner of a Tragedy, the effect wherof was that the pope was in
captivitie and the Church broughte under the foote, wherfore S. Peter appeared
and put the Cardinal [Wolsey] in authoritie to bryng the pope to his libertie, and so
set up the church agayn and so the Cardinall made intercession to the Kinges of
Englande and of fraunce, that they take part together, and by their meanes the pope
was delyvered. Then in came the french Kynges chyldren, and complayned to the
Cardinal, how the Emperour kept them as hostages[32] and wold not come to no
resonable point with their father, wherfore thei desyred the Cardinal to helpe for
their deliveraunce, which wrought so wyth the Kyng hys mayster and the french
kyng that he brought the Emperour to a peace, and caused the two yong princes to
be delyvered.

Also involved in the action, as the relevant account books reveal, were
personifications of Religion, Ecclesia and Veritas ('like iij novessis in
garments of sylke and vayells of lawne and sypers'), Heresy, False Interpretation and *Corrupcio Scriptoris* ('lyke laydys of Beeme, inpereld in
garments of sylke of dyvers collars'), the heretic Luther ('lyke a party frer'),
his wife ('lyke a frowe of Spyers in Almayn in red sylke'), Peter, Paul and
James, three sergeants and numerous others. The size of the cast alone, and
the cost of equipping it, give an indication of the importance afforded the
event by its patrons.[33]

---

[31] Hall, p. 735. The play seems to have been a formal response on the part of the English to an
entertainment based upon a similar theme, including within it a play entitled *The Ruin of
Rome*, performed at the French Court before an English embassy on 13 June 1527. P.R.O.
MS SP 1/42, fo. 74 (*L.P.* IV (ii) 3171).

[32] The French princes were held in Spanish custody as surety for the release of Francis I after
his capture at the battle of Pavia in 1525.

[33] *L.P.* IV (ii) 3564. The cost of making the apparel alone came to £5 4s 8d.

Here again the propagandist function of the play is readily apparent. In itemizing the more altruistic reasons for securing papal independence and linking that campaign, through the mediation of Wolsey, to efforts to secure the release of the French princes, it presented an effective case for continued Anglo-French co-operation in a period when England, owing to Henry's greater need, was rather more intent upon maintaining the alliance than was Francis I. But that Wolsey may well have gone beyond this general objective and used the play to make a case for his own indispensability (at a time when Henry was seemingly exploring other means of obtaining his divorce) is also suggested by his prominent role in the action. The French pageants which had greeted the Cardinal on his visit to Amiens earlier in the year had also afforded him a prominent role in their pacific iconography. And there was evident diplomatic advantage to be gained from promoting Wolsey as a figure of sufficient standing and authority to summon a conclave of cardinals which would administer the Church in the event of the Pope remaining a prisoner. But personal motives may well have loomed as large as national ones in this instance. As Edward Hall noted, 'at this play wisemen smiled, and thought that it sounded more glorious to the Cardinall than to the matter in deede'.[34]

Wolsey may well have had similar motives when, in December 1528, he patronized a series of French farces performed before the French ambassador, du Bellay. Whilst there was evident good sense in his portraying himself to Henry VIII as a supremely competent European statesman, and so an indispensable diplomatic aid, so there was equal value in appearing to du Bellay as the only minister with any sympathy for the French cause. And the patronage of French drama in the English Court provided one effective means of assuring the diplomat of his good will. For, despite the touch of condescending irony in du Bellay's report of the plays, he was nonetheless persuaded to report favourably of Wolsey's intentions.[35]

[I think] Wolsey would not be well pleased if I did not tell you of his causing farces to be played in French with great display, saying, in conclusion, that he does not wish anything to be here which is not French in deed and word.

It was, moreover, not only Wolsey who was alive to the political and propagandist potential of drama. The Cardinal was, perhaps, uniquely aware of, and adept at exploiting, the theatrical dimension to diplomacy, whether in the form of his patronage of plays or his own 'performances'

---

[34] Hall, p. 735. For a fuller treatment of this play, see Anglo, *Spectacle*, pp. 232–4. On the Pope's release Wolsey had a series of formal orations delivered in dramatic form, again lauding his own role, and that of Henry, in securing his liberty. *C.S.P.V.*, IV, 225, *L.P.* IV (iii), App. 140.

[35] *L.P.* IV (iii) 5133.

before foreign ambassadors.[36] But the actions of less flamboyant politicians confirm that drama was considered more generally to be a natural means of political expression for those with either the rhetorical talents to create it or the wealth to patronize it. Thus in early January 1531 Thomas Boleyn, Earl of Wiltshire and Thomas Howard, Duke of Norfolk, collaborated in the production of an interlude performed before the French ambassador, Claude la Guische. Both men were anxious to establish their own positions as leading ministers after Wolsey's fall, and so had repeatedly informed the French and Spanish ambassadors that Wolsey and his methods were now discredited and irredeemably a thing of the past.[37] A new dispensation now existed, they stressed, in which they were the important figures. To reinforce the point Wiltshire resorted to a dramatic presentation. As the Spanish ambassador, Eustace Chapuys, observed,[38] Wiltshire

invited to supper Monsieur de la Guische, for whose amusement he caused a farce to be acted of the Cardinal [Wolsey] going down into Hell.

Evidently la Guische was unamused, however, for Chapuys notes that he 'Much blamed the earl, and still more the Duke [of Norfolk] for his ordering the said fare to be printed'. But the diplomatic point had undoubtedly been made, as the diplomat's anger itself suggests. By putting on such a play, Wiltshire not only stressed the King's new, more hostile, attitude towards the Roman Church and all its agents, thus furthering the campaign of threats and counter-threats with which Henry was pressurizing the Pope for a favourable resolution of the protracted divorce proceedings, but also tacitly reminded the French of their own supposedly 'special relationship' with Wolsey, and their alleged involvement in his plotting immediately prior to his fall.[39] This effectively placed la Guische on the defensive in their diplomatic manoeuvres, and suggested the need to break with the past and rely upon new intermediaries with Henry, chief among whom would have to be Norfolk and Wiltshire themselves. Such points could not have been made in direct conversation without prompting a major diplomatic incident. By pursuing them in dramatic form the lords were able both to suggest and to enlarge upon them, risking nothing more serious in response than the charge of poor taste. Norfolk's curious decision to have the interlude printed suggests how effective he thought the strategy had been.

---

[36] Walker, *Skelton*, pp. 165–7.
[37] See, for example, *C.S.P.Sp.* IV (i), 373.
[38] Ibid., IV (ii), 615.
[39] L. R. Gardiner, 'Further news of Cardinal Wolsey's end, November–December, 1530', *B.I.H.R.* 57 (1984), pp. 99–107.

Rather more idiosyncratically, Henry VIII himself seems to have employed the dramatic form – or at least a consciously literary articulation of his ideas – as a means of expressing heart-felt political opinions. In the aftermath of the trial and execution of Queen Anne Boleyn in May 1536, he was said to have carried about with him a 'tragedy' of his own devising, relating the misdeeds of his former queen and her accomplices. This he sought to show to Chapuys and others during a moment of high passion.[40] Even if this document was not the dramatic text which the term 'tragedy' suggests to the modern reader,[41] it nonetheless provides a striking further illustration of the degree to which literary forms were seen as suitable vehicles for even the most important of political expressions. The use of conventional forms, fictive personae and voices gave one a freedom to explore political problems in a neutral medium, free from the accountability of more formal political discourse. The ability to have the finished work performed before others turned this meditative exercise into a powerful expository and persuasive tool.

The patronage of drama, then, gave powerful individuals like Northumberland, Wolsey, Norfolk and Henry VIII himself another effective vehicle for their opinions. It extended their capacity for influence into yet another medium and yet another arena. But drama, even political drama, was not a vehicle exclusively for the opinions of the great, although, as what follows will suggest, its content and rhetorical designs were largely determined by reference to those opinions. In arguing that most of the political drama of the period was the product of the Court and its environs, or of the courts in miniature of the provincial nobility, the chapters which follow will not claim that it was consequently entirely a tool of the King and his counsellors. The examples of courtly drama touched upon above have all been of a broadly propagandist kind, in that they reflected more or less directly the political ideas and directions of their patrons. Wolsey might patronize drama to reflect the current interests of English foreign policy, or Wiltshire and Norfolk might do so to further their own claims to Wolsey's role as leading minister. Yet even here, in the case of the first play mentioned (variously entitled by modern commentators either *Luther and His Wife* or *Of the Pope's Captivity*), things are more complex than they appear initially. It seems evident that Wolsey was able, in patronizing the play, to utilize the general theme of Anglo-French amity which the state

---

[40] *C.S.P.Sp.*, V (ii) 55, p. 127.
[41] 'Tragedy' in the late medieval period might denote any narrative charting a fall from prosperity and happiness to disgrace or death. Thus the stories related in Lydgate's *Fall of Princes* or Chaucer's *Monk's Tale* might all be termed 'tragedies', although none are dramatic in form. Chapuys himself, although he had not seen the text, guessed that Henry's 'tragedy' might have been 'certain ballades' of his own devising.

occasion required simultaneously to advance ideas of his own, asserting his own continued usefulness as a servant of the Crown, a point of significance primarily to himself. A play outwardly designed, and formally commissioned, to perform one function was tacitly diverted to encompass a second, rather different one. And in this respect *Luther and his Wife* is a model, albeit a very simple one, for many of the plays considered below. Such plays prove on close examination to be not baldly didactic – or not *only* baldly didactic. They provide a field for a complex interplay of political arguments and strategies, all of which are 'courtly', if by that we mean a product of the political centre, its elite groups and their affinities, but not all of which are complementary.

The plays performed at Court and in the halls of the nobility were certainly patronized by the Court elite, the great men and women of the realm. But they did not as a result reflect a single, 'courtly', viewpoint. Nor should we expect them to have done. Their authors were, as far as can be determined, not themselves leading ministers or aristocrats, but came from among the rather less exalted figures who worked in the service of such people. They were part of the educated rather than the social elite; scholars, clerics and minor courtiers; men whose views might not entirely coincide with those of their employers. And in this difference of outlook lay the potential for debate and attempts at persuasion. Such writers might use their work to argue points of their own, distinct from those required of them by their sponsors, and suggest new governmental initiatives or plead special cases.

The fact that the majority of these plays originate in what is often misleadingly described as a single institution, the Court, should not, then, imply that they will reflect a consensus on key political issues. Contrary to the assumptions of many pre-revisionist historians and contemporary literary scholars, it is now accepted that the Court did not form a single interest group. Against the general social ties which united its members one must set the specific disagreements and conflicts of interest which divided them. And in this period, as royal policy began to raise doubts about the status of the Church in England, new religious conflicts of conscience and interest were added to existing differences over diplomatic or social policies, economic, dynastic or regional issues and the inevitable clashes of personality, making the Henrician Court less unified still than its immediate predecessors. All of these issues created tensions within the Court and within its ruling class which were at least as important to its members as any putative class solidarity. In such an environment we should not expect either elite patrons or their clients to think with one mind or speak with one voice.

The English Court, as recent work on the subject is revealing, was not so much a political body as a political forum: an arena in which discordant ambitions might be exercised.[42] This is not to argue that it was necessarily riven with either open conflict or hidden intrigue, nor to agree with those scholars who suggest that political faction dominated its daily procedures. Such accounts seize upon the extraordinary incident or the partisan account of an ill-informed ambassador and treat them as typical of the normal running of the Court, rejecting the wealth of evidence attesting to the operation of more sober processes. Yet such divisions as did exist, and are always likely to exist in even the most harmonious institution, should not be ignored. But how, then, should the Court be characterized? By what mechanisms, whether formal or informal, did its members articulate their tensions and antagonisms and seek to justify their wider ambitions? How far were they free to voice their views and how far were they forced by censorship, whether external or internal, to compromise them and follow a 'royal line' on a given issue? And, if political expression was circumscribed, by what means was that circumscription effected, and how far might individuals evade or exploit the limits imposed upon them for their own ends? A careful and detailed analysis of the Henrician Court, its personnel and institutions is urgently needed if we are to gain an overall view of how the day-to-day business of political management was conducted, how particular policies were conceived and implemented and how they might subsequently be qualified and amended. Such a study is well beyond the resources of the present volume. But there is value, nonetheless, in a detailed examination of just one of the vehicles for expression available to ministers, courtiers and their clients, particularly if that vehicle deals, as drama does, with political, philosophical and moral issues, both explicitly and at length.

Only rarely does the historian of the Medieval or Early Modern periods come across documents in which individual writers consider issues of intense political interest both extensively and in detail. Too often attitudes are concealed by opaque injunctions, passing comments or cryptic memoranda or must be inferred by extrapolation from actions. In the play-texts examined below we will discover just such lengthy expositions of political themes, written for performance and consumption in the political heart of the realm. In this respect they provide an invaluable source for the study of

---

[42] See, for example, G. R. Elton, 'Tudor Government, the Points of Contact', III 'The Court', *Transactions of the Royal Historical Society*, 26 (1976), pp. 211–28. K. M. Sharpe, *Criticism and Compliment* (Cambridge, 1987) and the essays, particularly those by K. M. Sharpe and N. Cuddy, in D. Starkey, *et al.* eds., *The English Court from the Wars of the Roses to the Civil War* (London, 1987). For a stimulating account of a slightly earlier period, see Rosemary Horrox, *Richard III, a Study of Service* (Cambridge, 1989).

political opinion and debate at Court, and their examination is long
overdue.

COURT AND POPULAR: RIVAL DRAMATIC TRADITIONS?

Before continuing it is perhaps wise to offer some comments about the
purely courtly focus of this study. Much, if not all, of the evidence cited
above has been drawn from dramatic performances at the Henrician
Court and in its environs. And this will remain the focus of the chapters
which follow. This concentration upon the political centre is not accidental, but it raises important questions which need to be addressed before we
proceed further. Is this focus perhaps unnecessarily exclusive? Recent
literary scholarship has tended to stress the popular, even radically popular, implications of much late medieval literature. By concentrating upon
the political drama of the Court are we in danger of ignoring an alternative
and potentially more vibrant tradition of political drama existing beyond
it and perhaps even in opposition to it? Were there, perhaps, rival centres
of dramatic activity outside the Court which produced their own political
plays in which alternative ideas about the nature of society and the policies
of the Government were expressed and explored? Were there 'radical'
interludes as well as courtly ones?

As the preceding section will have suggested, this study is underpinned
by the general contention that drama of the sort we are considering here
was not a 'popular' medium, if by that we mean a form of literature
distinct from the culture of the ruling elites; expressive of alternative, or
even 'oppositional' ideas and sentiments. Even in the era of commercial
theatres the notion of such a drama is problematic.[43] In the pre-theatrical
period generally, and in the case of the early Tudor interlude particularly,
it is almost unthinkable.

Much has been written concerning the precise social status of certain
dramatic forms in the fifteenth and sixteenth centuries. In studies touching
upon the early Tudor period attention has focused upon the distinction
between what have been loosely termed 'elite' and 'popular' drama. Does a
play contain popular, 'folk', elements? Is it written in a coarse, 'low' style
and concerned with ribald themes? Or is it 'courtly', designed for an
aristocratic or scholarly coterie, written in the high style and concerned
with learned or refined ideas?[44] A continuum is often suggested with, at its

---

[43] For conflicting views on whether Caroline theatre contained within it a more popular,
oppositional tradition, see Sharpe, *Criticism and Compliment;* M. Butler, *Theatre and
Crisis, 1632–1642* (Cambridge, 1984); M. C. Heinerman, *Puritanism and Theatre:
Thomas Middleton and Opposition Drama under the Early Stuarts* (Cambridge, 1980).

[44] Bevington, *Mankind to Marlowe, passim*; R. Axton, ed., *Three Rastell Plays* (Cambridge,
1979), Introduction.

more popular end, a play such as *Mankind*, evidently written for a touring company for performance in provincial inn-yards or other public places, and, towards its elite pole, plays such as the 'goodly comedy of Plautus' played (probably in Latin) at Court in 1520.[45] But problems arise when one tries to draw any wider inferences from the mixture of supposedly popular or elite elements within a given play. How far can supposedly popular plays be seen as reflecting 'popular' attitudes, if by the latter one means the attitudes of the social ranks below the Court gentry and the urban patriciates? Can such plays be seen as reflecting a 'national' or regional culture distinct from that of the Court?[46] Or do they rather represent elite conceptions of what a popular audience would or should wish to see and hear? More generally, how far is it wise to draw firm distinctions about the audience envisaged for a particular piece relying purely upon the presence or absence of a high or low literary style? Might not elite audiences have appreciated both styles at different times or in different contexts? Or might one kind of elite audience have welcomed 'low' humour where another might not? The rudimentary nature of the surviving evidence means that one can offer only tentative answers to such questions. But certain broad conclusions can be reached which bring one closer to a general understanding of the processes at work.

Perhaps the most useful distinction to draw when studying the social origins of early drama is not that between allegedly popular and elite play-texts, but that between all those plays which appear to have been based upon texts *per se* and those localized, non-textual, plays and 'games' generated within individual communities which seem to have drawn upon purely oral traditions associated with specific occasions in the agricultural or religious calendar.[47] For, by the very fact of their written form, all the dramatic texts which we now possess are 'elite' creations. They were crafted by those literate individuals who formed only the highest echelons of educated society. Such men (and they were largely men) were not 'of the people'. Their knowledge of verse-forms and literary styles, their evident philosophical and religious learning, their access to writing materials and the printing presses, indeed, their very ability to write itself, marked them off from the vast bulk of the largely illiterate, uneducated, commons. And their social distinction is everywhere evident in the plays which they wrote. The only relevant question is thus whether the supposedly popular or folk

[45] R. Holinshed, *Chronicles of England, Scotland and Ireland*, ed., H. Ellis (6 vols., London, 1807–8) III, p. 635.
[46] Axton, *Rastell Plays*, p. 1.
[47] For introductions to such drama, see David Mills, 'Drama and Folk-Ritual', in *The Revels History of Drama in English*, I (1983), pp. 122–51; R. Axton, *European Drama of the early Middle Ages* (London, 1974), pp. 33–60; Chambers, *Medieval Stage*, I, pp. 89–273.

elements in these plays – the scatological humour, irreverent word-games and violent buffoonery – are actually reflections of genuinely popular ludic traditions, or simply examples of an alternative elite discourse, like Chaucer's 'low style', thought fitting for non-courtly characters or settings.[48] It may be that these elements were borrowed from popular festive practices, but it equally well may not. And as the only available evidence exists in the elite texts themselves, it is unwise to speculate too far beyond them.

Given the above, it would surely be unwise to ascribe much cultural or political significance to the distinction between elite and popular play-texts. Attempts have been made to see allegedly popular plays as express-ive of alternative political values, distinct from those of the governing classes.[49] But plays such as *Everyman* or *Mankind* hardly recommend themselves as evidence of a festive culture inherently subversive of the dominant aristocratic ideology. If these plays were indeed the work of scholars or clerics who were themselves part of that dominant social group, and were performed by acting companies wearing the liveries of noble patrons, then it would seem unwise to stress their 'popular' origins. And, given that the sort of 'popular' material to be found in a play like *Mankind* also appears in plays clearly written for the Court, it would seem dangerous to ascribe any particular cultural significance to them. What one sees in *Mankind* is surely a particular type of play, designed by an educated playwright, for a particular sort of performance, not the product of an entirely different set of 'popular' cultural assumptions.[50] There is nothing to say, for example, that its author might not subsequently have written more 'courtly' plays, or that *Mankind* itself, suitably modified, might not have been well received at Court.

But, if the distinction between elite and popular play-texts has little

---

48 Chaucer's 'popular' fabliaux tales were as much a part of the *Canterbury Tales* as the pious and 'gentle' tales and were aimed at the same elite readership. The latter would seem to have enjoyed both the ribald humour of the *Miller's Tale* and the chivalrous romance of *The Knight's Tale* without evident difficulty. A still more appropriate analogy is provided by the work of John Heywood, whose *Play of the Weather* (studied in detail in Chapter 5, below) offered the Court a drama which treated both classical themes and contemporary political issues, yet who also wrote coarse, dramatized, *flytyngs* and fabliaux such as *The Pardoner and the Friar* and *Johan Johan* (see, J. S. Farmer, ed., *The Dramatic Works of John Heywood* (London, 1905)).

49 For the association of the morality play with the carnivalesque, see M. Bakhtin's seminal *Rabelais and His World*, trans., H. Iswolsky (London, 1968), p. 15. See A. Gash, 'Carnival against Lent: The Ambivalence of Medieval Drama' in D. Aers, ed., *Medieval Literature, Criticism, Ideology and History* (New York, 1986), pp. 74–98, and particularly p. 80 for the suggestion that vernacular religious drama was 'an interface between literate and oral culture rather than an offshoot of the former'.

50 Note Bevington's assertion that '*Mankind* is the most indisputably popular play of the fifteenth century' (Bevington, *Mankind to Marlowe*, p. 48).

general cultural or social significance, does it, perhaps, carry a specific political interest? Might the use of different dramatic styles and registers indicate an attempt to find an alternative political voice? Albeit that the author was a member of an educated, social elite, might he not nonetheless have been voicing 'oppositional' political views? Could the use of a 'popular' dramatic mode suggest that the author wished to take his views 'out of Court' in order to find a more responsive audience elsewhere? Clearly it might. But a number of qualifications immediately suggest themselves. First, if one imagines an author searching for a 'popular' audience through a change of style, it is important to consider just how substantial a shift in his intended audience such a change might imply. It is interesting to note that John Skelton's radical shift in verse-form and register within his trilogy of satires against Cardinal Wolsey, from the complex linguistic games of the primarily rhyme-royal *Speke, Parott* to the simple, bold, assertions of the 'Skeltonic' *Collyn Clout* and *Why Come Ye Nat to Courte*, did not mark a comparably radical change in the social class of his intended audience. He turned from the primarily courtly and scholarly audience intended for *Parott*, not to the lower artisans and apprentices of London, but to their commercial and political masters, the merchant elite who ran the livery companies and occupied the major civic offices. It was the grievances and aspirations of the latter which he tried to mirror in the later satires, rather than anything more popular.[51] If Skelton's most 'popular' and coarse poetic style proves on closer inspection to be aimed at an audience only marginally less exalted in social and economic terms than that of his courtly poems (and indeed, at an audience whose own cultural aspirations were explicitly modelled upon those of the Court), then distinctions between varieties of literary culture based purely upon stylistic criteria are indeed in need of substantial revision.

Perhaps a more fundamental objection to the notion of 'popular' playwrights with oppositional political views is, however, to be found within the supposedly popular plays themselves. For plays such as *Mankind* are actually very conservative and conventional in their limited use of political subjects. It is the courtly plays which contain the sharpest material in this respect, as what follows will suggest. The interludes considered in this study are intensely political and express a variety of viewpoints distinctly at odds with many of the prevailing attitudes of the Crown. But these plays could hardly be described as popular or anti-courtly. Both the logistics of their production and their own dramatic form argue against such descriptions.

The Interlude, as we have seen, was a form of drama designed for

---

[51] Walker, *Skelton*, pp. 100–18.

performance in the great hall of a palace or manor house. By that very fact it was linked irrevocably to the patronage of the social and political elites. Only the Crown, the aristocracy, higher clergy and the civic authorities, Inns of Court, and livery companies could afford to stage the kind of occasions at which an Interlude might be played. And only they owned the types of buildings in which it might be performed. Thus, of its very nature, the Interlude was an exclusively elite form of drama, written for members of the governing classes and performed in an environment formed by and saturated with their values and attitudes. The writers who used such plays to discuss political issues did so conscious of these facts. If they wished to raise and promote controversial ideas, they did not take those ideas out of Court or outside London to incite dissent in the country beyond. They took them into the centre of political affairs. Their plays were designed for performance before those individuals who wielded power and influence in the Realm, and they sought, not to protest or to confront those individuals, but to sway and persuade them; to join a debate at the political centre. For it was there that the decisions were taken which would most readily effect the crucial political and religious concerns of the moment. An understanding of this fact has important implications, not only for the way we view the production of drama at Court, but also for our conception of Tudor politics generally.

CENSORSHIP, SOCIAL CONTROL AND A SUPPRESSED DRAMATIC TRADITION?

Although drama existed in many forms throughout the Realm, it is the contention of this study that it found its most political form in the political centre, at Court. There it would find its most knowledgeable and appreciative audiences, and there it might raise political issues among those individuals best placed to influence or resolve them. It is to the political and religious divisions within the social elites, within the Court itself and within the Government, that we should look, then, for the tensions which prompted such drama, not to wider social and cultural tensions between the elites and the commonalty, between centre and locality, Court and Country. If and where the latter existed, they generally found other, more immediate, forms of expression.

This is not to argue that drama outside the Court circle held no interest for courtiers and politicians. The sixteenth century provides ample evidence of the governing classes taking considerable interest in 'public' outdoor drama and acting to regulate it. But this should not be taken as evidence of a suppressed tradition of alternative, anti-establishment drama. Significantly it was usually the physical context of a dramatic performance which aroused governmental anxieties rather than any particularly subversive material in the play itself. And, when the subject matter was objected to, it generally proves to have been the external circumstances which made it so, not anything inherently radical within the play. And, once again, the precise auspices of a given play need to be carefully examined in order that texts produced by particular elite interest groups are not mistakenly assumed to be popular creations.

The official suppression of plays and play-going had a considerable history, even before the Reformation brought doctrinal scrutiny to bear upon them, resulting in the demise of the Corpus Christi cycles and catholic religious drama generally.[52] At times a doctrinal motive may be assumed for even pre-Reformation suppressions, as when, in 1515, the Chester play of the Assumption of the Virgin was put aside or, more assuredly, when, in 1532, the Town Clerk of Chester, William Newhall, deleted all references to Papal authority from the banns and proclamations heralding the town's play cycle.[53] But at others, the reasons behind the actions are less clear, as when the annual plays at Ipswich were 'laid aside' in 1518, 1519 and 1521, or when the playing of the Passion Play at New Romney was made subject to royal approval on the authority of the Sergeant of the Cinque Ports in 1517–18.[54] Why the central authorities should have been interested in these plays at these times (if indeed they were) is unclear.[55]

For a detailed exposition of the case for a particular suppression on other than doctrinal grounds, we must wait until 6 February 1545, when the City of London issued an ordinance suppressing unregulated dramatic performances within the City walls.[56] And in this case it seems clear that the authorities acted, not because such plays were spreading dangerous ideas abroad, but because the notion of unauthorised performance was itself the cause of anxiety.

It is likely that the audiences brought together by open-air plays

---

[52] For the latter, see H. C. Gardiner, *Mysteries' End* (Yale, 1946).
[53] *Revels History*, II, p. 9; Wickham, *Early English Stages*, II (i), p. 15.
[54] Ibid., p. 8.
[55] It is, of course, quite possible that what we are witnessing here is the result not of central interference but of local disputes or rivalries or, in the case of the action at Ipswich, of simple economic necessity.
[56] For a fine example of an attempt to suppress drama for overtly religious reasons, see Henry VIII's, undated, letter to the authorities in York, J. O. Haliwell-Phillipps, ed., *Letters of the Kings of England*, I, p. 354.

constituted some of the largest spontaneous gatherings known in early
Tudor England. Certainly reference to the only comparable events in
contemporary experience, ranging from street football games to
open riots, would hardly commend outdoor drama to the legislative mind.
Merely by their numbers and potentially irreverent behaviour, public
play-goers posed a challenge to the authorities which the latter
were unlikely to ignore. In a society which at least liked to think of itself as
closely regulated, the disordered jocularity of the play crowds inevitably
prompted concern, particularly as such crowds seemed invariably to
include precisely those social groups which proved most intractable to
the mechanisms of social control: the young; the poor; the unemployed
and miscreant apprentices. Hence the City fathers concentrated in their
proclamation, not upon the plays themselves, but upon their
audiences.[57]

Fforasmoche as by reason and occasyon of the manyfold and sundrye Enterludes
and common playes that nowe of late dayes have been by dyvers and sondrye
persones more commonly and besylye set foorthe and played than heretofore hathe
bene accustomed in dyvers and many suspycyous darke and inconvenyent plac[e]s
... to which plaies great parte of the youthe of the same Citie and many other light
idyll and evyll disposed persones daylye and contynuallye frequentynge hauntynge
and followynge the same playes have not onely bene the Rather moved and
provoked therebye to all proclyvyte and Redynes of dyvers and sondrye kyndes of
vyce and synne. And the said youthe by that occasyon not onely provoked to the
unjuste wastynge and consumynge of theire maisters goods and the neglectinge and
omyssyon of their faitheful service and due obedyence [but also] ... to the greate
decaye and hurt of the Common welthe of the said citie as of Archerye and other
lawfull and laudable exercyses.

It would, of course, be quite possible to argue that such public justification for the suppressions might mask a hidden desire to silence radical
political or religious voices.[58] But in the absence of any evidence that this
was the case it is surely wiser to accept the proclamation at face value. A
feeling that such gatherings were occasions for idleness and sin, coupled
with an anxiety that they were also both 'out of control' and on the
increase (and, perhaps as importantly, a realization that they brought in no
revenue for the civic purse) might provide more than enough justification

[57] The proclamation is printed in full as an appendix in Wickham, *Early English Stages*, II (i),
pp. 327–8.
[58] Note Chambers' sceptical assumption that in the case of the Elizabethan closure of the
theatres, concern at the spread of the plague was simply an excuse for 'a Puritanic attack
upon the theatres' (*Medieval Stage*, II, p. 111).

for suppression, without recourse to theories of covert political censorship.[59]

Such suppressions, as examples of attempts at social control on the part of a governing body, are, of course, broadly political in character. But they are political in a way which has little to do with the specific nature of the event suppressed. They are largely indistinguishable from such other actions to control the commonalty as legislation against sturdy beggars and vagrants, restrictions placed upon the free association of apprentices and so on. The fact that the occasions concerned here were dramatic performances does not seem to have created any particular concern on the part of the legislators. This in turn suggests that the plays themselves were not thought to be unduly contentious. There may have been a general feeling that they were immoral – a traditional but rather curious notion, given the highly moral nature of most surviving texts – but this was not the reason for the regulation. It was rather the occasion for a general assembly which these public plays provided which was the cause for concern. The sort of plays with which this study is concerned are, as we shall see, 'political' in a much more specific and pointed sense.

On the one occasion in which repressive action was taken as the result of words spoken on a public stage, those concerned, rather than inventing spurious social justifications for their actions, were entirely candid about their motives. The occasion was the 'May Game' played in a Suffolk village on May Day 1537. And, as Charles Brandon, Duke of Suffolk, informed Thomas Cromwell, the theme of the performance that year concerned 'a King [and] how he should rule his realm'.[60] Problems arose, Suffolk was

---

[59] See *Revels History*, pp. 7–9. The performance of plays in the open air had long been seen as an occasion for disorder and immorality. See, for example, the association in *Piers Plowman*, Passus V, lines 406–9, of the Shoemakers' 'somer game' with 'harlotrye', 'lesynges' and lies, all of which provided diverting entertainment for the sinful priest, Sloth. See also Richard Morison's letter to Cromwell cited at p. 11 above, which refers to 'playes of Robyn hoode, mayde Marian [and] freer Tuck' as occasions at which 'lewdenes and ribawdry' is 'opened to the people', and disobedience to authority is encouraged. See also Friar Melton's description of the potentially unruly behaviour of the crowds watching the York cycle (c. 1510), in A. F. Johnston and M. Rogerson, eds., *Records of Early English Drama: York* (2 vols., Toronto, 1979), I, p. 43. That it was, similarly, the fear of public disorder rather than any desire to stifle independent opinion *per se* that lay behind the theatrical censorship of the seventeenth century has recently been suggested by A. B. Worden, 'Literature and Political Censorship in Early Modern England', *Britain and the Netherlands*, IX (1987), pp. 45–62, p. 48. I am grateful to Dr G. W. Bernard for bringing Dr Worden's article to my attention before this book went to press. For an alternative and more conspiratorial view of censorship in this later period, see, Annabel Patterson, *Censorship and Interpretation: The Conditions of Writing and Reading in Early Modern England* (Madison, Wisconsin, 1984).

[60] *L.P.*, XII (i) 1212. Unlike Professor Wickham (*Early English Stages*, II (i), pp. 56–8) I am sceptical of J. P. Collier's claims to have found evidence of a performance in 1529 of 'a play of King Robert of Sicily' seemingly designed to discredit Henry VIII's divorce proceedings.

told, because one particular actor, who 'played Husbandry ... said many things against gentlemen more than was in the book of the play'. What these words were, or what happened next is unclear, but complaints were evidently made against the actor and Suffolk attempted to investigate. His report to Cromwell gives few further details, but it makes clear that it was, again, not the play itself which caused the problems, but the actions of the individual actor, who used the performance as an opportunity to air his own views. Under other circumstances such hostile comments about the gentry might have caused little concern. One recalls the often violently expressed *animus* against the gentry displayed by the Plowman in the courtly interlude *Gentleness and Nobility*.[61] But before a popular audience, in the tense months following the Pilgrimage of Grace, they took on a new significance. Hence Suffolk's informant took no chances and passed his report on to the Duke. And Suffolk himself relayed what would otherwise have been a trivial piece of news to the chief minister of the Crown.

Again, the problem was not that this was 'a dissident play',[62] from which we might extrapolate a whole tradition of dissident drama. The play itself may well have been unexceptionable. The dissident actor had, after all, to introduce his own words in order to make his point. And it was probably saying nothing which had not been said elsewhere. What was so worrying was the opportunity which the play provided for popular gatherings during troubled times.[63] And in this respect both the play, and the reaction to it from those in authority, would seem quite predictable. Those noblemen and gentlemen who represented civil authority in their localities were always wary of public gatherings. Whether they were occasioned by plays, open-air sermons or popular sports seems to have been only of secondary interest. What was worrying was the unsupervised and unregulated nature of the gathering. Thus to assume that every attempt to suppress a dramatic performance in this period was an act of political censorship, and that the lack of evidence of popular political drama is evidence of the success of such repression, would be unwise.

The examples of drama actually being singled out for suppression because of its subversive political content are few and almost exclusively elite in their auspices. The most famous occasion concerns Cardinal Wolsey's reaction to an interlude, or, as Edward Hall describes it, a 'goodly

---

[61] Axton, *Three Rastell Plays*, pp. 97–124.
[62] *Revels History*, II, p. 15.
[63] That it was the wider social implications of the event which worried Suffolk rather than the play itself is evident from his subsequent actions. The only actor whom he wished to question seems to have been the offending 'Husbandry', who was 'sent for' but had disappeared by the time the Duke compiled his report. Meanwhile other popular gatherings were immediately suppressed (*L.P.* XII (i) 1212 and 1284).

disguising', performed at Grey's Inn during the Christmas festivities of 1526–7. This play,[64]

was compiled for the moste parte, by master Jhon Roo, serjiant at the law, xx yere past, and long before the Cardinall had any aucthoritie, the effecte of the plaie was that lord governaunce was ruled by dissipacion and negligence, by whose mis-governance and evil order, lady Publike wele was put from governance: which caused Rumor Populi, Inward grudge and disdain of wanton sovereignitie, to ryse with a great multitude, to expell negligence and dissipacion, and to restore Publike Welth again to her estate, which was so done

Regardless of the fact that, as Hall claims, the play was 'compiled for the moste parte ... xx yere past' and well before his coming to authority, Wolsey evidently saw in it a contemporary significance which aroused his anger.

This plaie was so set furth with riche and costly apparell, with straunge divisis of Maskes and morriskes that it was highly praised of alle menne, savyng of the Cardinall, whiche imagined that the plaie had been divisid of hym.

He, being 'in greate furie', consequently summoned before him, not only the players involved, but also the unfortunate Roo, who was deprived of his coif and despatched to the Fleet along with one of the actors on the strength of this revival of his work.

Influential opinion evidently felt that Wolsey had over-reacted. William Warham, the Archbishop of Canterbury, referring to the incident in a letter to one of his chaplains, Henry Gold, declared himself to be sorry that such a matter should have been taken in earnest.[65] And, Hall suggests, others felt the same way.[66]

This plaie sore displeased the Cardinall, and yet it was never meante to hym ... wherefore many wysemen grudged to see hym take it so hartely.

Yet Wolsey may well have been justified in detecting a contemporary political purpose behind the play, albeit that Hall's assertion of its age may have been correct. For a multitude of sins may be concealed by the chronicler's vague phrase 'for the moste parte'. Does this suggest that new material was added, after the fashion of Husbandry's tirade against gentle-men, which gave an old text new meanings? Regardless of additions there was clearly considerable capital to be made from a judicious revival of a play on a germane subject at a moment of crisis, as the well-known example of the performance of *Richard II* (probably the Shakespeare play) to accompany the Earl of Essex's abortive rebellion in 1601 amply testifies. No doubt the same defence could have been made of that play. It had

---

[64] Hall, p. 719.   [65] *L.P.* IV (ii) 2854.   [66] Hall, p. 719.

evidently been written some years before. But Queen Elizabeth was under no illusions about its contemporary significance. 'I am Richard II. Know ye not that', she is reported acidly to have remarked to the Lincoln's Inn jurist, William Lambarde.[67]

For the Gray's Inn lawyers to revive a play such as that described by Hall, in which a popular tumult unseated ministers called Dissipation and Negligence, only months after royal demands for the Amicable Grant had been abandoned in the face of popular risings, strongly suggests a contemporary political purpose. And support for this supposition can be found in the account of the affair provided by the martyrologist John Foxe. Foxe suggests that 'in the play partly was matter against Cardinal Wolsey', and the potentially inflammatory nature of the piece was fully realized by the lawyers before the production began. For none of them 'durst take upon them to play the part which touched the said Cardinal' until the future protestant controversialist Simon Fish agreed to take on the role; a decision which was to result in his flight abroad in the face of Wolsey's anger.[68] One must read Foxe's narrative with some care in this instance, however, as the author clearly has an interest in maximizing the courage of his hero, Fish. The latter's death through plague robbed Foxe of the opportunity to add him to his list of martyrs for the reformed faith. Thus it is possible that what we see in the account of this earlier incident in his subject's career is an attempt to describe the next best thing to a heroic death. By insisting upon the known dangers of accepting the 'Wolsey' role, he invests Fish's decision to take it on with a significance close to a prefiguration of the martyrdom which would have given the story an appropriate conclusion.

Whatever Fish's precise role in the affair, however, it would seem plausible that the play would have been read as a satirical commentary upon contemporary events, at least in certain circles, in the aftermath of the failure of the Amicable Grant. And as Wolsey had publicly to accept the blame for imposing the demand without royal consent and take a carefully stage-managed rebuke from Henry as a consequence, it is not surprising that the Cardinal was more than usually sensitive to possible allusions to the event.[69]

Perhaps the most significant aspect of this incident in the light of our current concerns is, however, the fact that Wolsey was provoked to such fierce retaliation by a play performed in the political centre. It was in the Inns of Court, one of the most influential institutions of the realm, that Wolsey feared to be attacked. For in such places his reputation and his

---

[67] J. Nichols, *The Progresses of Queen Elizabeth* (3 vols., London, 1823), III, pp. 552–3.
[68] Foxe, *Acts and Monuments*, IV, p. 657.
[69] G. W. Bernard, *War, Taxation and Rebellion in Early Tudor England* (Brighton, 1986).

public image might be damaged most effectively. Should word of such a performance have reached the King and found favour, the Cardinal's position might well have been undermined. And it is equally significant that Wolsey acted so violently at the moment that he did. For the attack upon his reputation came at a time when he was particularly vulnerable in that area. He had accepted the blame for the Amicable Grant in order to deflect damaging criticism from the Crown. His political stock was thus particularly low. Had further criticism been levelled at him, it might have begun to appear to the King that his former asset was fast becoming a liability and that the best means of damage limitation was to jettison him entirely. Hence Wolsey needed to act quickly to suppress the play before it set an unwelcome precedent.

This specific example clearly has a wider significance. If the above is correct, it suggests that political drama of this sort was both specific and occasional. It gained its relevance and its potency from the expression of particular opinions at a given time and in a given place. The Grey's Inn play would have posed little threat to Wolsey had it been performed two years earlier, and would have caused him far less concern had it been produced, not by London lawyers but by a provincial acting company. It is instructive to note that the Cardinal's reaction to John Skelton's satires, which were far more direct and sustained in their criticism than Roo's play would appear to have been, was far more restrained. The crucial distinguishing factor would seem to have been that in 1521–2 Wolsey was rather less vulnerable to 'public' criticism than he was immediately after the failure of the Amicable Grant. Again the timing and the context of the criticism is all-important.[70]

Yet, as the individual studies which follow will suggest, the very notion of such plays being created outside the specific conditions which nurtured them is misleading. For their political content was the product of that environment. There would have been no reason to write a play like Roo's in a provincial town, except perhaps in those East Anglian and Kentish areas where resistance to the Grant was centred. For only in very specific areas was Wolsey's administration of the realm an issue at this time. Had the play been conceived, or even performed, elsewhere it would have lost its specific political resonance.

And the same is true of all the plays considered below. *Hick Scorner*, had it been written elsewhere, would not have carried the same implications as it held for the household of the Duke of Suffolk during the early 1510s. Similarly, John Heywood's *Play of the Weather* would not have been the same play had it been created anywhere other than in the royal Court during the religious and political controversies of the late 1520s.

[70] Walker, *Skelton*, Chapter 3 and Conclusion.

In order to draw out such specific political significances, one needs not simply to identify the topical allusions in a text, but to set them firmly in their contemporary context. This requires both a close reading of the text itself, and the sort of detailed historical analysis to be found in the chapters which follow. This will not simply provide an historical 'background' to the plays considered, but will suggest how literary text and historical context are part of a single political culture. This should, in turn, reveal the intimate associations between literature and history more generally in this period. With this strategy in mind, we can now turn to the first of the plays to be studied in detail, the anonymous interlude, *Hick Scorner*.

Chapter 2

IMPROVING LITERATURE? THE INTERLUDE OF *HICK SCORNER*

PLOT

In outline the interlude entitled *Hick Scorner* is a simple tale in the morality tradition, in which a representative figure, Free Will, inclines towards vice but is eventually won for virtue by the actions of good advisers. The play begins with the meeting of three virtues: Pity, Contemplation and Perseverance. Each describes his role in the salvation of mankind. The theological and ethical system which they articulate is fundamentally conservative. Pity defines himself as the kind of love which motivated Christ to intercede for humanity and which offers everyone the prospect of redemption.[1]

> Whoso me loveth damned never shall be.
>
> (line 26)

> ... all that will to heaven needs must come by me:
> Chief porter I am in that heavenly city.
>
> (lines 28–9)

He governs the other two; Contemplation, 'brother to Holy Church' (line 43), whose adoption of the solitary, heremetic, ideal paradoxically equips him for the active life as warrior of the Church Militant,[2] and Perserverance, the quality necessary to turn good intentions into a life of grace. The three lament the current parlous state of English society. People, Pity says, have no time for Contemplation. Priests ignore him and live 'uncleanly'. Poverty grinds down the commons, but gentlemen and lords offer no charity, preferring to marry off their heirs and clients to rich

---

[1] All line references refer to the edition in I. Lancashire, ed., *Two Tudor Interludes* (Manchester, 1980).

[2] Contemplation effectively represents both Christ and the Church in all its forms, regular and secular. 'I am the chief lantern of all holiness, / Of prelates and priests – I am their patron' (lines 48–9). 'To fight with Satan I am the champion / That dare abide and manfully stand' (lines 52–3). 'I am called Contemplation, / That useth to live solitary ... / I love not with me to have much company' (lines 63–4 and 67).

widows in lucrative marriages of convenience. 'All is not God's law', they conclude, 'that is used in land' (line 115). Thus lamenting, they leave the place.

Once the virtues have departed, the true protagonist of the play, Free Will, enters. He is a roisterer, who relates his experiences of the previous night spent drinking and whoring. Yet he is also representative of the catholic conception of the human condition.

> ... my name is Free Will
> I may choose whether I do good or ill.
> (lines 159–60)

He is met by Imagination, a compound of deceit and invention, who describes his adventures among the lawyers at Westminster and the great men in the shires, before both characters call for their comrade, Imagination's former cell-mate, Hick Scorner.

Despite giving his name to the play, Hick Scorner's contribution to it is relatively short. He enters the place, allegedly from a boat on the Thames, and reels off a long list of increasingly fantastic countries which he claims to have visited, moving thereafter to list the names of a number of sailing vessels which he says he saw sink in the Irish Sea. These vessels, many of which, as Ian Lancashire's research shows, were actually wrecked or run aground in the years immediately prior to the performance of the play, are said to have been carrying a crew of the more virtuous elements in society, all of whom were drowned. Meanwhile Hick's own vessel, the *Envy*, has landed, bearing a crew of five thousand vices. The three rogues propose to celebrate Hick's survival and the destruction of his enemies with a night in the Stews, but fall to fighting among themselves instead. Only the return of Pity reunites them, and then only in aggressive alliance against the virtue, whom they clap in irons before leaving for their night of debauchery.

Pity is left alone in the place to deliver a complaint about the sad state of the nation's morals, but is eventually released by his brother virtues, who resolve to search out Free Will and Imagination (no more is said of Hick, who disappears from the play) in order to convince them to repent. Thus, when Free Will does return, full of tales of a spell in Newgate and subsequent rescue by Imagination, Perseverance and Contemplation seek to persuade him to renounce his sinful life. At first he resists and threatens them with violence. But when confronted with the thought of his impending death and consequent damnation, he is induced to repent. This done, he and his new allies repeat the conversion process with Imagination, whose metamorphosis into 'Good Remembrance' brings the play to a close.

AUSPICES

The earliest known text of this short interlude is Wynkyn de Worde's black-letter edition printed at some point between 8 June 1515 and 5 September 1516.[3] On internal evidence the play seems to have been written only shortly before their first printing, most plausibly between August 1513 and August 1514, with Whitsun 1514 providing the most likely occasion for its first performance.[4] Like the other plays considered below *Hick Scorner* was evidently written for performance in a dining hall.[5] And from its seeming employment of East Midlands dialect and frequent knowing allusions to locations in London and Southwark it would appear to have been designed for performance there. Certainly the notional locale for the play's action is Southwark rather than the City, for Hick Scorner is said to arrive by ship *from* London, and Free Will leaves the place to obtain leg-irons and a rope from the King's Bench prison on Borough High Street, Southwark, an errand which leaves him absent for only twenty-six lines.[6] Moreover the drama is steeped in references to the Southwark area, the Stews and the Old Kent Road.[7]

This combination of dating and locale has prompted Ian Lancashire to suggest a performance in the great hall of a noble house in Southwark, of which there were only two of any note at this time; Manor Place (later Suffolk Place) the seat of Charles Brandon, Duke of Suffolk, and Winchester Palace, the London residence of Richard Fox, Bishop of Winchester and currently Henry VIII's Lord Privy Seal. As Lancashire argues, Suffolk

---

[3] A detailed exposition of the printing history of the play and much else besides can be found in Lancashire, pp. 1–96. I am indebted for much of what follows in this chapter to Professor Lancashire's pioneering and exemplary edition.

[4] Lancashire, pp. 22–4. As it is clearly based upon the earlier *Interlude of Youth*, it must post-date that play. The earliest convincing date for *Youth's* completion is August 1513; this therefore provides a *terminus a quo* for *Hick Scorner*. The allusion in the character of Hick to Richard de la Pole's prospective invasion of England (see below) is also helpful in this context, as only between May and August 1514 was this invasion a serious prospect. The play's origins can thus be located in the period May to August 1514. Lancashire's suggestion (p. 24) that the reference to Hick's broken 'poll' at line 450 alludes to an ignominious riot among de la Pole's German mercenaries during June–July 1514 seems less convincing.

[5] Free Will describes himself as a 'guest' at the performance (line 158) and invites the audience to 'fill the cup and make good cheer' at line 166. Both remarks suggest a dining-hall *milieu*.

[6] Lancashire, p. 33.

[7] Free Will and Imagination both claim to have slept at the Stews' side (lines 184 and 405). The latter also announces that he has been appointed Controller of the Stews and names two Southwark brothels which he will oversee, the *Bell* and the *Hart's Horn* (lines 898 and 901). References to Shooter's Hill and the gibbet at St Thomas-a-Watring (lines 543, 822 and 838) serve further to confirm a local knowledge on the part of the playwright.

seems by far the more likely patron of the two.[8] And a brief examination of the play-text confirms this suggestion.

Both the references to the Southwark area and those to the King's Bench prison suggest a performance in Manor Place. Unlike Fox, whose power-base and major sources of income were elsewhere, Brandon was much more obviously a 'Southwark man' at this time. Despite his East Anglian title and his favour at Court, Brandon's strongest links were still, during the first half of 1514 at least, with the London suburb. His noble title had been granted him only as recently as 1 February 1514, and he still faced a long struggle to establish himself in the eastern counties; a fact of consider-able importance for his political outlook, as what follows will suggest. He was far more securely established, both socially and economically, in Southwark.

With control of Manor Place came the office of Marshal of the King's Bench prison, a lucrative and influential title, for it enabled the holder to extract bribes and fees from his wealthier charges in return for an amelior-ation of their living conditions.[9] It also brought him into contract with the substantial citizens of the suburb through his work on local commissions and in other administrative functions. The local affinity which the Duke was able to build up through such contacts was, although small, to serve him well in these years. Thus when Free Will ran from the acting place to search for some fetters and returned, claiming to have obtained some from the King's Bench prison, the statement would, no doubt, have brought laughter in the Duke's household. Not only were the two buildings physi-cally close, almost facing one another across Borough High Street, they were also the twin poles of Brandon's local power.

A further link in the chains of prestige and influence linking the Duke to Southwark had been added during November 1511, when Henry VIII had bestowed upon him, in survivorship with Sir John Carew, the title of Marshal of the King's Household.[10] This appointment was no doubt chiefly a reflection of Brandon's influence with the King and was intended to bolster his status at Court. But it also brought some concrete, local, rewards. For the Marshal was *ex officio* also the keeper of the gaol attached to the court of Marshalsea (which heard cases arising from within the confines of the royal Court), a building located less than one hundred

---

[8] Lancashire, pp. 33–4.

[9] S. J. Gunn, *Charles Brandon, Duke of Suffolk* (Oxford, 1988), pp. 4–5. I am indebted to Dr Gunn's detailed researches into Brandon's career, published in the above and else-where, for much of the biographical material related in this chapter. I am also grateful for having had the opportunity to discuss Brandon and related matters with Dr Gunn on a number of occasions.

[10] Gunn, p. 4. Knyvet was to die within a year, leaving Brandon to exercise the office alone (see p. 57, below).

yards from the King's Bench prison.[11] With this charge came further opportunities for financial reward. For, although the number of prisoners passed on by the court of Marshalsea were few, a combination of prison overcrowding elsewhere and convenience prompted the sheriffs of both Surrey and Sussex and even the Royal Council itself in its judicial role to overlook statutory prohibitions and use Brandon's cells for their prisoners.[12]

For a number of reasons, then, Southwark bulked large in Brandon's life in a way which it did not in that of Bishop Fox. Hence the decision to set *Hick Scorner* in the suburb would have been quite natural if the play was to be performed in Suffolk's hall. Similarly, given the above, the play's otherwise curious concentration upon gaols and the paraphernalia of imprisonment and execution becomes more obviously relevant. For, if Brandon was anything in Southwark, he was a gaoler *par excellence*. Moreover, this aspect of his career was also, it seems, the subject of comment at Court, for he exploited it playfully during the tournament held at Windsor in February 1511, entering the field dressed in 'a long and course prisoners wede' and 'enclosid In a Towyr and led by a Jaylour holdyng a grete keye in his hand' with which Queen Katherine of Aragon was invited to release him.[13] In making such capital out of the discomforts of prisoners and the lengths to which they will go to escape punishment, then, the play again offers material singularly appropriate to Brandon's circumstances, and so likely to have amused an audience in his household.[14]

There is considerable evidence, then, to support the placing of the interlude within Brandon's household during 1514. And what is known of the Duke's household arrangements would further confirm this. Certainly Brandon sponsored a dramatic troupe during a slightly later period, for scholars of the history of drama have identified a number of references to his 'ludatores' and 'joculatores' touring East Anglia and elsewhere in the years 1521–45.[15] And it is quite reasonable to suppose that they were also active in the preceding period. There is also evidence of quasi-dramatic

---

[11] A sketch map which usefully illustrates the compactness of Brandon's Southwark power-base is printed in Lancashire, pp. 96–7.

[12] Gunn, p. 4.

[13] A. H. Thomas and I. D. Thornley, eds., *The Great Chronicle of London* (London, 1938), p. 372.

[14] The predominance of prison images in the play was evidently not accidental. In the play's source, *Youth*, there were some fifteen allusions to prisons, fetters or hanging, of which five were strictly necessary to the plot. In *Hick Scorner* there are thirty-seven, of which perhaps six are strictly functional.

[15] D. Galloway and J. Wasson, eds., *Records of Plays and Players in Norfolk and Suffolk, 1330–1640*, Malone Society Collections, XI (Oxford, 1980/1), pp. 12, 58, 113, 114, 225–6.

activities generated within the Brandon household itself. In the common-
place book of William Fellowe, Merlion Pursuivant, there is a record of
what appears to have been a disguising or dance with allegorical overtones
in the Duke's household during the mid-1520s. The younger men of
Brandon's affinity took such roles as 'Cur Noble', 'Valiant Desyr' and 'Bon
Pastaunce'; the women 'Mekenys', 'Beautie' and 'Dysport', in what was
evidently an imitation of the sort of entertainment Brandon enjoyed at
Court.[16]

Given the level of cultural activity suggested by this record, it is conceiv-
able that a member of Brandon's immediate household staff produced the
interlude. But it would be unwise to press too hard the candidature of any
particular individual.[17] What one can say is that the play clearly draws
upon Brandon's personal interests and activities in its choice of subject
matter and, as what follows will suggest, seems to direct much of its
didactic strategy towards him. In this it is of a piece with the other plays
considered in the following chapters. It is a persuasive document born out
of a particular set of political and cultural circumstances operating at a
given time. From the specific moral and religious interests which the play
seems to reveal it might be assumed that its author was a cleric. But this
would be no more than speculation. More certainly, as we shall see, he saw
his role as a playwright and purveyor of drama for his lord as analogous to
that of a spiritual counsellor as well as that of a political propagandist. In
that way he performed through his drama some of the functions of both
the household man and the cleric.

'HICK SCORNER' AS POLITICAL SATIRE

Perhaps the most obvious indications of Brandon's patronage of the play
are the very title of the piece itself and the curious relationship between the
eponymous character Hick and the rest of the action. As the summary of

---

[16] College of Arms MS R36, fo. 1v. I am grateful to Dr S. J. Gunn for this reference. The
names of the major male characters at least are borrowed directly from the Westminster
tournament of 1511 when four knights, three of whom bore the names 'Cure loyall'
(Henry VIII), 'Valiaunt desire' (Sir Edward Neville) and 'bon Voloire' (the Earl of
Devonshire), challenged before Katherine of Aragon. Hall, p. 517.

[17] Lancashire's suggestion (p. 34) that one Lewis Wynwood might have been the author, as
he had previous 'revels experience', remains highly conjectural. Wynwood's 'experience'
amounted to no more than the purchase of the materials for costumes for a mummery at
Greenwich in 1514, a task which fell within the purview of his normal role as the
purchaser of cloth for the Brandon household (*L.P.*, II (ii) 4448, p. 1501). Thus he need
not necessarily have been promising playwright-material. Even Lancashire's suggestion
that Wynwood 'functioned like Richard Gybson, one of the King's players and his revels
supervisor' (p. 85n) seems stretched.

the plot offered earlier indicated, the role that Hick Scorner plays in the interlude for which he provides a name is hardly fundamental. He appears approximately one third of the way through the play, speaks four set-piece comic speeches based upon lists (of countries, ships, virtues and vices) and then leaves the place, never to return. Although he is an integral part of the attack upon Pity, he does not return in the concluding episode to face retribution or undergo contrition. He is both part of the play and apart from it. His part is obviously an addition to the plot (no equivalent character appears in its source, *Youth*) but little effort seems to have been expended to integrate him into it. His very name sets him apart from the other characters. Unlike his fellow rogues, Free Will and Imagination, he is not an obvious personification of a theologically significant mental attribute. Nor does he represent a personal quality such as Pity, Contemplation or Perseverance. His is a proper name, albeit a proverbial one. If it is representative of anything it is his capacity to mock. He is Richard ('Hick') 'the Scorner'.[18]

Why should so awkward a character have been added to the tightly organized action of the original plot, particularly as it would have created additional strains upon the limited capacity for doubling of a small acting troupe?[19] The answer would seem to lie, as Ian Lancashire has demonstrated, in the significance of the name 'Hick' or Richard in the Brandon household and at the Henrician Court more generally at the time. For as the play was being performed, during the early summer of 1514, England was threatened with an invasion led by another 'Hick', Richard de la Pole, pretender to both the Suffolk dukedom and the English Crown.[20]

De la Pole had fled from England in August 1501 after the discovery of an alleged conspiracy against Henry VII. Whilst his other brothers were imprisoned, Richard travelled through Europe attempting to raise support for his family's claims to the throne. In Germany and Hungary he enjoyed little success. But Louis XII of France was more sympathetic.

Whilst England and France were at war the French King was prepared to support de la Pole's ambitions with men and money. And consequently the prospect of an invasion was looked upon with some disquiet by the authorities in England throughout the early months of the 1514

---

[18] Note the account of the provenance and continuation of the proverbial usage in Lancashire, Appendix II.
[19] As Lancashire suggests (p. 32), the text seems designed for use by a small, four-man, troupe.
[20] Much of what follows in the next two paragraphs is conveniently gathered together in Lancashire, pp. 239–42.

campaigning season.[21] Rumours that de la Pole was planning to cross to Scotland in the company of the Duke of Albany, the heir presumptive to the Scottish Crown, and an army of German mercenaries were passed on to the council on 5 June. Ten days later the invaders were said to be still waiting in Normandy for favourable weather.[22] Only with the completion of an Anglo-French peace treaty on 7 August did the threat recede and de la Pole withdraw to Lorraine.[23]

In portraying a character called 'Richard', who was in the process of 'invading' Southwark with a crew of five thousand vices, then, the play alludes to a matter of considerable current significance to an English audience in the first half of 1514. Moreover, that significance had an added personal element for Charles Brandon, as de la Pole was not only laying claim to the English Crown, but also to Brandon's newly won ducal title. The de la Poles had been formally deprived of the dukedom of Suffolk in 1493. But first Edmund (executed by Henry VIII in 1513) and then Richard continued to style themselves duke. Thus, when Henry VIII elevated Brandon to the dukedom on 1 February 1514, he did so, not only to reward a close companion with a prestigious and vacant title, but also publicly to establish the impotence of de la Pole's claims. By virtue of his title alone, then, Brandon was forced to consider Richard de la Pole his enemy. Personal ambition combined with loyalty to his king to make Brandon the one nobleman in England most hostile to the, so-called, White Rose's invasion plans.

The circumstances of de la Pole's prospective invasion and Brandon's position as the incumbent Duke of Suffolk clearly help to explain the intrusion of Hick Scorner into a play which, under other circumstances, would probably have been entitled 'the Interlude of Free Will' or 'Freewill and Imagination'. The appreciation of this topical element in the drama and its domination of the morality format which contains it would account for the otherwise curious decision to name the piece after what would appear on solely internal evidence to be a relatively minor character. An appreciation of the position of the play in relation to the Brandon

---

21 Lancashire is probably correct in concluding (p. 241) that it is 'hard to believe' that de la Pole posed any real threat to Henry's rule. But such assessments are easier with hindsight. During the summer of 1514 the prospect of an invasion would have seemed far more worrying, and the possibility that de la Pole might arouse popular support were he to land in Britain could not have been easily dismissed. After all, Henry Tudor had succeeded in winning the Crown under only slightly more promising circumstances.
22 *L.P.* I (ii) 2947; B.L. Cotton MS Caligula, E, I, fo. 26 (*L.P.* I (ii) 3004).
23 *L.P.* I (ii) 3029, 3129, 3165; B.L. MS Additional, 21,382, fo. 63 (*L.P.* I (ii) 3240); Hall, p. 569.

household and Tudor dynastic politics generally would have concentrated attention upon Hick's appearance almost to the exclusion of all else.[24]

Reading Hick's appearance in the light of de la Pole's claims also helps to elucidate some of the more baffling aspects of his role. The lists which constitute the bulk of his speeches seem less idiosyncratic, for example, if read against this background. The seventeen-line catalogue of the countries which he claims to have visited (ranging from the plausible – France, Ireland, Spain – to the fantastic – 'the new found isle' (line 315) and 'the land of rumbelow / Three mile out of hell' (lines 317–18)) obviously provides the materials for a comic tour-de-force in the hands of a skilful actor. But it also serves to undermine de la Pole's political credibility. For, as we have seen, much of his time during the past decade had been spent in fruitless diplomatic journeys through Europe, attempting to win practical support for his ambitions. By expanding these journeys to ludicrous extremes, the playwright turns de la Pole from a political threat into a figure of ridicule. And much of the dialogue with Free Will and Imagination pursues a similar strategy.

Hick is portrayed as leading, not an army of mercenaries, but a shipload of vices, the dregs of society,

> ... thieves and whores, with other good company,
> Liars, backbiters and flatterers the while,
> Brawlers, liars, getters and chiders,
> Walkers by night with great murderers,
> Overthwart Guile and jolly carders,
> Oppressors of people with many swearers.
>
> (lines 369–74)

He is not their military commander, but their whoremaster, running a brothel on the ship for his own profit. When Free Will and Imagination fall to brawling among themselves, he is unable to restore order and indeed proves a poor fighter, taking a buffet on the head for his pains and complaining pathetically to the audience, with what appears to be a heavy-handed reference to his historical analogue, that Imagination has 'made a great hole in my *poll*' (line 450).[25]

Hick's recital of the names of ships allegedly sunk during an expedition

[24] If the performance had proved a success in exploiting this topical subject matter, naming the play after its most obviously controversial character, and thereby stressing its political character, might well increase sales of the text. As only printed versions of the play survive it is impossible to know whether it was the original author or the first printer, de Worde, who decided to name the play in this form.

[25] My italics. The fact that Free Will refers, three lines earlier, to Hick and Imagination being 'in a mill *pool* above the arse' (line 447, my italics) would seem to confirm the specific intention behind the later line.

to Ireland provides a further strand in this strategy of denigration. As Ian Lancashire has shown, a number of the vessels referred to did actually sink or run aground in the years between 1510 and 1514.[26] The most notable of these was the *Regent*, a royal ship which had gone down in flames after a close engagement with the French warship *Cordelière* off Brest on 10 August 1512, killing one of Henry VIII's closest companions, Sir Thomas Knyvet and, *inter alia*, another courtier, Sir John Carew.

Joking references to the loss of the *Regent* would have been in poor taste anywhere in England during the early 1510s. Not only had the English Court lost one of its luminaries as a direct result of the action, but perhaps the most prominent courtier of Henry VIII's early years, Sir Edward Howard, had also died in a tragic sequel to the event. In a doomed chivalric gesture of the sort much admired by Henry's tilt-yard companions of these years, Howard had vowed to avenge the death of Knyvet or die in the attempt. And in April 1513 he was indeed to die as the result of a reckless boarding action during another sea-fight.[27] But if the loss of two of Henry's leading courtiers was greeted as a general calamity by the English political elite,[28] for Charles Brandon it had a particular poignancy. Brandon was a notable member of that small circle of royal jousting companions from which the two men had come, and had himself been involved in the earlier sea-battle. In the company of Sir Henry Guildford, another of the King's circle, he had been forced to watch from the deck of another ship as the *Regent* had sunk, taking Knyvet with it. Moreover, with Howard's subsequent death he had lost perhaps his closest personal friend.[29]

The passing allusion to the *Regent* in the midst of a comic speech would, then, have been especially pointed in its cruelty within the context of the Brandon household. To place it in the mouth of Hick Scorner consequently marked him out as a particularly vicious and unregenerate villain. As a result he becomes, not only an enemy of all virtue (and, by analogy, an enemy of the realm), but beyond the moral pale in a way largely unparalleled in previous morality drama.

In the play's direct source, *Youth*, and in other extant examples of the morality tradition, the vice characters are clearly marked off from their victims and from their adversaries, the virtues, by their love of excess, their evident coarseness, anarchy and numerous other stylistic indicators of

---

[26] Lancashire, pp. 245–53.
[27] Hall, pp. 533 and 537.
[28] Note the elegy for Howard in Alexander Barclay's fourth *Eclogue*, B. White, ed., *The Eclogues of Alexander Barclay*, E.E.T.S. (Oxford, 1928), pp. 169–80. See also *L.P.* I (ii) 1844.
[29] A measure of Howard's trust and affection for Brandon may be seen in his decision to name the latter as joint-executor (with Lady Howard) of his will. He also offered Brandon the wardship of one of his two bastard sons, Gunn, pp. 8–9.

folly in all its forms. In *Hick Scorner*, however, they are also characterized by a degree of social and moral depravity which is startling. There is a particularly black and macabre 'comedy' to the central sections of this interlude. As was mentioned above, the play-text is shot through with allusions to bondage and execution. Each of the vices boasts of his ability to cheat death and delights in his capacity to inflict suffering on others. All vice characters display these tendencies to some degree, but here the emphasis seems subtly different. The immorality of these vices is more substantial and vivid than that of, for example, New Guise, Nowadays and Nought in *Mankind*. For all their comic brawling there is literally a biting edge to their villainy; a hint of social realism which forces the audience to confront the actual physical cost of the crimes which they propose.

Whereas in *Mankind* the fighting is done with a spade and the impact is comic, in *Hick Scorner* it is knife-play to which the vices revert at times of crisis, and the consequences of this less sanitized violence are not avoided.

> Every man bear his dagger naked in his hand
> And if we meet a true man, make him stand,
> Or else that he bear a stripe.
> If that he struggle and make any work,
> Lightly strike him to the heart
> And throw him into Thames quite.
>
> (lines 413–18)[30]

This attention to the business of disposing of the body gives the violence a realistic aspect that reflects back upon its perpetrators. As with Hick's amused indifference at the loss of the *Regent*, it serves to isolate the vices from the rest of humanity and to give them an overtly evil quality not common among others of their type. And whilst Free Will and Imagination are both brought to repentance in the play and so reabsorbed within virtuous society, Hick remains unreformed. He has no place in the scenes of reconciliation. And this aspect of his role accords with the position of his historical counterpart, Richard de la Pole, in the eyes of Brandon's supporters. Again the aim is clearly to portray de la Pole as an irredeemable villain, a man who is at once both personally contemptible and a genuine moral and physical threat to society against whom the audience should protect themselves.

---

[30] The overt violence in *Youth* is restricted to the retelling of how Riot 'took' a youth 'on the ear' and stole his purse. The only vice figure in the morality tradition who even approaches the level of nastiness inherent in *Hick Scorner* is, perhaps, Mischief in the darker second half of *Mankind*, who boasts of killing his jailor and abusing his wife, although even here the actual details of the deed are not elaborated in the same way as in the passage quoted above.

GOOD COUNCIL: 'HICK SCORNER' AS A MIRROR FOR A DUKE?

In some ways, then, the play acts as an obvious reflection of Charles Brandon's political interests. By ridiculing de la Pole through the figure of Hick it performed an effective propaganda function whilst at the same time providing entertainment for its partisan audience. The concentration upon the business of imprisonment and the cruel humour at the expense of the imprisoned would no doubt also have prompted knowing smiles from Brandon and his affinity. But it would be premature to leave an account of the play's contemporary significances there. For there are aspects of its propaganda function which deserve closer attention. As with all propaganda it is important to consider the anxieties which stimulated it as well as the apparent confidence which it articulates. And by examining the complex relationship between Brandon's territorial ambitions and de la Pole's dynastic claims both aspects of the play can be brought into sharper focus. Moreover, there are also parts of the play which, on close inspection, prove to be far from supportive of Brandon's claims and sit uneasily with the idea of a 'propaganda' play in any simple sense of the word. In what follows both aspects of the play-text will be examined and it will be suggested that, for all the simplicity of its plot, *Hick Scorner* proves to be both morally and politically a more complex and interesting play than it initially appears.

Although at the time of the first performance of the play Brandon was one of a very select band of men who enjoyed both high noble title and the close confidence of the Sovereign, he was nonetheless very much a *parvenu* in Tudor aristocratic terms.[31] His rise to rank and favour had been meteoric. In 1503 he had been no more than a minor functionary, a Sewer for the Board's-end, at the court of Henry VII. By the time of Henry's death he had improved his lot noticeably, but still only modestly, to the rank of Esquire for the Body. It was with the accession of Henry VIII that his fortunes began to change markedly. His combination of sporting prowess, good looks and affability immediately recommended him to the new king and he was soon drawn into the group of royal favourites which included Sir Edward Howard, Sir Thomas Knyvet and the half-brothers Sir Edward and Henry Guildford. With royal favour came social and political elevation. On 6 October 1512 he was appointed Master of the Horse in succession to Knyvet, a post which formalized his status as Henry's companion in arms, as the Master acted as squire to the Sovereign on ceremonial occasions. With the coming of war with France in 1513 he was created Viscount Lisle and named High Marshal of the army with which Henry invaded France. Although his actual command was limited to the

---

[31] For this and what follows, see Gunn, pp. 5–27.

3,000 men of the vanguard of the King's ward, the marshalcy brought with it the far greater social distinction of nominal authority over all subordinate commanders, some of whom were of the high nobility. And by 1 February 1514 he had himself become one of their number. As Duke of Suffolk he was formally ranked the fifth most eminent peer in the land.[32]

So phenomenal a rise brought with it problems more fundamental than the sheer vertigo of success. In an age when ancient title and lineage were considered prerequisite for social respectability Brandon's arrival among the elite of the realm was bound to arouse both surprise and resentment. The Duke of Buckingham, the senior English peer, was said to have expressed privately his disgust at Brandon's elevation. Others were more open. The chronicler Polydore Vergil noted that 'many people considered it very surprising that Charles [Brandon] should be so honoured as to be made a duke', and Erasmus disparagingly compared the Master of the Horse to a drunken stable-hand risen above his station.[33]

It was not only resentment and name-calling which Brandon had to face, however. His new-found eminence also presented a number of serious practical problems. A noble title brought with it responsibilities as well as privileges, and none more so than the former title of the de la Pole Dukes of Suffolk. In accepting that particular honour Brandon was taking on, not only the normal social and political requirements of nobility, the need to keep up appearances, to dispense hospitality and act as a good lord to his neighbours, but also to supplant any vestiges of loyalty to the de la Poles and quickly and efficiently establish himself in the title. It is the duke's inability effectively to perform these last functions in the short term which, more than anything else, underlies the ridicule of de la Pole in *Hick Scorner*. Unable to demonstrate his superiority to the pretender in concrete political terms, Brandon seems to have commissioned the playwright to do so through the vehicle of dramatic propaganda.

Brandon's inability quickly to adopt and maintain the manner, style and functions of a nobleman had been evident even before his elevation to the ducal title. As Steven Gunn has shown, his lack of a loyal personal affinity had proved a liability when he acquired the title of Viscount Lisle in May 1513. Unable to insert men of his own into the key administrative offices on his new estates, Brandon was forced to rely largely upon those already there, regardless of their potentially suspect loyalty. And his inability to draw a personal following from among his tenants was revealed during the

[32] Ibid., p. 1.
[33] B.L. MS Egerton, 985, fos. 60–61v; *L.P.* III (i) 1284 (ii); P. S. Allen, ed., *Opus Epistolarum Desiderii Erasmi Roterodami* (12 vols., Oxford, 1906–58), I. 550–1 (*L.P.* I (ii) 2610); Gunn, p. 26.

military campaigns of 1513 and 1514, when he was to raise his troops, not from the Lisle estates, but through his royal offices in Wales and elsewhere and from the one area where he enjoyed real influence, the borough of Southwark.[34]

With the acquisition of the Suffolk dukedom these problems were to multiply many-fold. Brandon proved more than capable of matching his more experienced peers in the adoption of the paraphernalia of nobility. By 1513 he had, for example, already acquired the services of a Lisle Pursuivant.[35] But the financial and social bases for his new-found status proved harder to secure, particularly as the landed wealth upon which the de la Pole dukedom had rested came only slowly into his hands. The title itself had been accompanied by only one grant, in tail male, of the manor, castle and park of Donnington, Berkshire, with an annuity of £40 out of the counties of Norfolk, Suffolk and Cambridge.[36] Brandon's wealth effectively still rested at this stage upon his wardship of Elizabeth, Baroness Lisle, and the control of her estates which that gave him. On 1 February 1515 he was to gain almost all of the de la Pole estates, but even then largely only in the form of reversionary grants, requiring him to buy out the existing grantees.[37] His attempt to establish himself as a power in East Anglia was a long and hard-fought struggle. It involved not only the realization of his control over the former de la Pole lands, but also the shouldering out of Howard and de Vere influences which had spread into the former ducal lands after the de la Poles' disgrace. In 1514 this struggle was only just beginning and Brandon controlled no more than 4 per cent of the erstwhile Suffolk lands.[38]

Brandon's predicament was thus complex and demanded a correspondingly sophisticated strategy to overcome it. The most effective way to assert himself against both old pretenders and new interlopers alike was to reassert the cohesion of the Suffolk estates, attempting to reforge an affinity within them based upon old ducal loyalties, whilst simultaneously stressing the legitimacy of his own title and denigrating the person and claims of his de la Pole rival. In so doing he might capitalize upon deep-rooted local loyalties without arousing sympathy for the 'White

---

[34] Gunn, p. 24.   [35] Ibid., p. 25.   [36] *L.P.* I (ii) 2684(5).

[37] Because of the length of time between the de la Poles' removal from their dukedom and their replacement by Brandon, the estates as a whole suffered from a prolonged 'interregnum'. Into the power vacuum thus created moved a number of other families, most notably the Howards and the de Veres. Thus it was not simply the case that Brandon had to win over an existing de la Pole affinity. In the interim, power had fragmented, creating a far more complex situation. Suffolk was thus 'a new man with no old shoes to step into' (Gunn, p. 53).

[38] Gunn, pp. 31–42.

Rose'. The problem was as much one of image as of economic powers, as the methods Brandon used to tackle it reflect.

As soon as the grants giving him title to these lands had been made he instructed his agents to begin the arduous process of raising the money to acquire them outright. But, even before this, he had begun to assert his claims to the de la Pole legacy through more subtle means. As Steven Gunn has demonstrated, on his accession the Duke immediately refashioned his seal, which would be carried upon all his official correspondence, to include his arms, notably the Brandon lion rampant *queue fourchee*; a conscious evocation of the Chaucer lion rampant *queue fourchee* of the de la Pole seals.[39] In the absence of a powerful dynastic tradition of his own to draw upon, Brandon was seemingly attempting to hijack that of his rivals for his own ends. Nor apparently was the new duke averse to employing the other artistic and cultural resources at his disposal for political ends. His household entertainers, the acting troupe, trumpeters and bearwards who bore his name, were very active throughout East Anglia, outdoing the Howards' companies in the number of their performances in what may well have been a conscious policy of asserting Brandon's lordship through the locality against that of his potential rivals.[40]

And it is into this continuing effort to assert his authority in East Anglia which we might most profitably set the interlude of *Hick Scorner*. Although its original auspices were clearly in Southwark, it was quickly absorbed into the repertoire of the travelling acting companies, as its rapid publication in 1515/16 and its subsequent reprinting in 1525–9 seems to suggest.[41] Was it one of the plays which Brandon's 'ludatores' took on tour through the East Anglian towns? The logic of Brandon's position would suggest that it may have been.

Yet, if *Hick Scorner* is a 'propaganda' play, it is not so in any simplistic way. It criticizes Brandon's rival Richard de la Pole, certainly, and so plays its part in the furtherance of its patron's political and social ambitions. In this respect it no doubt performed the role which the Duke would have expected of it. But, like all morality plays, it is also a didactic piece. It seems to educate and improve its audience at the same time as it entertains and flatters them. And its moralizing content, like its political content, has a specific relevance to Brandon and to the circumstances of its first performance.

In a number of separate episodes within the play (the meeting of the

[39] Ibid., p. 40.
[40] Galloway and Wesson, *Records*, pp. 221–2, 225–6; Gunn, p. 53; I. Lancashire, ed., *Dramatic Texts and Records of Britain: A Chronological Topography to 1558* (Cambridge, 1984), pp. 376–7. The very limited amount of evidence prevents any certainty about this apparent trend, however.
[41] Lancashire, pp. 8–9.

virtues, Pity's complaint and Imagination's 'confession' of his crimes) characters itemize what they claim are the prevailing abuses of a sinful age. This is, of course, a timeless dramatic and literary motif, but it draws in a number of specific contemporary issues. The long-running debate over 'benefit of clergy' is alluded to in Imagination's claim that he and his cronies are 'clerks all and can our neck verse' (line 266). Abuses of the rights of sanctuary – which were to prompt Wolsey's campaign against this immunity in later years – are acknowledged in Contemplation's concern that the vices should not evade capture by that route (line 640). And the chequered career of the financier John Baptist de Grimaldi seems to have provided the material for Imagination's tale of a stolen horse at lines 270–96.[42] In this way *Hick Scorner* accommodates contemporary public issues within its treatment of more conventional abuses. But there is more immediately pertinent material to be found there too, which a close reading of the text in its contemporary political context reveals.

When Pity describes the woes of society, for example, he does so in terms which seem on the surface simply an uncontentious rehearsal of timeless general issues.

> I have heard many men complain piteously;
> They say they be smitten with the sword of Poverty
> In every place where I do go.
> Few friends Poverty doth find,
> And these rich men be unkind;
> For their neighbours they will nought do.
>
> (lines 103–8)

The unhappy lot of the poor had provided material for every satirist and social critic since classical times. Thus it is unsurprising that scholars have failed to identify a specific significance in these lines for the play's original audience. But that significance is nonetheless pointed, as what follows will suggest. And the lines' applicability becomes more obvious still as Pity goes on to describe a particular instance of rich men's 'unkindness'.

> Widows doth curse lords and gentlemen,
> For they constrain them to marry with their men,
> Yea, whether they will or no.
> Men marry for good[s], and that is damnable,
> Yea with old women that is fifty and beyond.
> The peril now no man dread will.
> All is not God's law that is used in land.
>
> (lines 109–15)

[42] Ibid., pp. 242–3.

As Ian Lancashire notes, this reference to (by implication younger) men marrying widows of 'fifty and beyond' had a specific and very topical relevance to Brandon.[43] For his name was being publically linked with that of Margaret of Savoy, the Regent of the Netherlands, during the early months of 1514. Rumours of an impending marriage had been started by Henry VIII when the King and Brandon, then merely Viscount Lisle, had dined with Margaret at Tournai during the French campaign of 1513. A polite exchange of compliments between Brandon and the Regent had been seized upon by Henry as the occasion for playful romantic speculation and the suggestion of a possible marriage was raised, 'seeing that it was the fashion of the ladies of England' to remarry 'at forty and three-score' (Margaret was herself a widow and well into middle age).[44] But the story took on a life of its own and soon got out of hand. By the end of the year the rumour was hard currency in London and bets were being laid upon the prospects. On 7 February 1514 the Venetian Ambassador, Badoer, was reporting the suggestion that Henry would 'give [Brandon] Margaret for a wife'. And by 29 July it was said that a marriage contract had been agreed between the two. News of the affair had even reached the Imperial Court.[45] The diplomatic repercussions of what had started out as a mischievous royal joke had quickly become more serious and Henry was forced to kill off the monster of his own creation with threats of death for the 'rumour mongers' when Margaret herself wrote to protest at the damage being done to her honour.[46]

There was thus an obviously comic aspect to Pity's allusion to men marrying older widows. Mention of this particular social 'abuse' could hardly have avoided reopening the long-running joke at Brandon's expense. But the reference also had its more serious side, and one which the Duke would have found less easy to dismiss with a laugh. For the hypothetical romance with Margaret was just one episode in Brandon's complex and unpleasant marital history.

As we have seen, many of Brandon's social and political problems arose from his being elevated to noble rank and authority further and more quickly than his power-base could sustain. And this problem carried with it a related financial dimension. Throughout his career Brandon was dogged by lack of money, a problem which his continued promotions did nothing to alleviate. Without the landed base to support his titles, the Duke was forever raising loans, needing to find the means in the short term to buy the estates which would yield profits at some point in the future.

[43] Ibid., p. 167n.   [44] L.P. I (ii) 2941.

[45] Ven. Cal., II (1509–19), 382, 464; Hall, pp. 566 and 568; L.P. I (i) 568; (ii) 2654, 2700, 2736, 3104.

[46] L.P. I (ii) 2941, 2654, 2701.

One way of bridging the gap between current income and expenditure was to exploit his favour with the King to obtain lucrative wardships. Another was to marry money. Both were cynically combined in his purchase from Henry (for £1,400 payable over seven years) of the wardship of Elizabeth, Baroness Lisle, the eight-year-old daughter of his dead friend Sir Thomas Knyvet. When Knyvet's widow, Muriel, died in December 1512, Brandon was free to milk her daughter's estates at will. He contracted to marry the child when she came of age, thereby enabling him to claim the title of Viscount Lisle, but probably never seriously intended to complete the match. The contract was sufficient, however, to keep the Lisle lands firmly under his control.[47]

Marriage in the Tudor period, particularly within the social elite, carried few of the romantic connotations cherished by modern sensibilities. Thus Brandon's exploitation of the young Baroness Lisle might have been forgiven him, were it not for the fact that this was simply one of a series of financially motivated marital adventures. As his biographer candidly observes, Brandon's marital history 'demonstrated an asset-stripping opportunism which even contemporaries found rather shocking'.[48]

He had originally abandoned one fiancée, Anne Browne, daughter to Sir Anthony Browne of Calais (despite the fact that she may well have been carrying his child), in order to marry her aunt, Dame Margaret Mortimer, a woman twenty years his senior, so as to obtain the estates of the Mortimer family and the lands inherited from the Marquess of Montagu which she brought with her. A number of these he quickly sold off or used as the security for loans, before having the marriage dissolved on grounds of consanguinity. These latter he promptly compounded by returning to the niece, Anne Browne, and marrying her.[49] After her death came the contract with the young Baroness Lisle, whose estates were used as the basis for his pursuit of the still larger prize of the Suffolk lands. Finally he was to marry Mary, the sister of Henry VIII, in a clandestine ceremony in France, and so gained nominal access to her substantial wealth as the dowager Queen of France. This last marriage is traditionally regarded as a great romantic adventure. But, given the above, it might as easily be seen as the apotheosis of Brandon's cynical use of marriage for his own ambitious ends.

For Pity to castigate those men who 'marry for good[s]' and to describe the practice as 'damnable', had, then, a very specific relevance in the context of the Brandon household. So too did the earlier allusion in the same speech to rich men's 'unkindness' to their neighbours and the poor (lines 107–8). For the financial overstretching which was the result of

47 Gunn, pp. 20–21.   48 Ibid., p. 28.   49 Ibid., pp. 28–9.

Brandon's social aspirations had forced him to employ a number of expedients far removed from the ideal, liberal, aristocratic lifestyle.[50] During the spring of 1514 he had illegally confiscated a cargo of papal alum from a Florentine merchant and extorted a 'fine' for its return, using the merchandise in the interim as collateral for a loan of 1,000 crowns. His 'unchivalrous meanness'[51] also extended to more mundane matters. In an effort to pare costs to a minimum he even instructed the under-steward of the Lisle estate of Chaddesley Corbett to purchase the parchment necessary for his audits out of his own wages; an expedient which, unsurprisingly, was strongly resisted. Evidently, behind the facade of a noble lifestyle, Brandon was forced to resort to a number of unbecoming strategies in order to make ends meet: a fact perhaps best symbolized by his behaviour on the occasion of his creation as a Duke.

At the ceremony he appeared in a magnificent gown of violet velvet trimmed with sable, valued at around £200. This no doubt had the desired impressive effect. But tradition demanded that the gown be given after the ceremony as a gift to Garter King-of-Arms. This Brandon was prepared to do in public. But, once the ceremony was complete, he immediately despatched a servant to reclaim the gown, offering Garter King instead a cheaper one, the money to buy a doublet and a £4 annuity.[52] Brandon's financial priorities could evidently not make exceptions, even for royal heralds.

Once the immediate social context of Pity's remarks is appreciated, then, they take on an entirely new significance. Far from being merely general comments they had a very individual relevance. Indeed, it is difficult to avoid the conclusion that the playwright was using the occasion of the play, not only to further his patron's political and social ambitions, but also to remind him, in as sharp a manner as possible, of the responsibilities which the realization of those ambitions entailed. If Brandon intended to be a great nobleman, the speech suggests, he should begin to act more like one and abandon his less chivalrous financial expedients. If the writer was indeed a member of the Brandon household, this 'lecture from below' serves as a useful reminder of the reciprocal nature of the bonds of patronage. The household man or client is prepared to serve his lord and bolster the latter's honour and dignity through that service. But the former also has his own honour to maintain, and to serve a lord who is seen to be acting dishonourably – failing to live up to the high expectations which the aristocratic ideal aroused – would reflect dishonourably upon the servant too. In a 'community of honour', honour was indeed communal property. Hence the playwright takes on the role of

50 Ibid., pp. 21–2.   51 Ibid., p. 21.   52 Ibid., p. 22.

the good counsellor, bringing unwelcome but necessary advice in warning
Brandon to amend his ways.

A combination of this awareness of Brandon's political and social
responsibilities and a concern for his eventual spiritual salvation seems to
underlie the playwright's warning. For Pity concludes his complaint with
religious rather than political guidance. Such erring rich men, he declares,
should not trust too greatly in God's mercy for their eventual salvation.
God is just as well as forgiving, and if the sinner does not merit a place in
Heaven, there is a danger that he will not get one. Mercy cannot be ensured
in every case.

> The peril now no man dread will.
> All is not God's law that used is in land.
> Beware will they not till Death in his hand
> Taketh his sword and smiteth assunder the life vain,
> And with his mortal stroke cleaveth the heart atwain.
> They trust so in mercy, the lantern of brightness,
> That nothing do they dread God's rightwiseness.
>
> (lines 114–20)

That this statement precedes the main action of a play dominated by
references to the arbitrary and even cruel aspects of human justice, and is
spoken, not by a character symbolic of divine correction or justice, but by
Pity, whose sympathies should be with the sinner, serve only to reinforce
its impact.

On closer examination, then, the play proves very much a two-edged
political weapon. Its didactic moral functions are not entirely subsumed
within its political purpose. There remain uncomfortable lessons for its
audience to learn. And this is nowhere more obvious than in the play's
most remarkable moment of apparent bad taste; the joking reference to
the sinking of the *Regent*, with its tacit allusion to the deaths of Brandon's
former companions.

The decision to refer to this event in this manner could have been no
light matter. For the playwright to have included the allusion he must have
had in mind a use for it sufficiently serious to justify the apparent risk. As
has been suggested, the intrusion into the comic business of so startling a
reference to a real and personal loss would clearly have placed its speaker,
Hick, beyond the moral pale. The Brandon household could not have read
his character favourably after that speech, however engaging his subsequent antics. But the emotional and moral resonances which the allusion
created may well have served another function too.

As with the pointed criticisms of noblemen who marry for money
and fail to practice the appropriate degree of charity and liberality, the
reference to the *Regent* seems likely to have been designed to prompt

Brandon to examine his own conduct and the path by which he had risen
to his current eminence. For the deaths of his fellow courtiers on the
Regent and thereafter were also the occasion of Brandon's own rise to
prominence at court. With the sinking of the *Regent* he lost a friend, but
gained a series of offices. Had Sir Thomas Knyvet not died, Brandon would
not have gained the former's prestigious title of Master of the Horse, and
the formal proximity to the King which it bestowed. Nor would he have
obtained the wardship of the infant Baroness Lisle, whose wealth gave him
the financial resources he so badly needed. Similarly, his appointment as
Marshal of the King's Household had been granted in survivorship with
Sir John Carew. With Carew's death in the sea-fight he gained sole control
of the office.[53] Moreover, it was only with the death of Sir Edward
Howard, who was at that point the nearest thing to a royal favourite at the
English Court, that Brandon began to rise to prominence within the circle
of the King's closest friends. With Howard gone, it was to Brandon whom
Henry looked as a comrade in arms. Thereafter he accompanied Henry in
the lists and in courtly disguisings more often than any other individual.[54]
As his biographer notes, with Howard's death, Brandon 'lost the one rival
who consistently outshone him in the court and in war', 'it was the fact
that Howard would not be coming home . . . that set the seal on Brandon's
rise'.[55]

The destruction of the *Regent*, then, for all its tragic consequences, was
also the event which, more than any other, provided the basis for Brandon's ultimate success as a courtier and companion of the King *par
excellence*. In reminding the Duke of this fact, the playwright achieves a
remarkable dramatic effect, combining a powerful demonstration of the
morally compromised foundations of his worldly success, with a startling
memento mori. Reference to the ship stresses that even in the life of the
most flamboyant of courtiers there is always the imminent prospect of
death. Worldly glory is both transient and grounded upon suspect foundations. Like the protagonist of the play, Brandon enjoys the free will to
choose or reject the virtuous lifestyle. But as Pity warns him, it is the
prudent man who abandons sin earlier rather than later. With the spoonful
of political sugar offered him in the play's attacks upon his rival, the Duke
was nonetheless obliged to endure some unpalatable moral and spiritual
medicine.

CODA: BEYOND CRITICISM?

The appearance of so critical a play in Brandon's household, of course,
raises new questions of its own. How could a playwright, even if he was a

[53] Ibid., p. 4.   [54] Ibid., pp. 8–10.   [55] Ibid., p. 9.

household officer or retainer, have hoped to get away with such apparently unsubtle criticism of his lord and still keep his job? If Tudor aristocrats were the 'over-mighty' and arrogant men of standard accounts, they surely would not have tolerated such implied criticism. But how, then, do we account for the play?

Perhaps much depended upon the accidents of individual personality. What might have been considered dangerous insubordination in the household of a man like Edward Stafford, Duke of Buckingham, may have aroused less indignation from a Brandon or a Howard. Yet there may also be a more fundamental explanation for the apparent problem.

Perhaps, as the previous chapter suggested, models of Tudor political activity which see poets, playwrights and other writers as necessarily potentially dissenting voices and so repressed and hedged around with censorship and danger are too simplistic to account for more than a minority of cases. Perhaps political debate was rather freer, within certain bounds, than we are prone to think. It is possible that the very act of writing or speaking within a literary or dramatic context gave one a licence otherwise unavailable. In an age when literature was seen as a didactic medium and employed for largely moral ends, perhaps unpalatable moral advice was a recognized part of the dramatic function and subjecting oneself to it seen (in part at least) as itself a self-improving act.

More obviously, the suggestion that the performance of *Hick Scorner* took place within Brandon's own household may provide the explanation for the playwright's apparent boldness. For this, despite the probably considerable size of the gathering, would have been an essentially private forum. For the play to voice criticisms of Brandon there was a very different prospect from it doing so outside the affinity, particularly in the household of another nobleman.

Within the household the retainer had a licence, even a duty, to speak his mind. The notion of 'good counsel' provided both the stimulus for offering harsh advice and a framework which partially neutralized its harmful implications. For all officers aspired to be good counsellors and the aspiring good-lord would pride himself on their presence within his entourage. One of the prime distinguishing characteristics of the virtuous prince, as advice literature proclaimed, was his capacity to employ such good counsellors rather than merely flatterers. In offering Brandon the plain-spoken advice of *Hick Scorner*, then, the playwright may not have needed to fear his lord's anger. For, however unwelcome its moral strictures, the play also proclaimed, by its very existence, Brandon's capacity to surpass his inadequacies. For only in the household of an essentially virtuous prince would such counsel be welcome. Moreover, the Duke could not react with hostility to the play, for this would appear to confirm his moral degeneracy. Rather he would welcome its criticism and thereby prove his essential virtue. If the play did indeed contain harsh medicine, that may, paradoxically, have made it all the more politically acceptable. For the willingness to take one's medicine suggested a proper concern for one's health, a point which should be borne in mind when considering the second play under scrutiny here, John Skelton's *Magnyfycence*.

Chapter 3

A DOMESTIC DRAMA: JOHN SKELTON'S *MAGNYFYCENCE* AND THE ROYAL HOUSEHOLD

THE AUTHOR

John Skelton (*c.* 1460–1529) was a scholar and poet whose life was spent in and around the Tudor Court, mainly on its margins. The high point of his career came in the last years of the fifteenth century when he became tutor to the future Henry VIII, then only the younger son of Henry VII. With the death of Henry's older brother, Prince Arthur, in 1502, the Prince became Heir Apparent, an elevation which brought him both a new household and a new schoolmaster. Skelton was dismissed with only a gift of 40s. and the living of Diss in Norfolk as a reward. Thereafter he spent his time attempting to secure a return to royal service through the production of verse and prose on apposite political themes. During 1513 he was briefly employed to write patriotic verses to celebrate Henry VIII's victories at Tournai and Therouanne, but it was not until 1523 that he received a major commission to write for the Court, paradoxically in the form of a request for propaganda verses against the Scots from Cardinal Wolsey, the chief minister whom Skelton had viciously satirized in a series of poems written in the previous years.[1] Thereafter Skelton's career fades into obscurity, until in 1528, the year before his death, he again wrote a commissioned work on a political theme, his *Replycacion* against two young heretical scholars, Thomas Bilney and Thomas Arthur, who had publicly abjured in 1527.

PLOT

Magnyfycence, Skelton's only surviving dramatic work, has long served as a snare for scholars in search of topical satire, who have seen beneath its moralizing allegorical façade a clear parable of Tudor high politics. The play concerns the fortunes of a prince, the Magnyfycence of the title, who, despite his claim to have set his court perpetually to rights under the guidance of his wise counsellor Measure, is eventually tricked into

---

[1] For a fuller account of Skelton's career as outlined here, see G. Walker, *John Skelton and the Politics of the 1520s* (Cambridge, 1988). For an alternative view, see H. L. R. Edwards, *Skelton: The Life and Times of an Early Tudor Poet* (London, 1949).

abandoning that prudent arrangement. Two fools, Fansy and Foly, persuade him to admit into his service a number of ne'er-do-well suitors, Crafty Conveyaunce, Clokyd Colusyon, Counterfet Countenaunce and Courtly Abusyon. These vices, by posing as virtues, lead him to banish Measure, and adopt the lifestyle and mannerisms of a dissipated braggart. They then proceed to complete his ruin, both moral and financial, by enticing him into an orgy of self-indulgence, which drives prosperity and contentment (in the form of Welthfull Felycyte) from the Court, and heralds the entrance of Adversity. At this point the vices depart, leaving Magnyfycence prey to Poverte, Dyspare and the suicidal promptings of Myschefe. He is only saved from self-destruction by the arrival of Good Hope, Perseveraunce and Redresse, who lead him to realize the foolishness of his earlier behaviour and educate him in the divine origins of true wisdom. Thus regenerated by his experiences, he returns to the Court accompanied by new, more responsible, companions.

DATING

Scholars have tended to agree that the play was written at some point in the years 1515–16, and marked the beginning of Skelton's satirical attack upon Cardinal Wolsey, Henry VIII's chief minister, which reached its height in the better-known satirical poems of 1521–2: *Speke, Parott, Collyn Clout* and *Why Come Ye Nat to Courte?*[2] In this view the ruinous promptings of the courtier-vices which denude Magnyfycence's treasury find their historical analogue in the equally foolhardy advice given to Henry VIII on the conduct of foreign policy in the years 1514–16. For at this time the Crown was pursuing a costly policy of financing the armies of the Holy Roman Empire and the Swiss Cantons to fight the French on England's behalf. Being unable to support a full-scale invasion of France of his own, Henry was attempting to counter French expansion by subsidizing her enemies. Yet the net result of this initiative was simply fruitless expenditure. For the recipients of these payments conducted their own affairs as they wished, eventually coming to terms with the French without

2 The classic exposition of this argument is in R. L. Ramsey, ed., *Magnyfycence*, E.E.T.S., Extra Series, XCVIII (London, 1908 for 1906), Introduction. It is followed by A. R. Heiserman, *Skelton and Satire* (Chicago, 1961), pp. 69–73, and M. Pollet, *John Skelton, Poet of Tudor England* (London, 1971), pp. 80–4. See also D. Bevington, *Tudor Drama and Politics* (Cambridge, Mass., 1968), pp. 5–9. Minor deviations from this consensus occur in P. Neuss, ed., *Magnificence* (Manchester, 1980), where a date in the early 1520s is favoured on stylistic grounds, and W. O. Harris, *Skelton's Magnyfycence and the Cardinal Virtue Tradition* (Chapel Hill, 1965), where Ramsey's date is accepted, but Wolsey's role in the play denied. E. S. Hooper, 'Skelton's "Magnyfycence" and Cardinal Wolsey', *Modern Language Notes*, XVI (1901), pp. 426–9, argues that Wolsey, rather than Henry VIII, is represented by Magnyfycence, a view with which Neuss (pp. 35–9) expresses some sympathy.

consulting their English backers.[3] Thus, it is asserted, Skelton, aghast at the folly inherent in throwing good money after bad in this way, designed *Magnyfycence* as a dire warning to Henry of the perils that awaited the spendthrift sovereign, and as an attack upon the supposed architect of English profligacy, Thomas Wolsey. In the antics of the vices, it is suggested, Skelton portrayed Wolsey's increasing dominance of both the King and his Court, and parodied the excesses of his personality and his costly diplomatic schemes.

This case has a certain logic to it, but it is based upon a number of highly dubious assumptions. The first concerns the dating of the play. For the above argument to convince, *Magnyfycence* must be a work of 1515–16. Yet the evidence does not allow such certainty. In reality the only firm date from which to work is a *terminus ad quem* of 1523. For in his semi-autobiographical poem, *The Garlande of Laurell*, printed in that year, Skelton listed 'Magnyfycence a notable mater' among his works.[4] Thus it may safely be assumed that the play had been written by that date.[5] Beyond this, all is conjecture. A passing reference in the text to the death of 'Kynge lewes of Fraunce' (line 280) led to Ramsey's contention that the play was contemporary with the death of Louis XII (died 1 January 1515), and that Fansy's reference to a watch kept on the Channel ports (lines 343–67) alludes to Anglo-French tensions which lasted from early 1515 to August 1516.[6] But no such inferences need to be drawn. Skelton was habitually imprecise in his allusions to continental events and personalities. In *Speke, Parott* he referred to Pope Julius II (d. 1513) as if he still lived (line 431), some eight years after his death. Thus the allusion to the death of Louis XII only provides the earliest date at which the text could have been completed. It could have been written at any time between January 1515 and October 1523.

Another major flaw in earlier arguments concerns the subject supposedly satirized. For Ramsey's case assumes far too great a knowledge on the poet's part of what were highly secret questions of foreign policy.[7]

Moreover, the identification of Wolsey as the target of the satire is problematic. For it is far from clear that criticism of the diplomatic initiatives of 1515–16 would have been interpreted as an attack solely upon the Cardinal. The aggressively anti-French policy pursued by the

---

[3] For these events, see J. J. Scarisbrick, *Henry VIII* (London, 1968), pp. 50–100.
[4] Line 1192. All references are to V. J. Scattergood, ed., *John Skelton, The Complete English Poems* (London, 1982).
[5] The first printed edition did not appear until *c.* 1530.
[6] Ramsey, pp. xxi–v.
[7] Skelton's lack of royal or noble patronage at this time seems to have left him without access to political information beyond that which was common knowledge. See, G. Walker, *John Skelton and the Politics of the 1520s* (Cambridge, 1988), Chapters 1 and 2.

Crown, of which the financing of mercenary armies was an integral part, was clearly as much Henry's project as Wolsey's. The extant diplomatic correspondence reveals a King very much involved in the formulation of policy and in its detailed implementation.[8] Thus, had *Magnyfycence* been performed during 1515–16, and had a connection been made between its content and current policies, it is more likely that the play would have been taken as straightforward criticism of the King rather than as criticism of Wolsey alone. This would have been far from Skelton's intentions. For all the evidence suggests that the poet was endeavouring to attract royal patronage at this time rather than seeking to deter it.[9] Skelton's loyalty to Henry VIII was considerable, if idiosyncratic. He had, after all, been his tutor during the future King's formative years, and retained a personal affection for him evident in his poems. Furthermore it suited the poet's vanity to appear to be the officially sanctioned spokesman of the Crown. This explains his habit of endorsing his poetry with the title 'John Skelton, *Orator Regis*' long after any royal commission had expired.[10] Thus, if he had decided to treat the events of 1515–16 satirically, it is likely that he would have continued to court royal favour by producing an *apologia* for current policies and a vigorous denunciation of the French, of the sort he had written in 1513,[11] rather than a drama which appeared critical of the English Court.

The assertion that Wolsey was the central target of the satire is also difficult to reconcile with the evidence of the play-text itself. For in it Skelton depicts a prince who is led to his downfall, not by a single Machiavellian minister, as might be expected were Wolsey the object of criticism, but by six vicious courtiers. The attempt to resolve all the various attributes and characteristics of these agents of Magnyfycence's corruption into a fragmented portrait of the Cardinal has led a number of scholars into exegetical contortions of quite heroic proportions. But none seems convincing. Could it not be argued, Ramsey enquired, that each vice personifies a separate aspect of Wolsey's personality?[12]

In Fancy we have the recklessness, in Folly the unwisdom of ... [Wolsey's] foreign policy. When Counterfeit Countenance enlarges on the fruitful theme of low-born upstarts, and Crafty Conveyance on perverters of justice, the Cardinal came at once to the spectator's mind. In Courtly Abusion we have the loose living, the

---

8 See, for example, *L.P.* II (i) 1244, 1863, 1928.
9 Walker, *Skelton*, Chapters 2–4.
10 The last poem written 'By the Kynges most noble commaundment' was the *flytyng Agenst Garnesche* (c. 1514). Skelton was still subscribing his poems 'Orator Regius' in 1528, the year before his death.
11 *Chorus de Dys Contra Gallos*, in A. Dyce, ed., *The Poetical Works of John Skelton* (2 vols., London, 1843), II, p. 191.
12 Ramsey, p. cx.

extravagant dress, and the consumate flattery, in Cloaked Collusion the dissimulation and artful breeding of dissension, and alike in all the courtiers the quar-
relsomeness, false courage and habit of forgetting old friends that Skelton wished
to ascribe to Wolsey.

Thus Ramsey concludes his case that the vices are a composite caricature
of Wolsey, whilst the virtues of the play, Measure and Sad Cyrcumspeccyon, are representations of those councillors such as the Duke of
Norfolk and Archbishop Warham who, in his opinion, opposed the Cardinal's policies.[13]

Such reasoning is hardly convincing. To see the abstract personifications
of Fansy and Foly as allusions to the foreign policy pursued by Henry VIII,
for example, is an entirely arbitrary decision. Nowhere in the play is it
suggested that the vices are concerned with political decision making,
whether international or domestic. Indeed the chief vehicle for such decision making, the Royal Council, is not mentioned. The vices' interests
and misdemeanours centre upon more mundane and traditional personal
indulgences performed within the royal household – a fact not without
significance for the identification of the satire's true object, as will be
suggested below. Nor do the specific 'similarities' between the vices and
Wolsey identified by Ramsey convince. The upstarts referred to by Counterfet Countenaunce are courtiers, but Wolsey was no courtier. His responsibilities as Lord Chancellor and head of the Council kept him at
Westminster during the Law terms, and his visits to Court were infrequent
– so much so that Skelton was to charge him, in *Why Come Ye Nat To
Courte?*, with attempting to turn his own household into a rival Court.[14]
Similarly the assertion that Wolsey would be recognized in any portrayal
of 'a perverter of justice' ill fits the evidence. As contemporary sources
suggest, and the research of John Guy confirms, Wolsey's problems in the
legal field stemmed in part from quite the opposite perception. It was as a
purveyor of swift and impartial justice that the Cardinal was popularly
known, with the result that the prerogative courts over which he presided
became counterproductively overburdened with litigants.[15]

Perhaps the most unlikely assumption, however, is that Wolsey would
be recognized in the character of Courtly Abusyon. The latter's entire
raison d'être, as his name declares, is to parody the latest court fashions.
He is 'a joly rutter' (line 752), a gallant, well versed in courtly dalliance, a
jouster and a dancer, whose wide slippers, flamboyant cloak, copious

13 Ibid., pp. cxx–i.
14 *Why Come Ye Nat . . . ?*, lines 399–415.
15 E. Hall, *Chronicle*, H. Ellis, ed. (London, 1809), p. 585. Rawdon Brown, *Four Years at the
    Court of Henry VIII* (2 vols., London, 1854), II, p. 314. J. A. Guy, *The Cardinal's Court*
    (Hassocks, 1977); and *The Court of Star Chamber and its Records to the Reign of
    Elizabeth I*, P.R.O. Handbooks, 21 (London, 1985).

sleeves and 'hose strayte tyde' (line 852) mark him out as the sort of sartorial peacock whom later generations would dub a fop. His one aim is to make a mark at court.

> Properly drest
> All *poynte devyse*,
> My persone prest
> Beyonde all syse
> Of the newe gyse,
> To russhe it oute
> In every route.
> (lines 842–8)

No less likely an analogue of the Cardinal might be imagined. Again, the vice is definitely a courtier, whilst Wolsey clearly was not. Abusyon is both a jouster and a dancer, whilst Wolsey was neither. And the latter's clerical garb, even at its most ceremonial, could hardly be compared with Abusyon's gaudy, ultra-modish, secular paraphernalia. The resemblance which Ramsey thought he had identified simply does not exist.

Thus, although some of the characteristics of the vices correspond vaguely to some of the faults ascribed to Wolsey by satirists and later critics, any attempt to establish a comprehensive correlation between the two can only end in failure. What similarities there are surely owe more to the stereotypical nature of satire and invective than to any specific intention to satirize Wolsey on the poet's part. Moreover, the assertion that the play criticizes the policy of subsidizing the enemies of France contains a more general flaw. For, whilst on the one hand it claims that the play attacks Wolsey's anti-French policy, it also asserts that the satire is carried by the identification of the Cardinal with the vices, many of whom are portrayed as Frenchified dandies, who favour French fashions and manners. Fansy, for example, announces that he has come from 'Pontesse' in France, and cites 'King lewes of Fraunce' as an exemplum of largesse, Abusyon and Colusyon break into French when speaking to each other, and the former sports 'This newe fonne jet, / From out of Fraunce' (lines 877–8). Wolsey is allegedly the inspiration for an anti-French policy, yet the characters which supposedly represent him are seemingly Francophile. The problems multiply the closer the thesis is examined.

Given the problems already encountered, it might seem unwise to attempt to reopen the debate over the political context of the play. Yet that context should not be ignored. *Magnyfycence* proves on close reading to be an intensely political play. It takes as its subject matter questions which contemporaries considered central to effective royal administration. What follows will examine these questions, and identify the ways in which

Skelton raises and deals with them. But, before considering these general themes, it is important to examine a more specific issue. For it seems likely that *Magnyfycence* was indeed occasioned by a particular political event: not the diplomatic manoeuvres of 1515–16, but a more domestic *cause célèbre* of 1519.[16]

THE OCCASION OF THE PLAY?
THE 'EXPULSION OF THE MINIONS OF 1519'

During September 1518 Henry VIII created a new and prestigious post in the royal household, that of Gentleman of the Privy Chamber, a title borrowed from the French Court of Francis I.[17] To this he appointed a number of his closest companions: Edward Neville, Arthur Pole, Nicholas Carew, Francis Bryan, Henry Norris and William Coffin. These newly elevated Gentlemen made much of their improved status, and were employed as Henry's emissaries to France as well as working within the Privy Chamber. Yet in May 1519, within nine months of their promotion, four of them, Neville, Carew, Bryan and Coffin, in company with a number of other courtiers, Sir Henry Guildford, his half-brother Sir Edward, Sir John Peachy and Francis Pointz, were dismissed from the Court and sent to posts elsewhere in disgrace. These expulsions caused a sensation at Court. The Venetian ambassador, Sebastian Giustinian, described them as among the most important events in years, and even Francis I was moved to remark upon them.[18] But neither contemporaries nor modern historians have been able to agree upon the significance of this event. What was the cause of this dramatic reversal in the fortunes of men who had, due to their familiarity with Henry VIII, been popularly dubbed the King's 'minions'? And what implications might the expulsion have for a reading of *Magnyfycence*? The suggestion that the play alludes to the expulsion is an illuminating one. But it is crucial to determine the nature

16 The possibility that *Magnyfycence* was a satirical treatment of the Court events of May 1519 was advanced by M. J. C. Dowling in her doctoral thesis, 'Scholarship, Politics and the Court of Henry VIII', University of London Ph.D. Thesis, 1981, pp. 104–8. An unpublished suggestion by Dr D. R. Starkey was cited as the source of this idea. To the best of my knowledge neither scholar has published further on the subject, and no reference to *Magnyfycence* appeared in the revised version of the thesis, published as *Humanism in the Reign of Henry VIII* (London, 1985). As will become clear, my own ideas differ from Dr Dowling's in all aspects but the dating and the occasion of the play. The suggestion subsequently resurfaced, seemingly independently, as a brief suggestion in I. Lancashire, ed., *Dramatic Texts and Records of Britain: A Chronological Topography to 1558* (Cambridge, 1984), p. 18. It has been advanced more recently in Alistair Fox, *Politics and Literature in the Reigns of Henry VII and Henry VIII* (Oxford, 1989), pp. 237–40.

17 D. R. Starkey, 'The King's Privy Chamber, 1485–1547', Cambridge University D.Phil. Thesis, 1973, pp. 97–108.

18 Rawdon Brown *et al.*, eds., *Calendar of State Papers Venetian* [hereafter C.S.P.V.], II, 1230, Rawdon Brown, *Four Years*, pp. 270–1.

and significance of the event before its implications for the satire can be properly understood.

It has been suggested that the removal of the minions was engineered by Wolsey in order to purge the King's Privy Chamber, the innermost sanctum of the royal household, of potential rivals and secure his own monopoly of royal favour.[19] Thus it has been argued that *Magnyfycence* is indeed a satire of Wolsey, but one which treats his actions in 1519, not 1515–16. The play, it is suggested, both dramatizes the purge and ridicules its architect, Wolsey; the latter through the characterization of Measure as a composite representation of both the Duke of Norfolk (the hero) and of Wolsey (the villain).[20] But such a suggestion fails to convince. Measure is hardly the ambivalent character which such a reading implies. Throughout the play he embodies the ideals of conduct against which the actions of the vices and Magnyfycence's own decline into folly may be charted. Thus it is difficult to see any criticism of Wolsey, however subtle, inherent in the character. Indeed, it is difficult to detect the Cardinal's presence in the play at all, which, given the above, would seem to argue against the possibility that the play was a satire of the expulsions. Yet the problem only exists if Wolsey is assumed to have been the architect of the purge, and this, as I have argued elsewhere, seems not to have been the case.[21] Rather, the expulsions were the result of an entirely different initiative.

From the account of the affair provided by the chronicler Edward Hall it seems clear that the minions' fall was the result, not of Wolsey's jealousy, but of the action of a number of the leading figures at Court who had become antagonized by the young men's behaviour. As Hall records, the minions became particularly objectionable after their return from a diplomatic mission to Paris, which seems to have degenerated into a fracas initiated by Francis I.[22]

Duryng this tyme remained in the Frenche courte Nicholas Carew, Fraunces Brian and diverse other of the young gentlemen of England and they with the Frenche Kyng roade daily disguysed through Paris, throwyng Egges, stones and other foolishe trifles at the people, which light demeanoure of a Kyng was muche discommended and gested at. And when these young gentlemen came again into England, they were all Frenche, in eatyng, drynkyng and apparell, yea and in Frenche vices and bragges, so that all the estates of Englonde were by them laughed at: the ladies and gentlewomen were dispraised, so that nothing by them was praised, but if it were after the Frenche turne, whiche after turned them to

[19] Dowling, 'Scholarship', pp. 104–6; D. R. Starkey, *The Reign of Henry VIII: Personalities and Politics* (London, 1985), pp. 79–80, and *thesis cit.*, pp. 110–14.

[20] Dowling, 'Scholarship', p. 107.

[21] G. Walker, 'The Expulsion of the Minions Reconsidered', *The Historical Journal*, 32, 1 (1989), pp. 1–16.

[22] Hall, pp. 597–8.

displeasure ... and [they] so highly praised the frenche Kyng and his court, that in a maner they thought litle of the Kyng and his court, in comparison of the other, they were so high in love with the frenche courte, wherefore their fall was litle moned emong wise men.

The minions' extravagant behaviour, their condescending, disparaging, manner, and especially the overfamiliar way in which they treated their King, Hall suggests, began to alarm the members of Henry's council, who felt that such loutish activities and such disrespectful behaviour were bringing the Crown into odium. In a society where display (literally magnificence) was taken as an index of political power it was clearly dangerous to have a group of influential individuals publicly belittling the culture of the Court and comparing it unfavourably with that of a rival state, particularly at a time when Henry was, however half-heartedly, presenting himself as a potential candidate for the Imperial election.[23] Thus, fulfilling their role as the sovereign's natural advisers, the councillors approached Henry with their criticisms and persuaded him that the offending individuals should be disciplined if the reputation of the Court was to be restored.

Having decided upon the removal of the minions, however, King and council were faced with a problem. The expulsions would clearly attract considerable attention, and so could not be conducted without comment. But how should such a major alteration in the personnel of the Court be presented to the nation and to the resident diplomats who were only too ready to pass on news of such events to their employers? For his councillors to present criticisms of the King's companions (and, by implication, of his lifestyle) to him in private was one thing. For such criticisms to circulate at Court unchecked was quite another. There was an obvious danger in allowing Henry to appear as a man who had to be rescued by his councillors from the bad influence of his companions. Thus the account of the purge which was released to the ambassadors and to the wider public seems to have been carefully constructed to present the King in the best possible light.

Whether the calculations suggested above were ever openly discussed by Henry and his councillors, or whether they were made privately by the King himself prior to his decision to act against the minions, can only be guessed at. But it was clearly decided at an early stage in the proceedings that the expulsions would be presented to the public as a determined and positive act of policy. Hall's version of the story, which seems to reflect an

---

[23] I owe the suggested connection with Henry's Imperial ambitions to my former Special Subject student, Joanne Parsons.

official or semi-official account, was clearly designed to reflect only praise upon Henry. It recalls how,[24]

certain young men of [the] ... privie chamber, not regardyng ... [Henry's] estate nor degree, were so familier and homely with hym, and plaied suche light touches with hym that they forgat themselves: which thynges although the Kyng of his gentle nature suffred and not rebuked nor reproved it: yet the Kynges counsaill ... thought it not mete to be suffred for the Kynges honor.

The ill-effects of the minions' dominance, and the possible implications of that dominance for the reading of Henry's character are not dwelt upon. The account stresses Henry's reaction to the councillors' approach which is portrayed as authoritative and decisive. He informed them, Hall states,

that he had chosen them of his counsaill, both for the maintenaunce of his honor, and for the defence of all thyng that might blemishe thesame: wherefore if they sawe any about hym misuse theimselfes, he committed it to their reformacion.

The period of 'enormities and lightnes',[25] during which the minions dominated the court, is thus described as very much a thing of the past. Even as their unhealthy influence over the King was acknowledged it was being skilfully converted into evidence of Henry's virtue. Their removal was portrayed as part of a significant change, both in Henry's attitude and in the atmosphere at Court. No longer was the King content to tolerate vice and inefficiency among his courtiers. He would now take an active role in the reform of Court and country. As Hall noted, the minions were replaced as Henry's personal attendants by 'four sad and auncient Knightes', the more sober and experienced Knights of the Body, Sir Richard Jerningham, Sir Richard Weston, Sir Richard Wingfield and Sir William Kingston, and 'diverse officers were chaunged in al places'.

The Duke of Norfolk, so often Henry's spokesman to the foreign ambassadors at Court, was also sedulously spreading this account of a newly reformed monarch. As he told Giustinian, the minions had led Henry into 'incessant gambling', but now, 'on coming to himself, and resolving to lead a new life, he [the King] of his own accord, removed these companions of his excesses'.[26] What had begun as criticism of Henry's lifestyle became, as it was prepared for public consumption, a paean to his responsibility and strength of character. And the effectiveness of this shrewd propaganda can be judged from the fact that, as far away as Paris, Francis I had heard that there was 'a new world in England' now that the minions had been exiled.[27]

---

[24] Hall, p. 598.   [25] Ibid., p. 598.
[26] Rawdon Brown, *Four Years*, II, pp. 270–1.   [27] *C.S.P.V.*, II, 1230.

However cynical and diplomatic the origins of this account of the affair may have been, Henry seems quickly to have adopted the desire for reform as a serious political initiative.[28] A number of memoranda were drafted which identified areas of the administration, both within the Court and beyond, where Henry, 'like a noble, wise and politic prince', thought that changes were necessary.[29] And significant measures were undertaken in areas in need of immediate reformation. The root of the problem, the disordered and undignified Privy Chamber, was subjected to particular scrutiny. Not only were the erring minions removed and replaced by more suitable attendants, but the finances of the Privy Purse, as administered by the Chief Gentleman of the Privy Chamber, the Groom of the Stool, were reorganized, and the functions and responsibilities of the officers of the Chamber and Privy Chamber formalized, with the majority of the staff of the latter being granted regular wages for the first time.[30] A similar spirit motivated new reforming initiatives in the administration of wardships, in new ordinances for the prestigious Order of the Garter and a new policy for the government of Ireland.[31]

The significant fact to note from all this is that the expulsion of the minions was not a covert palace revolution engineered by Wolsey, but an act of government conducted amid considerable public excitement and accompanied by fanfares which were clearly orchestrated by the Crown.[32] Rather than attempt to conceal the purge, the government actively promoted it as evidence that Henry was, after a brief lapse, once more a King in command of his vocation. Part of the official enthusiasm for the circulation of this story could, no doubt, be attributed to a desire to counter and suppress other accounts of the affair which attributed less attractive motives to the expulsions – some hinted at hostility to France, others at Wolsey's ambitions for a monopoly of power – either of which would be damaging to the Crown if it took hold. But, whether genuine reforming enthusiasm or political expediency was the prime motive, it seems clear that an 'authorized version' of the expulsion story existed, and was circulated at Court and elsewhere. This fact, rather than any desire to criticize

---

28 Walker, 'The Expulsion', pp. 8–10.
29 B.L. Cotton MS Titus B 1, ff. 188–90.
30 D. R. Starkey, 'Court and Government', in Starkey and C. Coleman, eds., *Revolution Reassessed* (Oxford, 1986), pp. 39–40; and *thesis cit.*, p. 121.
31 Walker, 'The Expulsion', pp. 8–10.
32 Public interest in the expulsion is attested to by Hall's decision to devote three paragraphs of his Chronicle to it (the trial and execution of Anne Boleyn warranted only two, Henry's marriage to Jane Seymour just two and a half lines) and by ambassadorial references to the rumours and controversy which it excited, both in England and abroad, *C.S.P.V.*, II, 1220, 1235. As Thomas Boleyn reported, everyone was full of the news in Paris, *L.P.*., III (i) 246.

Wolsey, would seem to explain most satisfactorily Skelton's decision to write *Magnyfycence* in 1519.

For the entire period between 1509 and 1521, the poet was intent upon regaining the level of royal patronage which he had enjoyed under Henry VII prior to 1502 (the year in which he was dismissed as a tutor to the future Henry VIII).[33] To this end he seems to have taken upon himself the role of an unlicensed apologist for the King, attempting to justify and eulogize his actions to courtly and popular audiences alike. In 1513, during the special circumstances of the French war, when the government perceived the need for such poetic propaganda, he may have produced such works with royal approval. But after this brief flirtation with favour he returned to freelance work, ever hoping to attract by self-promotion and conspicuous acts of loyalty the royal commissions which he felt he deserved.

Was *Magnyfycence*, then, another of Skelton's attempts to win royal favour, this time by dramatizing the Crown's account of the expulsion of the minions? Was he attempting to envelop the original political act in an allegorical framework which made apparent the issues raised by the removal of the young men and the subsequent reforming initiatives, with a view to attracting the attention of the government and demonstrating the political potential of his services? Again the case hinges upon the likely date of the play, and upon its plausibility as a reflection of the events of 1519.

The similarities between the plot of *Magnyfycence* and Hall and Norfolk's accounts of the expulsions are many and obvious. In both cases a King is described as surrounded by dissolute wastrels who threaten to ruin him financially and corrupt him morally. Both the minions and the vices become the close companions of the Prince, his 'household men', who use their intimacy with him to obtain honours, wealth and offices (line 1941, see also lines 612–13 and 639–40, where the domestic nature of the vice's service is further stressed). Like the minions, who frequently supported Henry VIII in martial tournaments,[34] the vices are keen jousters, who pepper their conversation with tiltyard terms (lines 1180–1). And like those Gentlemen who returned from the French Court 'all Frenche, in eatyng, drynkyng and apparell, yea, and in French vices and bragges',[35] the vices sport the latest 'newe fonne jet / From out of Fraunce' (lines 877–8), exchange quips in bastard-French (lines 748, 750–1, 1197), and swear by 'the armes of Calys' (line 675) and 'Kynge lewes of Fraunce' (line 280). Both accounts present a Court fallen into disorder under the influence of

[33] Walker, *Skelton*, Chapters 2, 3 and 5.
[34] Starkey, *thesis cit.*, pp. 89–90.   [35] Hall, p. 597.

these individuals, which is restored to order only by their removal and replacement by more responsible advisers – in the Henrician Court the 'sad and auncient' Knights of the Body, in Skelton's fiction, Sad Cyrcum-speccyon, Good Hope and Redresse.

Clearly both the number of characters involved and the purely domestic locus of the action support the suggestion that the vices satirize a group of courtiers rather than a single minister such as Wolsey. It is also possible that there are specific references in the text to individuals involved in the expulsions.[36] Yet speculation on such specific correspondences between Skelton's characters and Henrician courtiers is dangerous. For too often a line, or even a word, taken out of context can suggest identifications which disappear on closer scrutiny. What does seem convincing, however, is the general association between the minions and the vices. The former's over-familiar 'light touches' with Henry do seem to be paralleled in the liberties which Foly takes with the King, and in Fansy's disregard for Magnyfycence's authority.[37] Similarly the moral resurrection of the pro-tagonist in the final scenes closely resembles Henry's declared resolution to 'live a new life', free from 'the companions of his excesses'.

Ultimately it is, of course, impossible to prove a connection between the events of 1519 and the subject matter of *Magnyfycence*. Beyond the suggestive coincidences there is no hard evidence, apart from stylistic similarities with Skelton's later satires,[38] to date the play in 1519 rather than 1515 or 1516. Yet, on the balance of the evidence currently available, it seems the most plausible of the historical readings of the play. And, as will be suggested below, many of the general questions raised by the expulsion of the minions are considered by Skelton in *Magnyfycence*. The latter is very much a household play, and has to be read in that light if it is to be fully understood, regardless of its possible links with specific events.

SATIRE OF HENRY VIII IN 'MAGNYFYCENCE'

But, if the above is substantially correct, a further problem arises. If the play was indeed a dramatic treatment of the expulsion of 1519, could it really have been written to attract royal patronage, given the apparently less than flattering light which critics have suggested it casts upon the central character? If Magnyfycence was a dramatic representation of Henry VIII, would not the King have been horrified to see himself depicted as a fallen tyrannical braggart led into lecherous thoughts and irrational

---

[36] Dowling, 'Scholarship', pp. 105 and 109.
[37] Note Magnyfycence's initially hostile reaction to Fansy's jocularity in lines 304–5. 'You are nothynge mete with us for to dwell, / That with your lorde and mayster so pertly can prate'.
[38] Neuss, *Magnyfycence*, pp. 17 and 34–6.

behaviour by his companions? Could the author really have expected to win royal favour with such a play? Critics have generally assumed that he could not. As William Nelson asserted, 'if King Henry ever saw the play, he must have recognised himself, and found it hard to forgive its author'.[39] Similarly David Bevington was certain that 'the most daring topical meaning in *Magnyfycence* is ... [the] implied criticism of Henry VIII'.[40] Yet a close examination of the play-text suggests the contrary.

First it must be noted that, despite critical assertions concerning the daring nature of his political theme, Skelton was doing nothing revolutionary in portraying dramatically a King fallen into vice. Indeed his treatment of Magnyfycence was far less critical of the institution of monarchy than earlier dramatic representations of kings.[41] In moral and liturgical drama mortal kingship (as opposed to the divine kingly ideal) generally performed an unenviable allegorical function, being used to illustrate the epitome of futile worldly ambition and pride. As such it stood at the opposite moral extreme to the Christian virtues of humility and spiritual detachment, and was execrated accordingly. In Medwall's *Nature* the protagonists adopt the trappings of royalty purely because elevation to the royal estate provided the most extreme example of worldly success. To bring a monarch to despair and poverty thus powerfully exemplified the fragility of worldly fortune by demonstrating its operation in its most extreme form. No such simplistic critical framework underpins *Magnyfycence*. Skelton's treatment of his protagonist considers Kingship on its own terms. Indeed, given that the mortal king most commonly portrayed on the medieval stage was Herod, Skelton's play could well be read as an attempt to rescue monarchy from the calumnies of previous dramatists, rather than as a daring critique of either the institution or the person of Henry VIII.

The playwright's licence to offer unwelcome truths in the form of 'good counsel' which was explored in the preceding chapter also has an obvious role to play here. In portraying Henry critically, Skelton could always plead that it was ultimately in the Sovereign's best interests that he did so. Good advice was not always flattering. Thus the genre in which Skelton was writing offered its own inbuilt safeguards. But even given these generic considerations, the playwright seems, unlike the author of *Hick Scorner*, to have gone out of his way to minimize the play's harmful implications. In the details of the characterization of the Prince, and in the mechanics of his fall, *Magnyfycence* provides a portrait which ultimately reflects only

---

[39] W. Nelson, *John Skelton, Laureate* (New York, 1939), p. 138.

[40] D. Bevington, *Tudor Drama and Politics*, pp. 60–1.

[41] See, for example, the characterization of World in *Mundus et Infans*, or Rex in *The Pride of Life*, O. Waterhouse, ed., *The Non-Cycle Mystery Plays*, E.E.T.S., Extra Series, CIV (London, 1909).

praise upon its subject. The crucial point to note is that, if he was drama-tizing the expulsion of 1519 after the event, Skelton was appealing to the 'redeemed' Henry, the King who had himself implied criticism of his own conduct during the ascendancy of the minions, through his declaration that he would 'lead a new life' thereafter. Thus Skelton, in dramatizing such criticism, was doing no more than mirroring the King's own publicly expressed position. Yet even in doing this the poet so constructed his play as to minimize the direct criticism of the Prince, and to maximize the corrupting role played by the minion/vices, whom the King's statements had tacitly declared to be 'fair game'.

Magnyfycence's fall into error is so handled as to suggest tacit praise for the King's good features even as it criticized his political mistakes. As will be demonstrated, it is only through his decision to adopt what he takes to be the noble practice of largesse that he falls into sin. Moreover the King is absent from the drama during the greater part of the middle portion of the play. For the thousand or so lines of the vices' dominion over the action, as their folly and corruption are made all too obvious, he, like Anima, the protagonist of the play *Wisdom*, is conveniently 'off-stage', and so is not associated with their grosser antics. He returns only to preside over the last scenes of corruption which precede his repentance and recovery. And upon his return his character, like that of Anima, is signally transformed.[42]

Magnyfycence re-enters the drama as a stereotypical morality-play tyrant. Suddenly his speech is heavy with the alliterative arrogance associ-ated with the Satan and Herod characters of liturgical drama.

> ... I am prynce perlesse, provyd of porte,
> Bathyd with blysse, embracyd with comforte.
>
> (lines 1471–2)

> I drede no daunger; I dawnce all in delyte:
> My name is Magnyfycence, man most of myght.
>
> (lines 1493–4)

> ... no man on molde can make me aferd.
> What man is so maysyd with me that dare mete,
>
> (lines 1505–6)

The conscious archaism of 'mold' rather than 'earth' in the final lines signals the poet's allusive intentions here most clearly. The fallen Magny-fycence is not only fashioned in the morality tradition, he is a clear pastiche of the morality tyrant, speaking in the archaic alliterative verse of the cycle plays. Nothing that has gone before has prepared the audience for this

[42] See *Wisdom* in Mark Eccles, ed., *The Macro Plays*, E.E.T.S., 262 (Oxford, 1969), pp. 113–52.

complete transformation of character. It is as if Magnyfycence, like Henry VIII, was indeed no longer himself now that he is under the influence of the vices. And this change from character to caricature further reduces the play's implied criticism of the King. By presenting his audience with so obvious a stereotype at the very moment at which a personalized lampoon of Henry VIII would have been most satirically effective, the poet consciously prevents them from making the specific associations between the King and his dramatic figure which he had encouraged hitherto. Thus even where the King had himself implied that mistakes had been made, Skelton chose to divert and minimize the critical implications of his play. All this suggests most strongly that the poet was striving to prompt a favourable reaction from the Crown rather than to attack it.

It must be remembered that the most enduring effect of any drama is likely to be that created by its final scenes. And the final image of *Magnyfycence* is that of an ideal monarch, restored from folly, combining reason with the Christian virtues and surrounded by sound advisers. Critics have suggested that such a conclusion ill-fits what has gone before and unbalances the play. It would have been far better dramatically, it has been argued, if these scenes of reconciliation and restoration had been omitted, and the play completed with the flight of the vices and the arrival of Dyspare. Thus the allegory would have been presented in a far more powerful manner.[43] But to argue thus is to ignore the political functions of the play. For, if the above is correct, *Magnyfycence* was written to explain how the King was restored to his current virtuous condition – to chart allegorically the rise of the minions, and to justify their expulsion to make way for Henry's 'new life'. To truncate the play at lines 2283 or 2322 would imply that the King was morally ruined by his experiences. The arrival of Redresse and the other virtues demonstrates that he is once more the just prince. Hence the last scenes were essential if the play was to succeed, both in allegorizing the events of 1519, and in attracting royal patronage.

It is in these final scenes that the renewed authority of the King is displayed. For, having been schooled in fortitude by the virtues,[44] he once more takes the commanding role in the drama which he had exercised in the opening scenes. It is the actor playing Magnyfycence who speaks most obviously for the play's 'maker', Skelton, here. He orchestrates the final moralizing, commanding each of the virtues to offer his own interpretation of the lesson the play offers, and indicating the order in which they

---

43 Ramsey, p. xxviii. Neuss (p. 30) asserts that 'the advent of Good Hope ... and the resulting arrival of Redresse, Sad Circumspection and Perseverance are unsatisfactory on every level of the play'.

44 See, Harris, pp. 71–126; and below, pp. 77–9.

should do so (lines 2480–1). And it is he who judges the merits of those interpretations (lines 2505–6). As with Henry VIII who, it was said, had himself taken the decisive role in the expulsions and the subsequent reforms, so with Magnyfycence, who declares his own conversion to moral regeneration.

> ... hooly to perseveraunce my selfe I wyll bynde,
> Of that I have mysdone to make a redresse,
> And with Sad Cyrcumspeccyon correct my wontonnesse.
>
> (lines 2507–9)

Finally, the actors turn to the audience, and each summarizes the message of the play, drawing together the Christian themes of the folly of 'worldly vaynglory' (line 2514) and the mutability of fortune (lines 2515–51). Again it is Magnyfycence who concludes the matter. Unlike the other characters, who had spoken only for themselves, he now offers an informal epilogue on behalf of the entire company.

> This matter we have movyd, you myrthys to make,
> Precely purposyd under pretence of play,
> Shewyth wysdome to them that wysdome can take.
>
> (lines 2552–4)

The audience is presented here, not only with a wholly restored Magnyfycence who is both virtuous and wise, but with a character who dominates the acting area. If doubts had been raised in the earlier scenes concerning his fitness to rule, they are dispelled now. It is unnecessary for the virtues to pass judgement on his recovery, for Magnyfycence's conduct and bearing, and their tacit acceptance of his authority, have long since signalled his regeneration to the audience. Thus, in portraying Henry VIII as Magnyfycence, Skelton clearly fashioned a vehicle for praise of the King, rather than for criticism. The King who emerged from the play was strengthened by his experiences. His fall into folly was educational in its effects rather than corrupting. Such a play, appearing in 1519, could only have complemented the account of the expulsion of the minions promoted by the Crown.

But, if the intention behind *Magnyfycence* was political, how was that intention executed? On a practical level, what were the circumstances of the play's performance? And how did the poet utilize his material? How do Skelton's drama and contemporary politics inform each other?

'MAGNYFYCENCE': POLITICAL THEMES AND PHILOSOPHY

The search for the sources of the philosophical positions adopted in the play has long exercised scholars. As early as 1908 Ramsey declared that he had located them in the *Nicomachean Ethics* of Aristotle. All that Skelton had done, Ramsey claimed, was take the characteristics ascribed by the philosopher to the quality translated as 'liberality' and dramatize them in the character of Magnyfycence.[45] This view has been challenged, most notably by W. O. Harris, who suggested that there was no evidence of direct borrowing from the *Ethics* in the play, and that it was rather to Thomas Aquinas and the cardinal virtue tradition that Skelton looked for his philosophical inspiration.[46] There, Harris argued, the poet found the quality of fortitude, upon which he based the protagonist of his play.

This attenuated argument has led to some illuminating work, but must remain unresolved if advocates of the latter position insist upon the complete rejection of Ramsey's ideas. For it is surely the case that both scholars are partially correct. The philosophical traditions of Aquinas and Aristotle are hardly mutually exclusive, and *Magnyfycence* is informed by both. But each serves a separate function. Skelton presents his audience with both the moral education of a man, and the political education of a prince, and the moral schemes governing each are clearly distinct. The question fundamental to all morality drama: 'How ought we to behave?' is addressed within a theological framework, and prompts a conventional Christian conclusion. All worldly possessions, the play declares, are transient. Therefore the Christian man, alert to the welfare of his soul, ought to set his eyes upon spiritual goals, and through the cultivation of fortitude, remain indifferent to the extremes of worldly fortune: wealth and poverty. Thus Magnyfycence is first tested by the sins of gluttony and luxuriousness, the products of his misuse of prosperity, and then by the spiritual despair of *accidia* and the temptation of suicide, resulting from his fall into poverty and the recollection of his past sins. Only after his failure in the face of both contrary temptations is he prepared for the arrival of Good Hope and Perseveraunce and his subsequent education in fortitude.[47]

In so far as Magnyfycence's personal education is fundamentally Christian, the play is little different in form and outlook to the other morality dramas of the period. But Skelton is not primarily concerned here with issues of personal morality as they affect Magnyfycence's soul. Spiritual questions form a coherent sub-theme to the play, but they are nonetheless marginal to the action. The central issue which Skelton dramatizes concerns the education of his protagonist in the conduct of royal government, and here Aristotelian principles dominate.

Prior to the King's entrance into the play the acting area is occupied by a thoroughly Aristotelian debate between Lyberte and Welthfull Felycyte

---

[45] Ramsey, pp. xxxii–iii.   [46] Harris, pp. 3–11.   [47] Ibid., pp. 97–109.

over which of them represents the greater virtue. This argument is quelled by Measure, the King's chief counsellor, who insists that both are of equal value, provided that they are regulated by himself. Thus, from the outset, the audience is presented with a dramatization of the realized Aristotelian ideal of wealth and Lyberte guided by Measure.[48] By having him ally himself with Measure, Skelton shows Magnyfycence to be the incarnation of Aristotle's liberal man. And, having established the protagonist and his Court in Aristotelian terms, the poet then uses the principles outlined in the *Ethics* to plot their downfall. As Aristotle stated, the observation of the mean in managing wealth avoids two vices, 'prodigality or extravagance on the one hand: illiberality or meanness on the other'.[49] In falling under the influence of Fansy Magnyfycence abandons that mean and, as events readily demonstrate, falls into the first of the vices, prodigality. For the Prince who dismisses his advisers and showers offices and titles upon those vices who tempt him into gluttony, lust and thoughtless extravagance is surely a type of Aristotle's prodigal, whose[50]

gifts are ignoble and given for an ignoble purpose and in the wrong spirit: nay they sometimes enrich people who *ought* to be poor. They never think of giving to persons of good character, but lavish their favours on toadies or anybody who ministers to their pleasures. That is why most prodigals are intemperate as well. Making the money fly, they plunge into dissipation regardless of expense, and having no standard by which to regulate their lives, they fall into mere sensuality.

By rejecting the regulating standard provided by Measure, Magnyfycence does indeed fall into mere sensuality, favouring the courtly vices who minister to his pleasures. It is his consequent wanton expenditure upon his favourites, governed only by Fansy, which brings on his financial and personal collapse, as the vices dissipate his fortune until they 'have ryfled hym metely well' (line 2170) and his coffers are empty (line 2163). It is at this point, as Harris observes, that he is taught the virtue of fortitude in the face of Adversyte and Poverte. But this is not the point stressed by the poet.

[48] Liberality, stated Aristotle, 'may be defined as a disposition to observe the mean in dealing with material goods'. J. A. K. Thomson, ed. and transl., *The Ethics of Aristotle* (Harmondsworth, 1955), p. 109. The point is made in terms closer to Skelton's own in Lydgate's translation of the pseudo-Aristotelian *Secrees of Old Philisoffres*. 'There is a mene paysed in ballaunce/ Atwiken hym that is a greet wastour, / To kepe a meane by attemperaunce, / That ech thyng be paysed by mesour'. R. Steele, ed., *Lydgate and Burgh's Secrees of Old Philisoffres*, E.E.T.S., LXVI (1894), lines 771–4.

[49] *Ethics*, p. 109. Thomas Elyot elaborated this notion in terms directly relevant to Skelton's play. 'If vertue be an election annexed unto our nature, and consisteth in a meane, which is determined by reason; and that meane is the very middes of two thynges visciouse, the one in surplusage, the other in lacke, Then nedes must benificence and liberalitie be capitall vertues, and Magnificence procedeth from them, approachynge to the extreme partes. And may be tourned in to a vice if he lacke the bridle of reason'. T. Elyot, *The Boke Named the Governour* (London, 1531), f. 139.

[50] *Ethics*, p. 114.

The central moral is provided by both the departing Lyberte and the newly returned Sad Cyrcumspeccyon. Each returns the attention of the audience to the political debate conducted in the opening lines, and stresses that it was Magnyfycence's failure to maintain the liberal mean in the distribution of largesse (rather than his failure to display fortitude in the face of extremes of fortune) that was his crucial error. As Lyberte scoffs,

> Cockes armes, syrs, wyll ye not se
> Howe he is undone by the meanes of me?
> For yf Measure had ruled Lyberte as he began,
> This lurden that here lyeth [Magnyfycence] had ben a noble man.
> But he abused so his free lyberte,
> That nowe he hath loste all his felycyte:
> Not thorowe largesse of lyberall expence,
> But by the way of fansy insolence.
> For lyberalyte is most convenyent
> A prynce to use with all his hole intent,
> Largely rewardynge them that have deservyd;
> And so shall a noble man nobly be servyd.
>
> (lines 2109–20)

Both Redresse and Sad Cyrcumspeccyon reiterate this point, couching in explicitly Aristotelian terms the need to avoid extremes in expenditure.

> ... of noblenesse the chefe poynt is to be lyberall,
> So that your largesse be not to prodygall.
>
> (lines 2487–8)

> Lyberte to a lorde belongyth of ryght,
> But wylfull waywardnesse must walke out of the way;
> Measure of your lustys must have the oversyght,
> And not all the nygarde no the chyncherde [miser] to play.
> Let never negarrshyp your noblenesse affray;
> In your rewardys use suche moderacyon
> That nothynge be gyven without consyderacyon.
>
> (lines 2489–95)

Both at the opening and the close of his play, then, Skelton presents his audience with arguments which seem to paraphrase passages from the *Ethics*. That he did so in order to stress the political aspects of his play rather than its purely moral implications might seem paradoxical. But the paradox would not have been evident to a Tudor audience. For the Aristotelian ethical prescriptions were taken in the later medieval period, not simply as notes towards a code of correct personal conduct, but as profound statements of specific political guidance. The virtues and vices of royal housekeeping had been considered and articulated in those very terms for a century or more. Indeed, the central lesson of the drama, that ideal conduct involves the observation of a measured mean between unwelcome extremes of over-expenditure and niggardliness, was the central motivating principle behind a long-running attempt to regulate expenditure and conduct within the royal household. Again Skelton's manipulation of what initially appear to be moral commonplaces proves, when considered in its contemporary context, to be a succinct and quite overt political statement. The language of the moral drama, gleaned ultimately from Aristotle, was also the language of domestic politics as expressed in contemporary documents.

That the King ought to live magnificently within his household was an established principle of medieval politics. As Sir John Fortescue declared,[51]

it shall nede that the Kyng have such tresour, as he may make new bildynges when he woll, ffor his pleasure and magnificence; and as he may bie hym riche clothes ... stones ... and other juels and ornamentes convenient to his estate roiall ... and do other such nobell and grete costes, as bi sitith his roiall majeste ... Ffor yff a king did not so, nor myght do, he lyved then not like his estate, but rather in miseire, and in more subgeccion than doth a private person.

The keystone of such magnificence was held to lie in observing the mean between extravagance and parsimony, in a fitting degree of outlay tempered with measured economy. Such a dictum governed all the household ordinances and regulations of the fifteenth and early sixteenth centuries, the sheer number of which attest to the importance attached to the issue by contemporary legislators.

Harris's argument, that Aristotelian principles cannot govern the play as the poet nowhere borrows directly from the *Ethics*, fails to convince, not least because Skelton did not need to have read the *Ethics* to have been thoroughly saturated in the teachings of the philosopher. He need only have looked to the writings of the late medieval and early Tudor administrative theorists and legislators to have found Aristotle's ideas reiterated and interpreted in a household context. And as a royal tutor during the reign of Henry VII, responsible for educating the future Henry VIII in the principles of good behaviour and sound government, he would have had both good reason and every opportunity to consult such works.

When Edward IV and his council attempted to reform the royal household in 1478, it was in the language of the Aristotelian mean and of personal virtue that they expressed their political desires. 'We take consideration', the warrant for the household ordinances announced,[52]

That no thing was more behovefull for the good and politique administracion of alle that to suche a household might appertaigne, than that the same shuld be

[51] Sir John Fortescue, *The Governance of England*, ed., C. Plummer (Oxford, 1985), p. 125.
[52] A. R. Myers, *The Household of Edward IV* (Manchester, 1959), p. 212.

established upponne certayne ordonaunces and dirrecions grounded principaly upon the two virtues that be mooste requisite in suche maner guyding and rulyng. First, as it is knowen notorily that in politique administration of outward goodes and expenses that the two extremytees be vicious, whereof that one is by excesse and superfluyte, and the other vice is by defaute and skarsete, and the meane of both the vices is the vertue wherby every suche administracion oweth to be modered and guyded, and so is liberalite dewe meane betwix avarice and prodigalite, whiche in regard to that vertue be extremytees vicious. We, ne willing that oure said household be gyded by prodigalite, whiche neyther accordeth with honneur, honeste, ne good maner, ne on that other partie, that it be gyded by avarice which is the werse extremite ... We have taken [therefore] ferme purpose to see and ordeyne thadministration of our said householde ... to be grounded and established upon the forsaid vertue called liberalitee.

Not only was the household governed by Aristotelian principles, its entire organization was based upon such guidelines. Just as the Aristotelian liberal man would exist upon a modest income and a moderate expenditure, so, according to the numerous household ordinances issued by the late medieval kings, should a balance be struck between undue exaction and undue expenditure.[53] Indeed in the, so-called, *Black Book* which regulated the household of Edward IV, that balance was institutionalized in the offices of the household. For the King's Chamber, that portion of the household corresponding to the nineteenth-century household 'above stairs', consisting of the Presence Chamber and the numerous private apartments of the monarch, was described as the *Domus Regie Magnificence* (the Household of Magnificence), whilst the Household proper (the office called by that name, equating to the household below stairs, comprising the public and service wings of the household) was described as the *Domus Providence* (the Household of Providence).[54] The Household of Magnificence, administered by the Lord Chamberlain, concerned itself with display and consumption and acted as the showcase of royal splendour and power, whilst the Household of Providence, administered by the Lord Steward was concerned with economy, designed to feed and clothe the Chamber and 'provide the utmost royal magnificence at the lowest possible cost'.[55]

Time and again in the household ordinances the need for measure is cited as paramount: measure in the individual operations of the complementary households of magnificence and provision, and measure *between* the two households in order that neither more was spent than could be afforded, nor more gathered than was required to be spent. 'The King will

[53] For 'liberality consists in the observance of due measure in the getting as well as the giving of wealth', *Ethics*, p. 112.
[54] Myers, p. 89.
[55] Myers, pp. 86–7, 141–2; P. Williams, *The Tudor Regime* (Oxford, 1979), p. 50.

have his goodes dispended', the *Black Book* declared, 'but not wasted'.[56] The key elements in that measured household were order and economy. Waste and superfluity were to be cut to a minimum, or ideally, eliminated altogether. It was thus vital that offices within the household were filled by those capable of performing their tasks ably and honourably. Many of the household ordinances concentrated upon the need to find officers who were both efficient and virtuous enough for royal service. The Eltham Ordinances of 1526 made the point most clearly in the declaration that,[57]

to the intent the King's Highness may be substantially served in his chamber and household, by such personages as be both honest in their gesture and behaviour, and also expert in such roomes and offices as be deputed unto them; considering also the great confusion, annoyance, infection, trouble and dishonour, that enseweth by the numbers as well of sicklie, impotent, inable and unmeete persons, as of rascalls and vagabonds, now spred, remayning and being in all the court [the Vice Chamberlain should undertake to dismiss the latter to make way for the former]

As the vices gradually make their entry into *Magnyfycence* it is easy to recognize in them, not only the vicious villains of the morality tradition, but more significantly such unmeet persons as the ordinances warned against. They exhibit a catalogue of personality traits inimical to good rule and order. They abhor reason and wisdom, the qualities most prized in good household officers,[58] and elevate sheer caprice ('Fansy') as their motivating principle. They are precisely the dishonest, spendthrift flatterers which ordinance after ordinance condemned. By introducing them to the Court of Magnyfycence, Skelton depicts a household fallen into a form of government entirely contrary to the collective wisdom of the household legislators. The ruin of the Prince's household in the hands of these incompetent self-servers is inevitable.

Yet appointment to household office was not simply a question of efficiency. In a personal monarchy the Crown was the fount of all patronage. Thus the surest means of advancement for the subject was to secure access to the Sovereign in order to press his or her case for favour. Failing that, he or she gained the favour of someone who themselves had that access and who would act on their behalf. Hence the individuals with the greatest opportunity to provide for themselves, and for others, were those close household servants and intimate companions of the King who, like the minions of 1519, were in continual attendance upon him. To a significant extent, therefore, national affairs became domestic affairs, as the

---

[56] Myers, p. 87.
[57] Society of Antiquaries, *A Collection of Ordinances and Regulations for the Government of the Royal Household Made in Divers Reigns* (London, 1790), p. 146.
[58] The *Black Book* of Edward IV, for example, declared that the Lord Steward should rule and guide the household 'by his reson', and amend dishonourable or unprofitable practices 'as shale seme his wisdom' (Myers, pp. 142 and 145).

quest for wealth and influence was played out within the royal household. Although there were other means of access, other channels for counsel, and other centres of power, the need to have at least one friend in the private staff of the King was recognized by even the most powerful of noblemen and bureaucrats. This process placed a great burden upon both the King who had to dispense the favours, and his servants. Hence who the King chose as his closest attendants was a carefully weighed political decision which generated a whole body of literature offering theoretical and practical advice.

As the quest for patronage and favour was so crucial an aspect of Court life, it needed close regulation. The royal household was carefully organized in order that access to the King was limited – not with the intention of denying those with legitimate suits the means to advance them, but to ensure the smooth running of the system by eliminating frivolous suits and malicious or mischievous individuals.[59] Those ministers and courtiers who enjoyed the coveted access were enabled, indeed expected, to act as a mean between the Sovereign and his subjects. They maintained the dignity of the Crown by keeping the King free from the clamour of would-be suitors, yet ensured that the business of the administration could be carried on. Hence the politics of royal patronage became institutionalized in the architecture and administrative structure of the Court, with access to each suite of rooms, the Great or Outer chamber, the Presence chamber and the Privy chamber (in order of selectivity) strictly regulated, and their staffs carefully briefed on whom to admit and whom to refuse.[60]

Such was the theory. The system relied upon a carefully constructed protocol of privilege and deference. When it worked correctly the result would be an harmonious blend of order and freedom. When it was perverted by self-interest, as became the case in *Magnyfycence*, corruption and rivalry replaced order and the Sovereign became the prisoner of his own servants. Thus the royal household was considered in many ways the

---

[59] For attempts to regulate access to the Sovereign in the reign of Edward IV, see B.L. Harleian MS 642, f. 180; printed in Myers, p. 201. For those in the reigns of Henry VII and Henry VIII, see *Ordinances*, pp. 109–241.

[60] Starkey, 'The King's Privy Chamber', Chapter 1. The Eltham Ordinances of 1525 appointed, regarding the 'Outward Chambers', that 'one of the yeoman wayters shall dayly take charge of the door of the same, not permitting or suffering any person to enter, but such as by his discression shall be seene good and meete for that place: nor any gentleman's page to come within the same chamber except it be to speake with his master: and his message done, incontinently to depart' (*Ordinances*, p. 152). The Privy Chamber was more selective. It was declared necessary for 'the King's Highnesse [to] have his privy chamber and inward lodgeings reserved secrett, at the pleasure of his grace, without repaire of any great multitude thereunto: it is therefore ordeyned, that noe person, of what estate, degree or condicion soever he be, from henceforth presume, attempt, or be in anywise suffered or admitted to come or repair into the King's privy chamber, other than such onely as his grace shall from time to time call or command' (ibid., p. 154).

testing ground of a regime. The King who could govern his own household
suggested that he could govern the nation. The King who failed to keep his
own house in order was deemed a failure. These are the terms which
govern Skelton's play. Magnyfycence is a man, certainly, who must resist
the psychological temptations which endanger his soul, but he is more
importantly a prince, and the result of his struggle will effect his subjects
and his realm. Just as the individual psyche of Everyman provided a model
for humanity, so the royal household provides a microcosmic type of the
commonwealth in *Magnyfycence*. As Adversyte tellingly informs the protagonist as the conclusion of the play approaches, his downfall was
brought about by his inability to control his courtiers.

> ... I stryke lordys of realmes and landys
> That rule not be measure they have in thyr handys,
> That sadly rule not theyr howsholde men.
>
> (lines 1938–40)

Similarly his restoration to virtue is signalled by his acceptance of new,
sound courtiers in the form of Cyrcumspeccyon and Redresse.

Magnyfycence is thus firmly based in the theory and procedure of the
royal household.[61] It takes as its theme the recruitment, and subsequent
removal, of unsuitable courtiers to illustrate the value of conventional
wisdom on the subject and draws heavily for its theoretical base upon the
principles which governed household administration. The relevance of all
this to the dismissals of 1519 is clear. By setting the removal of the minions
in the context of an Aristotelian debate on true Kingship, Skelton presented the purge as clear evidence of Henry's status as a magnificent
sovereign. In so doing he offered a clear and effective *apologia* for the
King's actions. Yet the play does more than simply justify and allegorize
the events of 1519. By dramatizing the operation of Aristotelian principles
in a household context the play demonstrates how the Court ought to

---

[61] Even the incidental details of the plot betray a keen interest in and knowledge of household
procedures and problems on the part of its author. When the poet has the vices decide, for
example, that Foly shall become 'mayster of the masshe fat', and 'kepe the brewhouse
boule' (lines 1319–24) he draws upon both a traditional morality motif and his own
knowledge of household affairs. An association with alcoholic excess was frequently used
in moral drama to indicate a character's vicious tendencies. Usually the point is made by
reference to a tavern, but as Skelton's dramatic locus is the royal household, he refers
instead to the royal cellars. The allusion is not simply emblematic, however, as an
examination of the household ordinances reveals. For the appointment of the Butler of Ale
and his subordinate grooms, who had 'speciall charge under the saide sergeant [of the
cellar] for the keping of ... ale, bere, or such other stuf, and ministracion thereof', was,
given the potential for misrule evident in his responsibilities, a sensitive one. That the royal
ale cellars were notorious nonetheless is indicated by a pointed instruction in the *Black
Book* that 'Hit fittithe the grete officers of [the] countynghouse, oftin tyms and sodenlye,
to visite the officers and offices [of the Butlery of Ale] to se and know if any riotous rulis be
usyd within for the Kynges hurt, and to amend hit'. Myers, p. 182.

operate. By writing the theoretical implications of the household reforms so large, Skelton made it difficult for the subject of this *encomium* to fall back again from the high standards set by the 1519 declarations. Like many another vehicle of praise, the play also acted as an example to be lived up to. It provided a didactic mirror for the prince rather than just a reflection of his actions. Indeed, it is difficult not to read the play as an attempt by the poet, for whom the question of (re)appointments to household posts was a very relevant one, to jog the conscience of the King and prompt him to carry through the personal and administrative renovation which he had promised.

Perhaps paradoxically, a close study of *Magnyfycence* also proves to be extremely informative concerning the theory and practice of political advice and the protocol of political discourse in the Tudor period, although the play was probably not performed before the royal household, and ultimately did little either to restore its author to royal favour or to confirm the King in his resolution to 'lead a new life'.[62] It stands, nonetheless, as a model of political advice literature. Like the 'text-book' cricket stroke performed a split-second after the ball has passed, it is instructive even in failure.

That Skelton chose to offer Henry VIII a subtle encomium rather than a political treatise or a sermon is significant. In choosing that mode of expression he followed a familiar path. Others would use such vehicles for ideas far more critical of their intended recipients than the modest suggestions of continued enthusiasm for reform which seemingly underlie Skelton's text. This was not because Tudor monarchs would not entertain anything which looked like a lecture from their subjects, and so bred a sycophancy which dominated all forms of expression. As the previous chapter suggested, Tudor statesmen, even princes, might expect to receive quite severe criticism under certain circumstances. That political discourse between subject and sovereign took such forms as these illustrates deeper assumptions about political behaviour in the period.

It is a matter for debate whether Tudor and Stuart monarchs and their governments saw their role as anything beyond simply continuing to be. Certainly they did not see a need to formulate clear, far-sighted, policies, and the Whiggish notion of the progressive evolution of newer and better administrative systems was anathema. Hence for a subject to offer anything approaching a manifesto of action for royal consideration was ultimately pointless. The Crown had no need of policies, it simply reacted in the short-term to specific challenges, occasionally with unlooked-for

---

[62] By the early 1520s the Court had reverted to its unregenerate state, Henry was threatening to turn self-indulgence, in the form of hunting, 'into a martyrdom' (*L.P.* III (i) 950) and new ordinances had to be issued in 1526 to start the reforming process over again.

long-term consequences. But this is not to say that Tudor princes and their ministers were entirely lacking in idealism. Ideals they had, relating both to themselves and their environment. There existed very clear views about how certain individuals, and certain institutions, should act, and these served as models against which to measure current conduct. Henry VIII, for example, had a clear idea of the responsibilities and character of an ideal king, a sovereign who acted as the father of his people, their leader in war, and guardian and patron in peace. And frequently his actions may be judged as attempts to exemplify this ideal.

From such models sprang the concept of Reformation, the return to the ideal from the debased current practice. Hence the hostility to the concept of progress. For, by definition, all such 'advancement' would be away from the original ideal, which was conceived of, not only as a notional Platonic form, but also as a concrete reality located in time, inevitably in the past. What was needed was not an advance into a new dispensation, but a return to past practice. Hence the religious reformers called, not for a new pure Church to replace what they saw as a corrupt old one, but a return to an ideal practice associated with the Apostolic ministry. And hence Henry VIII's concept of royal honour was not consciously innovative or unique to himself, but retrospective, harking back to previous exemplars of greatness such as Henry V and Edward III.

The modes of expression available to the subject utilized the ideal of Monarchy cherished by Henry VIII in different ways. The petition for redress of grievances engaged with that part of it which stressed the Sovereign's role as protector of his subjects and paterfamilias. The King had no obligation to provide for the improvement of the life of his people in any progressive way. But he was obliged to maintain their rights and privileges against the encroachment of others. Thus the appeal for action based upon a notional loss of rights was likely to be heard, where the suggestion of positive improvements might be dismissed as presumptuous.

Central to this process was the question of honour. It conferred honour upon the Sovereign to conform to the ideal of kingship: that honour was tarnished if he failed to do so. Hence the discussion of political questions was conducted within a rhetoric of honour and dishonour. It was honourable for a king to preside over an ordered household, to have the means to live magnificently, and to have contented, loyal subjects. If his household was chaotic, his coffers empty, or his subjects discontented, it brought dishonour upon him. Hence the willingness to reform institutions, or to improve the lot of his people (if they were thought to merit it) sprang not from a regard for social welfare *per se*, but from the need to remove a blot upon the royal honour. The wise subject appreciated this and articulated his petition in appropriate terms.

The writer of an encomium also articulated the request for change in the language of honour and reformation. By presenting the Sovereign with a vision of the ideal, the author tacitly challenged him to live up to it.[63] *Magnyfycence* did not attempt to tell Henry VIII what he should *do*, it merely reminded him what he should *be*. By drawing upon the same Aristotelian ideals of behaviour and demeanour which motivated the ideal sovereign of Henry's imagination, the play both encouraged and reinforced his own resolution to reform himself. The play and the reforming measures of 1519 acted symbiotically.

Whereas *Magnyfycence* dramatizes a Court regulated by decorum and deference which falls into disorder and is subsequently restored to its original state, the reality of the Tudor Court, even at its most reformed, was of an overcrowded and generally indecorous institution. The numerous household ordinances attest not only to a continuing commitment on the part of the administration to the ideals of good household government, but also to the continued failure of the reality to live up to those ideals. No matter how theoretically selective the various royal suites were in terms of admittance, in practice they were invariably besieged by suitors and packed with varying degrees of the Tudor great and the good. Even the Presence Chamber, supposedly the most formal public room in the royal palaces, in which the majesty and mystery of Kingship was symbolized by the ever-present throne covered with a cloth of state, and in which due reverence was paid on those occasions when the Sovereign himself chose to appear there, was frequently indistinguishable from the Great Hall or the other 'public' chambers, as a contemporary drawing showing Henry VIII dining there amply illustrates.[64] In the chamber are at least seventeen persons, some serving the King, others paying him no attention whatsoever, conducting their own conversations or standing idly about. Documentary accounts of events in the Privy Chamber suggest that this number of occupants was also far from exceptional in the ultimate retreat for a

---

[63] Note Erasmus's observation to Jean Desmarez, that 'Those who believe panegyrics are nothing but flattery seem to be unaware of the purpose and aim of the extremely far-sighted men who invented this kind of composition, which consists in presenting princes with a pattern of goodness, in such a way as to reform bad rulers [and] improve the good', 'no other way of correcting a prince is as efficacious as offering the pattern of a truly good prince under the guise of flattery to them', R. A. B. Mynors and D. F. S. Thomson, eds. and trans., *The Correspondence of Erasmus* (2 vols., Toronto, 1975) II, 81. For a wider study of the poetics of praise, see O. B. Hardison, jr, *The Enduring Monument: A Study of the Idea of Praise in Renaissance Literary Theory and Practice* (Chapel Hill, 1962).

[64] British Museum, 1854–6–28–74 (after Holbein). That the Privy Chamber was frequently crowded was observed by S. J. Gunn, 'Charles Brandon, Duke of Suffolk, A Magnate among Minions', paper read to the Institute of Historical Research Sixteenth- and Seventeenth-Century History Seminar, 7 February 1984. I am grateful to Dr Gunn for the opportunity to cite this paper.

monarch in search of solitude. In the contrast between Skelton's dramatically presented ideal and the readily apparent contemporary reality lay a spur to reforming action every bit as effective as an impassioned cry for redress.

Magnyfycence was, however, seemingly not performed at Court. Where then might it have been presented? And how were the theoretical considerations outlined above presented in performance? What follows will examine these questions in detail.

'MAGNYFYCENCE' IN PERFORMANCE: ARENA AND AUDIENCE

What little may safely be said about the evolution of the play and its subsequent performance must be inferred from internal evidence. This means that a number of crucial questions concerning its early history cannot be answered with certainty. The most vital of these concern the audience for its first performance(s). Where, and before whom, was the play performed? And what does this imply about its political stance and significance?

Perhaps the safest assumption that can be made concerns the locale of the first performance. For the play clearly seems to have been written for an audience in or around London. Only there would the play's political allusions have been fully understood, and only in the vicinity of the Court and in diplomatic circles would Henry's personal and administrative 'reformation' of 1519 have been of interest. Moreover, the setting for the action within the play is apparently in the London area, close to both the City itself and a royal palace. For the text contains a number of local topographical references aimed at a City audience, whose sensibilities the poet, himself a resident of Westminster, was well able to judge.[65]

But, if the play was first performed in or close to London, who formed its audience? Perhaps the most likely possibility is Paula Neuss's suggestion that it was intended for performance in a livery company's hall, perhaps even that of the Merchant Taylors' Company, which was the butt of the poet's ironic humour at line 1404.[66] The alternative, that it was played at Court, or in the hall of a nobleman or leading courtier, seems, despite the play's theme, less likely.

There is little in the play text which suggests that a court performance was envisaged. Unlike the lavish productions which normally graced Court occasions, *Magnyfycence* seems to have been written to a very modest budget. It employs none of the costly properties or staging devices

---

[65] Note the familiar references to the '[Merchant] Taylers Hall' (line 1404), the 'halfe strete' (line 2263) and 'Tyburne' (lines 423 and 910).
[66] Neuss, p. 43.

of more elaborate productions and, apart from the costumes of the vices, maintains an impressive economy of dress and acting personnel.[67] Perhaps significantly, all the parts required by the play may be performed by four men and one boy: the traditional composition of the touring company.[68] Does this suggest that Skelton had such a troupe in mind when writing? It is useful to contrast the play with works known to have been designed for Court performance, such as John Heywood's *Play of the Weather* (printed in 1533) or the anonymous *Respublica* (1553), which called for ten and eleven actors respectively. Such economies of casting as Skelton employed suggest that, unlike the writers of these later works, he did not enjoy the backing of a royal or noble patron or access to a large body of potential actors.

Similarly the audience is addressed by the actors as 'syrs' (line 1896) and 'maysters' (line 1044). This need not, of course, be conclusive, but, were the King or members of the nobility expected to be present, it is surely likely that they would have been afforded their correct titles. This again tends to support the suggestion of a performance before a London livery company.

There is further circumstantial evidence to support this possibility. There is no evidence to link Skelton with any acting company. Thus, if he were not writing for the Court, and so did not have the Gentlemen or Children of the Chapel Royal, or the King's Players placed at his disposal, it is difficult to see how he might find the actors he needed. But the livery companies frequently employed professional companies to perform for them on their feast days.[69] Hence it is possible that the commissioning company acted as broker in this instance and brought playwright and actors together to create this production of the play.

The possibility of such a performance would satisfy the conditions for performance outlined above. It would provide an audience in the London area capable of appreciating the political subtleties of the play, who would have the resources to back the kind of modest production suggested by the

---

[67] Contrast the modest equipment necessitated by *Magnyfycence* with the 'traverses' and numerous extras required by *Godly Queen Hester* or Heywood's *Play of the Weather*.

[68] Ramsey, pp. xiix–l.

[69] G. Wickham, *Early English Stages* (3 vols., London, 1959–81), III, p. 56. Unfortunately the Merchant Tailors' archive lapses in this area for the entire period 1485–1544. Thus it is impossible to substantiate the suggestion that they commissioned the performance. Neuss, pp. 42–3. But from as early as 1404 or before many companies had hired acting troupes. See Lancashire, *Dramatic Texts and Records*, p. xx. This process continued throughout our period. In 1516, for example, the Drapers' Company hired the King's Players to perform two plays. In the previous year they had employed John Slye and his company for the same task. Similarly the Goldsmiths and the Merchant Taylors commissioned the choirboys of St Pauls' and the boys of the Merchant Tailors' school. Wickham, III, p. 56.

play text.[70] It would also provide a performance close enough to the Court for word of Skelton's efforts to be carried there, which was seemingly his intention.[71] This need not necessarily imply that the company concerned actually commissioned the poet to write a political play. It is more likely that Skelton received a general commission, and chose to use it to further his own ends, producing a play which would both entertain and instruct his immediate audience and continue his campaign to regain royal favour. The result was a doubly persuasive drama. Even as it sought to justify Henry VIII's actions to the governors of his capital city, it also contrived to appeal to the King himself on behalf of its author. In so doing it proved itself, not only technically, but also politically, an extremely accomplished creation.

'MAGNYFYCENCE' IN PERFORMANCE: POLITICAL THEMES AND PHILOSOPHY IN ACTION

In *Magnyfycence* the place (the *platea* or acting space which served as a stage in those halls and arenas which had no provision for a raised platform) takes on a political dimension. The space in which the action is enacted, and the movement of the characters across it, are, of course, crucial elements in all plays. They have both mimetic and symbolic functions. In other works they might be manipulated to signify the fortunes of, or indicate psychological truths about, the characters presented. When Marlowe presents Tamburlaine forever on the march, crossing the stage, making and striking martial camp, he provides his audience with both a suggestion of the tyrant's material fortunes – a sense of his constantly expanding empire – and an indication of his psychological state – his restless ambition and aspiration. In *Magnyfycence* Skelton utilizes movement across the place, and the spatial relationships of the characters within it, for political ends, to suggest truths of political conduct rather than internal states. In the physical interaction of monarch, courtiers and anti-courtiers, the play provides a symbolic representation of the theory of conduct in the early modern Court.

As has been suggested, the fall of Magnyfycence is explicitly shown to be the consequence of his failure to regulate the workings of his household.

[70] The notion of a merchant audience here would also help to explain an otherwise curious aspect of Skelton's later satirical poems. After the completion of *Speke, Parott* and *Collyn Clout* (in 1522), he chose, perhaps surprisingly, to write *Why Come Ye Nat To Courte?*, the last of the satires of Wolsey, from the perspective of the City's merchant community (Walker, *Skelton*, Chapter 3, part 3). If the poet had already enjoyed the patronage of a livery company in 1519, however, the decision to court such patronage again would be readily understandable.

[71] That the Court generally and the King in particular were well informed about dramatic performances outside the Household seems highly likely. See below, pp. 226–7.

This proposition is explored and demonstrated through a number of interconnecting scenes, each of which represents a stage in the corruption of the politics of patronage.

The first of these scenes involves the acceptance by Magnyfycence of the services of two suitors, Lyberte and Felycyte. Here, through his use both of language and of dramatic space, Skelton reveals the exemplary nature of his Prince and his Court.

Having restored order to the stage (at line 160) by reconciling the arguing suitors, Measure prepares the audience for the entrance of the Sovereign, whom he formally announces, in order to clear the aisle of spectators.

> Nowe pleasyth you a lytell whyle to stande:
> Me semeth Magnyfycence is comynge here at hande.
> (lines 161–2)

Magnyfycence's entrance and bearing are fitting for a sovereign whose Court is governed by virtue and decorum. His introductory speech is free from the self-defeating bravado of his subsequent fallen state. Announcing himself to suitors and audience alike, he declares,

> To assure you of my noble porte and fame,
> Who lyst to knowe, Magnyfycence I hyght.
> (lines 163–4)

He immediately takes command of the acting space and, noticing the strangers, requests to know their names.

> But Measure, my frende, what hyght this mannys name?
> (line 165)

Significantly, given Aristotle's dictum that the liberal man is characterized by his capacity to identify fitting objects for his beneficence,[72] it is the virtuous Felycyte whom he selects for introduction rather than the morally neutral Lyberte.

The correct protocol is followed throughout the encounter. Magnyfycence does not approach the suitors directly before they have been recommended to him. It is Measure who is asked to identify the strangers, and it is he who returns their reply to the King. Accepting the role of patron of the two men, he recommends them as fitting servants for the Crown.

> Syr, though ye be a noble prynce of myght,
> Yet in this man you must set your delyght.
> (lines 165–6)

[72] *Ethics*, p. 110.

Only once they have been formally introduced and sponsored by the trusted counsellor does Magnyfycence offer them words of welcome. Only when the correct etiquette of introduction has been followed are the two able to speak, naming themselves afresh to the King and offering him their service.

Measure has thus acted as 'a merry mene' (line 380) throughout this opening section of the play. Not only does he represent a moderate mean between extremes of conduct, he also acts as a mean between individuals, a channel of access for fitting aspirants to place and office. He exemplifies in his person both an ideal of conduct, and a practical example of that ideal in action in its courtly context.

Taking Measure's counsel, Magnyfycence suggests that he will adopt the suitors into his household as

> Convenyent persons for any prynce ryall.
> Welthe with Lyberte, with me bothe dwell ye shall.
>
> (lines 173–4)

Yet, because Measure has acted as their benefactor and referee, it is into his keeping that the King entrusts them. Having begun as the honest broker, recommending their merits to the Sovereign, he is now to act as guarantor of their future conduct. The King has admitted them into his service provisionally, but his political acumen is demonstrated by this further prudent step taken to ensure their good behaviour.

> To the gydyng of my Measure you bothe commyttynge,
> That Measure be mayster us semeth it is syttynge.
>
> (lines 175–6)

Measure accepts the charge with magnanimity.

> Whereas ye have, syr, to me them assygned,
> Suche order I trust with them for to take,
> So that welthe with measure shalbe conbyned,
> And lyberte his large with measure shall make.
>
> (lines 177–80)

Only once this assurance is given, and both probationers agree to abide by Magnyfycence's 'ordinance', does the King formally grant them a position in his household, welcoming them with the words

> Then may I say that ye be servauntys myne.
>
> (line 183)

The allegorical dimension to all this needs little elaboration. Skelton presents a man in full command of both himself and his calling, who assures the continuation of his wealth and happiness (Welthfull Felycyte) by tempering his freedom of action (Lyberte) with a concern for propriety

(Measure). But, although there is an obvious moral element to the drama, the terms in which that personal allegory are worked out are those of household administration. It is not that Skelton uses household terms and protocol merely as a metaphor for psychological statements. Magnyfycence is revealed as a just man and a just prince precisely through his regulation of his household. Unlike *Everyman* or *Mankind*, *Magnyfycence* presents, not a personal struggle which re-enacts a spiritual one, but a personal struggle considered as part of a political one.

It must not, of course, be forgotten that drama is essentially a visual medium. And undoubtedly the rhetoric of patronage, recommendation and service which underlies this scene was reinforced by the physical actions of the players, thus giving it a potent visual dimension. As Magnyfycence entered the place, not only would the audience be alerted to clear the aisle by Measure's cry of 'Magnyfycence is commynge here at hand', but the actors would themselves move away from him.[73] Thus the gulf between the two would effectively demonstrate the aura of majesty surrounding the virtuous sovereign. Later, once Magnyfycence has been tempted into corruption by the vices, this crucial distancing will collapse, serving as an emblematic rendering of the failure of his Kingship. For the present, the distant position adopted by the suitors serves to emphasize the true magnificence of the protagonist.

Having appraised the situation, Magnyfycence summons Measure to him. The latter's role as an intermediary then becomes manifest as he speaks for the two suitors waiting out of earshot at the far side of the place. Only after the recommendation does the King's summons permit Lyberte and Felycyte to cross the divide: hence the need for them to reintroduce themselves. Magnyfycence and the audience had already heard their names from Measure, but the suitors themselves were not privy to this conversation: a further indication of their lowly rank. As good subjects they can only await their Sovereign's pleasure. Only when convinced of their worthiness does Magnyfycence grant them leave to become active in 'his' space, and they approach. The ideal Sovereign's complete control of his household is thus exemplified, King and subject having become respectively the active and passive elements in a brief dumb-show of the manipulative qualities of the Crown.

Thus in the first 183 lines of the drama Skelton has provided both an exposition in debate form of the principles of good government and a visual demonstration of those principles in action. The characteristics of the ideal household are revealed to be deference to authority (exemplified in the protocol of patronage), the virtuous use of largesse (revealed in

---

[73] R. Southern, 'The Techniques of Play Presentation', in N. Sanders *et al.*, eds., *The Revels History of Drama in English*, II (London, 1980), pp. 80–2.

Magnyfycence's adoption of Felycyte and Lyberte) and the rule of reason
and order (figured in the authority granted to Measure as the King's chief
minister). What follows is the progressive dismantling of this ideal system,
as the household is turned into a perverted reversal of itself through the
corrupting influence of the vices.

The first of the vices to appear is Fansy, who enters in the guise of the
noble virtue 'Largesse'. The contrast between his conduct and what has
gone before could not be more pointed. Cutting through the protocol of
recommendation and acceptance he enters the place unannounced and,
boldly crossing it towards the King, requests leave to speak (lines 252–3).
This overturning of proper conduct arouses both shock and anger among
the courtiers. Felycyte demands to know

> From whens come you, syr, that no man lokyd after?
> (line 255)

Magnyfycence, astounded at the stranger's presumption, adds,

> Or who made you so bolde to interrupe my tale?
> (line 256)

By claiming to be Largesse, Fansy seems to warrant a place at Court;
thus he manages to placate Felycyte (lines 270–6). But Magnyfycence
remains unconvinced. Fansy is clearly working within the accepted Aristotelian notion of liberality when he suggests that

> ... without largesse noblenesse can not rayne
> ... without largesse worshyp hath no place,
> For largesse is a purchaser of pardon and of grace.
> (lines 265, 267–8)

Yet the falsity of his argument is demonstrated by all he says and does.
Unlike the audience, Magnyfycence does not see that 'Largesse' wears a
fool's costume under his courtly robes, but the King is sufficiently astute to
be suspicious of his claims. Largesse, Fansy suggests, 'is he that all prynces
doth avaunce' (line 279). But his entrance alone demonstrates his unfam-
iliarity with princes and the procedures of their Courts, whilst his manners
and language (he accuses Magnyfycence of having been 'blowen ... full of
wynde' by 'covetyse' (line 290)) reveal him to be firmly in the tradition of
the irreverent vice. Everything about him is false. His argument that
'Largesse is a purchaser of pardon and of grace' degrades the Aristotelian
virtue to the point where it becomes simply a means of cynically courting
heavenly reward. His costume is a sham. Even his name is false, as his
diminutive stature emphasizes, for the part was played by a boy. Thus
'Largesse' is the smallest figure in the play.

Uneasy in the face of these deceptions Magnyfycence appears to see through the pretence and seems on the point of banishing Fansy from the Court.

> What! I have aspyed ye are a carles page.
> (line 288)

> Go shake the, dogge, hay, syth ye wyll nedys!
> You are nothynge mete with us for to dwell,
> That with your lorde and mayster so pertly can prate!
> Get you hens, I say, by my counsell.
> I wyll not use you to play with me checke mate!
> (lines 303–7)

To this point, then, Magnyfycence has proved himself to be the model King. He has accepted into his service the worthy suitors Lyberte and Felycyte, leaving them in the keeping of Measure who will curb Lyberte's anarchic tendencies, and he is unconvinced by the charlatan Fansy. Yet it is at this moment that his fall into folly begins. Significantly that fall is initiated by a perversion of the patronage system, the cornerstone of household politics. For Fansy, on the point of dismissal, produces what purports to be a letter of recommendation from the King's trusted counsellor Sad Cyrcumspeccyon. Although it later transpires that this testimonial is a forgery, neither Magnyfycence nor the audience have reason to deny its authenticity at this moment. Thus 'Largesse' seems to merit a place at Court after all. The prince is deceived by a corruption of the system upon which he has to rely. Hence, although he still resists offering Fansy a post immediately, he is willing to take him to the palace to interrogate him further. Fansy has thus gained the crucial access to the person of the monarch which he sought. Hereafter he will corrupt Magnyfycence at his leisure. With this one act the dam has been breached. Soon the Court will be awash with vicious interlopers.

Thus through two examples of patronage in action, the one correct, the other fraudulent, Skelton presents his audience with first a view of the perfectly regulated Court, then one of that Court infiltrated by vice. Subsequent scenes plot the further fall of King and Court into folly and tyranny, depicting a thoroughly corrupt household through a debased parody of the patronage system demonstrated in the opening lines.

As we have seen, access to the monarch, the admission or refusal of suitors, and distance or proximity to the royal person, were the key issues of domestic politics examined in Skelton's play. How far the Sovereign emerged from his private rooms to greet an individual, and how far that individual was permitted to penetrate into the Sovereign's domain were signal marks of favour. The opening lines of the play portrayed that spatial interaction in its perfect form. The proper distance between King and suitors was established, and then bridged by the intermediary Measure. The role of each of the characters was established by protocol and tacitly accepted by all concerned. The King's ability to summon the suitors to him demonstrated his superiority, their obedience in awaiting that summons demonstrated their humility. As the play progresses this tacit consensus over the wielding of authority degenerates into mere anarchic posturing.

In a clear parody of the earlier scene the vices Crafty Conveyaunce and Clokyd Colusyon each attempt to demonstrate their capacities to act as powerful patrons to the aspiring suitor Courtly Abusyon. Having offered to recommend Abusyon to Magnyfycence, Colusyon refuses to compromise his new-found dignity when Conveyaunce enters the place imperiously 'poyntyng with his fynger' (between lines 778 and 779), and calling him with a peremptory 'hem, Collusyon' (line 779). Faced with this summons Colusyon chooses to ignore it, despite Abusyon's attempt to draw his attention to it. As he has not moved, Conveyaunce attempts to call him again.

> Nay, come at ones, for the armes of the dyce.
> (line 781)

This provokes Abusyon, who is not yet initiated into the protocol of the Court, to express surprise at Colusyon's behaviour. 'Cockys armys', he swears, 'he hath callyd for thee twyce' (line 782). But still Colusyon will not move.

The problem arises because, in the absence of the central authority manifested in the person of the King, each vice claims preeminence. Neither will compromise his pride and play the suitor, crossing the space between them at the other's behest. For to do so would be to concede precedence and dignity, and so lose face in the eyes of the suitor Abusyon. Thus Colusyon replies to the latter's observation,

> By cockys harte, and call shall agayne!
> To come to me I trowe he shalbe fayne.
> (lines 783–4)

Each character accuses the other of pride, yet neither will move. As a result they simply trade insults from opposite ends of the place.

> Abusyon: What! Is thy harte pryckyd with such a prowde pynne?
> Colusyon: Tushe! He that hathe nede, man, let hym rynne.
> Conveyaunce: Nay, come away, man! Thou playst the cayser.
> Col: By the masse, thou shalt byde my leyser.
> Con: Abyde, syr, quod he! Mary, so I do.
> (lines 785–9)

The vices here parody the proper use of regal dignity and concern for honour exemplified by the unfallen Magnyfycence. But it is a measure of the already corrupted state of the household at this point that Abusyon is impressed by their ludicrous display. Faced with two such pompous individuals he is unsure which is the greater patron ('I ne tell can / Whiche of you is the better man' (lines 801–2)).

It is curious to note that previous commentators have been puzzled by the object of the vices' intrigue. Why are they expending so much energy in finding places at Court? Precisely what object are the plotters hoping to achieve by their machinations?[74] In actuality, of course, 'plot' and object are one and the same. Their intention, like that of the many hundreds drawn to the Court in the early Tudor period, was simply to seek a place there, and to gain access to the King. That was sufficient prize for even the most ambitious of men, for it was the key to wealth and influence. There is no need to search for a grander design behind the characters' scramble for places in the household. As in Skelton's previous excursion into Court satire, the vices' object is simply to obtain 'bowge of court', for from it all things flowed.[75]

To obtain a position provided both the opportunity to press for further royal grants for oneself, and the chance to petition on behalf of one's friends. Thus one became sought after oneself, and with clients came status. Hence all the vices are delighted when Fansy and Crafty Conveyaunce gain 'a room' in the household. As Counterfet Countenaunce confides to Clokyd Colusyon, the other vices' success provides a vehicle for his own rise to favour.

> ... these twayne
> With Magnyfycence in householde do remayne;
> And there they wolde have me to dwell.
>
> (lines 612–14)

This is confirmed by Crafty Conveyaunce who gleefully reports that

> Fansy and I, we twayne,
> With Magnyfycence in householde do remayne;
> And counterfeted our names we have
> Craftely all thynges upryght to save...
> Magnyfycence to us begynneth to enclyne,
> Counterfet Countenaunce to have also,
> And wolde that we sholde for hym go.
>
> (lines 639–42, 644–6)

---

[74] Heiserman, pp. 108–9.   [75] *The Bowge of Courte*, Scattergood, *Works*, pp. 46–61.

Similarly Courtly Abusyon declares his intention to find a place at court.

> Mary, with Magnyfycence I wolde be retaynyd.
>
> (line 763)

There is thus no unified conspiracy at work in the play. What is portrayed is simply the chaotic scramble for offices that characterized the corrupt Court.[76] Abusyon is already intent upon entering the royal household when he encounters the other vices. Their meeting is not prearranged. The entrance of this aptly named vice merely exemplifies the full debasement of the system of patronage which the vices had achieved. Unlike the ideal example of the patron provided by Measure, who through genuine regard for the well-being of the Sovereign and the commonwealth, recommended those suitors best suited for royal service, Abusyon's attitude towards patronage is entirely cynical and self-interested. He announces his intentions quite openly in soliciting favour from Colusyon.

> I am of fewe wordys. I love not to crake.
> Beryst thou any rome? Or cannyst thou do ought?
> Cannyst thou helpe in faver that I myght be brought?
>
> (lines 775–7)

He is also candid about his willingness to swap patrons if he might benefit as a result. Once Crafty Conveyance begins to appear as influential as Colusyon, Abusyon is at a loss who to approach, a dilemma which, as we have seen, brings him into conflict with his original sponsor.

> Colusion: What sayst thou, man? Why dost thou not supplye, [supplicate]
> And desyre me thy good mayster to be?
> Abusyon: Spekest thou to me?
> Col: Ye, so I tell the.
> Ab: Cockes bones! I ne tell can
> Whiche of you is the better man,
> Or whiche of you can do most.
>
> (lines 797–803)

In these scenes Skelton presents the parody of patronage employed by the vices, which is in reality simply the practice of naked self-interest. In a final tableau he depicts the corrupt state of the fully fallen Court by having Magnyfycence himself preside over a cruel perversion of the process of recommendation.

Whilst Measure provided the active element in the process of recommendation, it was a means of bringing the virtuous into royal service.

---

[76] For the continuing battle waged by the senior household officers to prevent courtiers and household servants drawing in gangs of undesirable hangers-on with them, see, for example, Myers, p. 87 and *Ordinances*, p. 148.

Once he is supplanted by Fansy and the vices he becomes the passive victim of a form of anti-patronage which frustrates the advancement of the virtuous and promotes deception and villainy.

Having been removed from office, Measure approaches one of those now in favour, Colusyon, hoping to gain an interview with the King at which to beg for a reprieve from his banishment. Colusyon, in return for a bribe, accepts the role of patron and promises to speak to Magnyfycence on Measure's behalf. Then in a scene which is the direct antithesis of the opening audience, Colusyon, the anti-patron, takes Measure's suit to the King.

Placing Measure in the position of the impotent suitor, distanced from the King and out of earshot of the proceedings, Colusyon crosses the space between subject and King, promising the former that he will act as his spokesman.

> Stande styll here, and ye shall se
> That for your sake I wyll fall on my kne.
> (lines 1629–30)

Just as he had welcomed Measure in the earlier scene, Magnyfycence now welcomes Colusyon. The latter begins in the manner of the genuine patron, speaking in the aureate style employed earlier by Measure himself.

> Please it your grace at the contemplacyon
> Of my pore instance and supplycacyon,
> Tenderly to consyder in your advertence –
> Of our blessyd Lorde, syr, at the reverence –
> Remembre the good servyce that Mesure hath you done,
> And that ye wyll not cast hym away so sone.
> (lines 1633–8)

Yet, although the motions of supplication and recommendation are gone through, it becomes clear that Colusyon's true intention is to speak against rather than for his client. Magnyfycence suggests that, despite his own reservations, he is prepared to grant the suit.

> My frende, as touchynge to this your mocyon,
> I may say to you I have but small devocyon.
> Howe be it, at your instaunce I wyll the rather
> Do as moche as for myne owne father.
> (lines 1639–42)

Shocked at his success, Colusyon swiftly changes tactics, and begs leave to 'rowne' secretly in Magnyfycence's ear, out of earshot of the other suitor present, Abusyon. Living up to his name and making full use of the privilege of private access to the Sovereign, Colusyon then covertly gainsays all that he has previously said on Measure's behalf.

Syr, so it is, this man is here by,
That for hym to laboure he hath payde me hartely:
Notwithstandynge to you be it sayde,
To trust in me he is but dyssayved;
For, so helpe me God, for you he is not mete.
I speke the softlyer because he sholde not wete.[77]

(lines 1649–54)

Whilst posing as the good patron, then, Colusyon actually frustrates his client's suit. The hypocrisy of his pose – and the extent of Magnyfycence's connivance in it – are revealed by his request that the King go through the motions of granting Measure an interview to conceal his treachery.

Colusyon: It were better he spake with you or he wente,
That he knowe not but that I have supplyed
All that I can his matter for to spede.
Mag.: Now, by your trouthe, gave he you not a brybe?
Col.: Yes, with his hande I made hym to subscrybe
A byll of recorde for an annuall rent ...
... [Yet] I shall waraunt you for me,
And he go to the devyll, so that I may have my fee,
What care I?

(lines 1662–7, 1669–71)

Mag.: Well, for thy sake the better I may endure.
That he come hyder, and to gyve hym a loke
That he shall lyke the worse all this worke.
Col.: I care not howe sone he be refused,
So that I may craftely be excused.

(lines 1680–4)

Unable to hear the substance of Colusyon's speech, Measure is convinced by the vice's dumb-show gestures of supplication (lines 1693–7) and so is entirely unprepared for the hostile reception which he receives from his prince.

The expulsion of Measure is the final symbol of vice triumphant in the play. And significantly it is the manipulation of one of the fundamental instruments of household and Court administration (and, moreover, an instrument central to the ceremonial functions of the Court), the Audience, which brings about his downfall. Just as questions of household management dominate the moral scheme of the play, so a series of dramatic explorations of the possibilities for good and evil inherent in the procedures of public audience provide its structuring principle.

[77] 'So that he should not hear.'

Although *Magnyfycence* may not be, as was once thought, the first secular Morality play in the English language,[78] it is nonetheless a play uniquely saturated with the culture of its secular setting, the Henrician Court. Unlike most previous writers, Skelton displays an awareness of the dramatic potential in Court ceremonial, and in the philosophical bases of Household administration. Whereas Morality drama prior to *Magnyfycence* had employed dramatic techniques to explore private issues of morality and personal salvation, Skelton employs those techniques to consider public issues, making full use of the coincidence of setting to convert the 'business' of Household management and courtly protocol into the action of his play.

Unlike the creators of the Corpus Christi cycles, whose works needed to be performed in the limited space on and around their pageant wagons, the writers of interludes were provided with a significantly larger arena in the Tudor Great Hall.[79] Furthermore, that space, with its dais and the seats of the elite diners at one end and the screens and the domain of the servants at the other, was already inscribed with its own political significances. Again, Skelton seems to have been the first writer to utilize these significant features, by not only creating a 'differentiation of acting space' within the hall (that is, by having different parts of the hall floor represent different locations in the play), but by giving that differentiation a political dimension. Thus Magnyfycence occupies the dais end of the place when he holds his Court, and the suitors must await his pleasure at the screens end. Conversely, his moral decline and subsequent spoliation by Adversitie and Poverte are accompanied by a migration down the hall towards the screens. Through this innovative use of the acting space and of the symbolic potential of dramatic action, the play raises issues, and suggests dramatic techniques for exploring them, which were to be taken up by those subsequent playwrights whose work we shall consider in the following chapters.

[78] That distinction must be afforded to Medwall's *Fulgens and Lucrece*, see F. L. Boas and A. W. Reed, eds., *Fulgens and Lucrece* (London, 1926).

[79] This is not to deny that the authors of the cycle plays were also skilled in their use of their particular settings. As Martin Stevens has recently argued, the authors of the York cycle in particular made considerable use of the space available on their pageant wagons, in the city streets and in the various other urban locations available to them. There too the symbolic and iconographic potential of the acting places (each carrying its own civic and religious significances) was effectively utilized by the performers. M. Stevens, *Four Middle English Mystery Cycles* (Princeton, 1987).

Chapter 4

CONSERVATIVE DRAMA I: *GODLY QUEENE HESTER*

AUTHORSHIP AND DATE

The *Enterlude of the Vertuous and Godly Queene Hester* was not printed until 1561, but it is clearly a work of an earlier period. Previous commentators have suggested dates between 1522 and 1527. But, as what follows will demonstrate, it forms a part of the attack upon Cardinal Wolsey at his fall in 1529. A close reading of the text reveals the numerous similarities between it and the political charges laid against Wolsey at this time, which both help to date the play more closely than has hitherto been possible, and illuminate its subject matter in ways unnoticed by earlier critics.

The play has much in common with *Magnyfycence* in that both plays contain allegorical treatments of contemporary political issues. Moreover, both contain stylistic similarities, which have prompted the suggestion that Skelton may also have been the author of *Hester*. Yet this seems unlikely. Stylistic similarities there are, but they are only intermittently evident, and the bulk of the play suggests a different hand. It is more likely, given the conclusions reached below concerning the dating and subject matter of the play, that the author was consciously adopting Skelton's style at certain points for satirical effect. This was, not as some early studies have suggested because he was a protegé of the poet, or a member of 'the political and literary school or party of Skelton',[1] but because Skelton had, with *Collyn Clout* and *Why Come Ye Nat to Courte?* (1521–2), established a popular satirical mode suitable for the treatment of ecclesiastical issues, and which had proved an effective vehicle for attacks on Cardinal Wolsey in particular. Just as the successful satirical texts of previous centuries, such as *The Canterbury Tales* and *Piers Plowman*, and spawned their own imitators, so during the late 1520s and 1530s

---

[1] W. Bang, unidentified citation, in W. W. Greg, ed., *The New Enterlude of Godly Queene Hester* (Louvain, 1904), p. xi.

Skelton's satirical style became the model for religious satirists anxious to win an audience.[2]

But if the author of *Hester* cannot be identified with a known individual, the subject matter of the play helps to identify his general standpoint and the nature of his intended audience. The interlude is ostensibly a recapitulation of the Old Testament Book of Esther. The heroine of the title (here named Hester) is chosen for his queen by King Assewerus (Ahasuerus or Artaxerxes of Persia). At first she conceals her Jewish origins. But when Aman, the newly appointed chancellor, gains Assewerus' connivance in a plot to massacre the Jews, she reveals her true race at a banquet prepared for the King, and pleads for a royal reprieve for herself and her people. The King, shocked that he has been misled by Aman into so vindictive an act, grants her request, and has Aman executed on the gibbet he had prepared for Hester's foster-father, Mordecai. Elements of the biblical story are omitted from the interlude. Both the callous dismissal of Esther's predecessor, Queen Vashti, which opens the story, and the massacre of the enemies of the Jews which concludes it, are excised, in order to maximize the audience's sympathies for Hester, and for the fate of the Jews. And new elements are added in the form of a satirical conversation between the vices Pride, Ambition and Adulation, and the introduction of a further vice, Hardy Dardy, who seeks employment in Aman's service. But the broad sweep of the original narrative is retained. A closer reading of the detailed treatment of that narrative, however, quickly reveals that the interlude is rather more than a simple rehearsal of the biblical story for moral or theological effect.

Many of the incidental details in the drama are curiously inappropriate. The location of the story should, of course, be Old Testament Persia. But little effort seems to have been expended by the author to create a credible biblical society. On the contrary, the text insists at many points on the contemporary English locus of the action. The reader is presented with a society familiar with friars (line 502), pursuivants (line 156) and park keepers (line 657).[3] When Aman uses a legal weapon to humble a rival, it is not to the Persian law that he looks, but to the very English 'statute of apparell' (line 378). And when war is mentioned, it is not a biblical foe of the Persians who is feared, but 'eyther ... Scotland or France' (line 479). These anomalies need not in themselves demonstrate a covert political motive behind the play. Contemporary references of often startling

2 W. Barlowe, 'The Burial of the Mass', printed as *Rede Me and Be Not Wrothe*, ed., E. Arber (London, 1871). For the derivative work of later writers see, for example, the anonymous 'Image of Ypocrysy', in F. J. Furnivall, ed., *Ballads From Manuscripts*, Ballad Society (2 vols., London, 1868) I, pp. 167–274, and Luke Shepherd, *The Upcheringe of the Masse* (c. 1548), S.T.C. 17630.
3 All references are to the text in Greg, see n. 1, above.

inappropriateness litter the medieval Miracle cycles. But these allusions are not the only idiosyncratic elements in the play. The Jews themselves, whose plight forms the substance of the plot, are also oddly defined. Some of the practices ascribed to them seem appropriate to biblical Jewry, others do not. Like the people of the original story, the Jews of *Hester* are 'scattered abroad and dispensed among the people in all ... provinces', practising their own laws.[4] But the duties of these Jewish 'households' (lines 956–7) and communities are to dispense charity and hospitality to the poor and needy (lines 943–4) and to pray and conduct ceremonies for the benefit of the wider community (lines 1096–1102). In addition the author mentions their going on pilgrimage (line 790) and at one point presents them singing hymns (line 861). Reference to such practices makes it evident that the play is something more than a simple narrative of the sufferings and triumphs of biblical Jewry. In fact it casts in the role of the persecuted Jews the religious orders of the last years of the 1520s.

What the play provides, as what follows will exemplify, is an attack upon Cardinal Wolsey for his intrusion into the affairs of the religious houses and into the prerogative rights of the secular clergy. It has recently been claimed that the play was a product, not of the fall of Wolsey in 1529, but of that of Thomas Cromwell some eleven years later. By this account the play was written in 1541 to praise the Duke of Norfolk and his niece and protegée, Catherine Howard, for their role in Cromwell's downfall. But this seems unlikely. There are few, if any, resemblances between Aman and Cromwell, whilst those between Aman and Wolsey are both numerous and striking.[5] The more significant points of similarity will be drawn out in the remainder of this chapter, but it is perhaps worthwhile to summarize a number of the most obvious here.

---

4 King James Bible, Book of Esther, 3:8.
5 There are also less direct echoes of Wolsey in the play. A number of the satirical epithets aimed at the Cardinal in Skelton's poetry and elsewhere resurface in descriptions of Aman. He is 'this ravenous wolf' (line 820), and this 'carnifex' (line 840). Skelton's jibes at the *vitulus*, or 'bull calf', may also be alluded to in the reference to 'the bull or the calf' (line 550). Compare the above with, for example, Skelton, *Speke, Parott*, lines 59, 347–52, 377–80; *Why Come Ye nat to Courte?*, Dechastichon, lines 1–10. Compare also the attacks upon Aman's domination of the law courts in lines 399–416, with the criticisms of Wolsey's administration of the court of Star Chamber in *Why Come Ye Nat To Courte?*, lines 184–204 and 314–45. For the claim that the play treats the fall of Cromwell, see, I. Lancashire, *Dramatic Texts and Records*, p. 22 and, more recently, A. Fox, *Politics and Literature in the Reigns of Henry VII and Henry VIII* (Oxford, 1989), pp. 240–5. Fox's assertion that Mardocheus must be a figure for the Duke of Norfolk, as the playwright has altered his relationship to Hester, from the cousin of the original, to uncle seems a slight basis for discounting the weight of evidence pointing to the earlier dating. It is surely more likely that the need to give Mardocheus, the figure of loyalty and good sense in the play, greater gravity and seniority in contrast to the 'upstart' Aman led to the change. I am grateful to Dr S. J. Gunn for a number of the suggestions advanced above, and for the chance to discuss the play with him on a number of occasions.

Aman, like Wolsey, and unlike Cromwell, is explicitly created Chancellor of the realm by King Assewerus, and thus gains control of the law courts, a fact which gives rise to a number of allegations of legal malpractice in the play. Unlike Cromwell Wolsey was himself the target for just such allegations of malpractice, particularly over his exercise of Equity in the prerogative courts. Thus it is significant to note Aman's defence of his use of Equity at line 601, an issue which would have had no significance in an attack upon Cromwell. Aman, like Wolsey, is also created the King's Lieutenant (line 627) and is referred to familiarly by the King as his 'father' (lines 1131–2), a term far more fitting to Henry VIII's relationship with Wolsey than to that with Cromwell. Moreover, Aman is criticized for causing food shortages, a charge similarly levelled at Wolsey in the late 1520s, whilst Aman's vision of his King as the arbiter of international politics and diplomacy (lines 695–701) also follows very closely Wolsey's own public statements concerning the aims of English foreign policy. All of which strongly suggests that it was Wolsey and not Cromwell who stands behind the figure of Aman. Moreover, had Cromwell been the target of the play, then the attacks upon Aman would surely have centred upon charges of heresy and sedition rather than upon hostility to the monasteries. For Cromwell's alleged religious radicalism was the factor which most obviously distanced him from Norfolk, and which formed the basis of the charges against him at his fall. The monastic dissolutions criticized in the play were both fully supported by the King and connived at by the Duke himself, the latter profiting handsomely from his share in the spoils. An attack upon the dissolutions would therefore be an unlikely way to court the favour of either Norfolk or the King. As to allegations of radicalism against Aman in the play, these are conspicuous only by their absence. The Chancellor's orthodoxy is nowhere questioned, and indeed his chief weapons are said to be 'bulls' (line 430), hardly the instruments of the anti-papal Cromwell. All of this surely places the play in the late 1520s, rather than in the markedly different religious climate of the early 1540s.

POLITICAL THEMES: WOLSEY AND THE RELIGIOUS

In 1524 Wolsey began the suppression of a series of small English religious houses, whose incomes he transferred to the Oxford college which he was in the process of founding. Between 1524 and 1529 a combination of papal bulls and royal warrants authorized him to suppress a total of twenty-nine houses, in order to realize a yearly income of 3,000 ducats towards the maintenance of Cardinal College. It is in the light of these suppressions that the defence of the religious contained in Hester's ostensible defence of the Jews is to be read.

Yet it is important to note at the outset that the justification of the religious houses presented in the play is not a conventional retort to charges laid against them by their critics. In the vast majority of satirical attacks upon the religious and their communities, and in the findings of the episcopal visitations and government-inspired investigations, a clear corpus of critical ideas can be identified. For the traditional satirist, the abuses practiced in the monastic houses and convents were largely sins of the flesh, predominantly those stemming from gluttony, vanity and lechery. The monks of satirical literature overate. One recalls Chaucer's Monk, suspiciously 'ful fat and in good poynt'[6], or the ironic question posed by the author of the anonymous poem 'The Simonie',[7]

> Where shal men nu finde fatter or radder of leres?
> Or betre farende folk than monekes, chanons and freres?

They dressed like princes,[8] kept horses and hounds for hunting, and birds for hawking,[9] and ignored the strictures of their rules. Their sexual, promiscuity made a nonsense of their vows of chastity,[10] and, rather than devote their time to study, they scorned scholarship, choosing to learn only the limited number of texts necessary for the exercise of their office, and those by rote.[11] Such charges recur throughout numerous works of anticlerical satire, across three centuries and from most of the countries of western Europe. And, far from confounding such stereotypical accounts, the visitation records of the period tell much the same story. Houses of religion were by no means all corrupt, but where abuses were noted, they tended to be precisely those castigated by the satirists. Whether because the commissioners' expectations and perceptions were governed by their reading, or because the erring religious simply lacked imagination, adverse visitation commissioners' reports frequently read like paraphrases of satirical poems. Allegations of sexual irregularity, of drunkenness and gluttony, of permitting dogs, hawks and other animals to be kept in the monastic buildings, of failure to observe the hours, or to attend services, or to uphold the bar upon women in the precincts of the house abound.[12]

---

6 G. Chaucer, 'The General Prologue' to *The Canterbury Tales*, line 200, in F. N. Robinson, ed., *The Complete Works of Geoffrey Chaucer* (Oxford, 1979).

7 'The Simonie', lines 153–4, in T. Wright, ed., *The Political Songs of England, From the Reign of John, to that of Edward II* (London, 1839).

8 See Chaucer, 'General Prologue', lines 193–203.

9 Ibid., lines 168, 190–2, and J. Mann, *Chaucer and Medieval Estates Satire* (Cambridge, 1973), pp. 24–5.

10 See, for example, 'Why I can't be a Nun', edited by F. J. Furnivall in *Transactions of the Philological Society* II (1859), pp. 138–48.

11 D. Erasmus, *In Praise of Folly*, transl., J. Wilson, ed., P. S. Allen (Oxford, 1925), p. 126.

12 D. Knowles, *The Religious Orders in England* (3 vols., Cambridge, 1955–71), III, 'The Tudor Age', pp. 64–86.

It is thus interesting that neither the criticisms of the religious orders voiced in the play by Aman, nor Hester's defence of their vocation place any stress upon these traditional complaints. The only assertion which seems to bear any relevance to contemporary criticisms of monasteries or monasticism would seem to be Aman's declaration that the religious live by their own laws rather than the King's.

> More over the preceptes of your [the King's] law,
> They refuse and have in great contempte
> They wyll in no wise live under awe,
> Of any prince but they wil be exempte.
> (lines 737–40)

But any attempt to see this passage as a conscious foretaste of the criticisms of clerical privilege voiced in such documents as Christopher St German's *Treatise Concerning the Division Between the Spirituality and the Temporality* (1532–3) or the House of Commons' *Supplication Against the Ordinaries* (of 1532) would be mistaken.[13] For the allegation is a direct paraphrase of a charge laid against the Jews in the biblical original.[14] Of the new material added to the story by the author, the vast majority relates to a separate issue, the question of charity. Both Aman's attack upon and Hester's defence of the religious revolve around their alleged failure to provide alms and hospitality to outsiders. Assewerus declares that he was convinced to act against the Jews when Aman

> ... signified unto me that the Iewes did
> Not feed the poore by hospitalitie
> Their possessions he sayde, were all but hydde,
> Amonge them selves lyvyng voluptuouslye.
> (lines 943–6)

The results of those suppressions are described by the vice Ambition in similar terms. Aman, he claims, has 'eaten' the food of the poor. Previously

> had they releefe, bothe of breade and beefe,
> And eke drynke also,
> And now the dore standes shet, and no man can we get,
> To worke neither to fyghte.
> (lines 475–8)

> As for domine vobiscum, I dare say nothinge but mum.
> (line 482)

---

13 C. St German, *A Treatise Concerning the Division Between the Spirituality and Temporality*, in J. B. Trapp, ed., *The Complete Works of St Thomas More*, IX, Appendix A, pp. 176–212. For the Commons' Supplication, see *L.P.* IV (iii) 6043(7); V 1016 (1–3).
14 Esther, 3:8.

Hester's defence of the religious takes a similar line. In her first major speech in the play she implicitly declares her support for the religious when telling the King how prosperity can best be distributed fairly through the commonwealth.

> where goddes servyse and hospitalitie
> Doeth decaye, and almes to the poorall,
> There maye be welth in places two or three.
> But I assure you the most part in generall
> Neither have meate nor money, nor strength substancial
> Fytte to doe you service...
>
> Let God alwaye therefore have hys parte
> And the poore fedde by hospitalitie
> Eche man his measure, be it pynte or quarte,
> And no man to muche...
>   (lines 311–16, 318–21)

In arguing against Aman later in the play she returns to her theme.

> as for hospitalitye.
> Of the Iewes dwellinge in your regyon
> It is with them as alwayes hath bene
> Sins the beginning of their possession
> Which god to them gave, of his mere mocion.
> Eke great knowledge both of catell and of grayne
> That none to them like household coulde maintayne.
>   (lines 950–6).

> Since god therefore hath begunne theyr housholde.
> And ay hath preserved theyre hospitalitie,
> I advise noman to be so bolde,
> The same to dissolve what so ever he be,
> Let God alone for he shall orderly
> A fine *ad finem*, both here and there
> *Omnia disponere suaviter*
>   (lines 964–70)

Allegations of lapsed hospitality or charity had been made by visitation commissioners in the past, and were to be made again during the 1530s, but they were never a major element in criticisms of the religious life *per se*, or of specific institutions, in the way that charges of immorality or of financial irregularity were. Why then should the author have spent so much time in defending this aspect of the regular vocation here?

Interestingly, although the *failure* to provide charity was only rarely cited *against* houses, their charitable function was often cited in their favour by their apologists. Thus, in criticizing Cardinal Wolsey's financial exactions from the monasteries, the authors of the, so-called, Lords'

Articles, a catalogue of criticisms of Wolsey's regime, drawn up at his fall in 1529, argued that[15]

where good hospitality hath been used to be kept in houses and places of religion of this realm, and many poor people thereby relieved, the said hospitality and relief is now decayed and not used, and it is commonly reported that the occasion thereof is, because the said Lord Cardinal hath taken such impositions of the rulers of the said houses ... as they be not able to keep hospitality as they were used to do, which is a great cause that there be so many vagabonds, beggars and thieves.

Seven years later Robert Aske, the 'Great Captain' of the Pilgrims of Grace, justified his opposition to the suppression of the monasteries on the grounds that[16]

the abbeys in the north partes gaf great almons to pour men and laudable servyd God ... [whereas] no hospitality [is] now in thos places kept ... Also diverse and many of the said abbeys were in the montaignes and desert places [where both bodily and spiritual refreshment were otherwise scarce] ... also strangers and baggars of corne as betwix Yorkshir, Lancashir, Kendall, Westmoreland, and the bischopreke [of Durham], was ... greatly socored both horsse and man by the said abbeys, for non was in thes partes denyed nether horsemeat nor manesmeat, so that the peple was greatlie refresshyed by the said abbeys, wher now they have no such sucour.

The need for monasteries to act as travellers' rests and centres of poor relief in remote and inhospitable places was also cited in their defence at the Dissolution. The sympathetic commissioners at Ulverscroft, Leicester-shire, for example, reported that the house there 'stendith in a wildernesse in the forest of Charnewood, and refressith many pore people and waye-faryng people',[17] and it may well have been the importance of Bayham Abbey as a provider of hospitality in the harsh woodlands of the Weald which prompted the local inhabitants to take up arms to defy Wolsey's suppression commissioners in 1525.[18]

How much truth there was to support this perception of religious houses as wholesale dispensers of charity is unclear. It seems that rates of chari-table provision varied from house to house and from region to region. Whereas the small monastic house at Northallerton, Yorkshire, spent £28, from a gross annual income of only £59, on the relief of twelve individuals, the monks of St Mary Graces, London, spent only £3. 8s. and 4d, whilst

15 Lord Herbert of Cherbury, *The Life and Reigne of Henry the Eighth* (London, 1649), Article XIII, p. 268.
16 'The Confession of Robert Aske', *E.H.R.*, V, 1890, pp. 551–73, p. 551.
17 A. Savine, 'English Monasteries on the Eve of the Dissolution', in P. Vinogradoff, ed., *Oxford Studies in Social and Legal History*, I (Oxford, 1909), p. 241, n. 2.
18 J. J. Goring, 'The Riot at Bayham Abbey, June 1525', *Sussex Archaeological Collections*, CXVI (1978) pp. 1–10. It is interesting that Edward Hall stated that the abbey was 'verie commodious to the country', E. Hall, *Chronicle* (London, 1809), p. 702.

the house at Cranborne, Dorset, spent just 10s.[19] But, whatever the reality, the perception was the crucial point played upon by defenders of the monasteries. References to hospitality and charity were frequent because these functions were an aspect of the monastic vocation which everyone would agree was worthwhile. In the 1530s, when the arguments of the religious reformers attacked the entire theological basis of monasticism, their charitable functions provided their defenders with one justification for their continuation of which even the most ardent reformer could not cavil. More specifically, in the context of the suppressions of the 1520s, this argument was of even greater utility. In this case both suppressors and suppressed shared a common belief in the value of properly regulated monastic houses. The only grounds for suppression were questions of detail. Were the individual houses concerned fulfilling their functions adequately? Or could their wealth be better employed for the good of the commonwealth in Wolsey's Oxford college, or other projects? The assertions contained in *Hester,* and in those of the Lords' Articles which criticized Wolsey's dissolutions, addressed this issue directly, suggesting that the resources of the religious houses *were* employed for the benefit of the commonwealth. And they did so in the most effective terms possible. For, unlike prayers for the dead, the preservation of relics or any of the other less tangible services provided by the monastic orders, the relief of the poor was a social service which was both easy to appreciate and readily observable on a daily basis.

Hester thus provides a carefully thought out apology for monasticism based upon the social utility of the monastic houses. But why should monastic suppressions have aroused the interests of a satirical writer in the 1520s? True, these years had seen Wolsey's suppression commissioners at work. But such activity was hardly new. Bishop Alcock of Ely had suppressed the nunnery of St Radegund to found Jesus College, Cambridge, in 1496. Richard Fox, Bishop of Winchester, had endowed the newly founded Corpus Christi College, Oxford, with the revenues of houses suppressed in 1517. And John Fisher, Bishop of Rochester, had endowed his college, St John's, Cambridge, with the property of two nunneries in 1524.[20] Nor were the houses suppressed by Wolsey in the 1520s particularly large or significant institutions. They were small houses, generally on the margins of independent viability. Only four contained more than eight occupants, and only five enjoyed an income in excess of £100 per annum.[21] Yet Wolsey's suppressions do seem to have aroused an unusual amount

---

[19] Savine, 'English Monasteries', p. 235. As these figures refer only to mandatory alms claimed against income in the *Valor Ecclesiasticus* they are likely to be minima rather than records of actual expenditure on charitable provision.
[20] Knowles, pp. 157–8.   [21] Ibid., p. 161.

of protest and opposition, both at the time and subsequently, at his fall. The townsfolk of Tonbridge, Kent, felt sufficient affection for their local priory to petition Archbishop Warham for its salvation,[22] whilst at Bayham in Sussex local men went as far as forcibly to restore the canons to their abbey, in clandestine defiance of the suppression commissioners.[23] Such acts clearly indicate a degree of local support for the houses concerned. Thus it is possible that the author of *Hester* was reflecting spontaneous local opposition to the suppression of a specific house. But it seems more likely that the play was written somewhat later, after the houses had been dissolved, as part of a more general attack upon the engine of the suppressions, Wolsey's legatine authority. For what is perhaps more interesting is that criticism of the suppressions surfaced again, as we have seen, at Westminster, after Wolsey's fall from grace in 1529, as one of the charges levelled at the Cardinal in the Lords' Articles. Among these articles, which share a number of suggestive coincidences of theme and approach with the text of *Hester*, was the assertion that [24]

the said Cardinal hath not only, by his untrue suggestion to the Pope, shamefully slaundered many good religious houses and good virtuous men dwelling in them, but also suppressed by reason thereof, above thirty [*sic*] houses of religion.

It would be possible to see the inclusion of such charges in both the Lords' Articles and the text of *Hester* as simply a reflection of how widespread was popular concern at an obvious iniquity. Might it not be argued that Wolsey was suppressing perfectly good religious institutions in order to finance a college that was little more than a monument to his own vanity, and that popular opinion recognized the fact and protested? Similar suggestions have been offered in the past.[25] But a close reading of the texts concerned, and an examination of the political context in which they appeared, suggests that the situation was more complex than this. Indeed, both the Lords' Articles and *Hester* seem to be the product of specific political motives held by a particular interest group.

The allegations against Wolsey gathered together by the authors of the Articles of 1529 are an idiosyncratic collection, combining substantial political charges with personal grievances, conventional assertions of wrongdoing and wild accusations of secret malice. These could hardly be the concerted grievances of any one group, nor a reflection of popular opinion, nor even a true representation of the views of any one of the signatories. They are too diverse for that. Rather they seem to be a collection gathered at short notice on an *ad hoc* basis.

22 *L.P.* IV (i) 1470–1, 4920.
23 Goring, 'The Riot at Bayham Abbey'.
24 Herbert, Article XIX, p. 269.
25 See, for example, A. F. Pollard, *Wolsey* (London, 1929), p. 217.

An extended group of councillors was assembled and provided with a brief to produce formal criticisms of Wolsey by a King anxious to use the Cardinal's fall to put pressure upon the Pope, and upon the English clergy, to further his campaign for a divorce. These criticisms, gathered together as a set of articles, were formally compiled on 1 December 1529, possibly as the first step towards a subsequently abandoned Bill of Attainder. But the first draft of these indictments may have been compiled as early as the end of July 1529, almost immediately after the failure of the Blackfriars Court. What it is important to note, however, is that, whenever the original draft was compiled, the initiative in Wolsey's condemnation lay with Henry, not with the councillors themselves. As Edward Hall observed, it was only when 'the nobles and prelates perceived that the Kings favor was from the Cardinal sore minished' that 'every man of the Kynges Counsaill beganne to laye to him suche offences, as they knewe by hym'.[26]

In their haste to comply with Henry's wishes, the attendant lords and commoners seem to have collected suggestions from a number of interested parties, and presented them as their own, with only the minimum of editorial attention. Despite the generally anti-clerical intentions behind the document, and despite the fact that it was eventually signed only by laymen,[27] it is clear that the signatories' parliamentary colleagues, the bishops and the abbots of the greater monasteries, were also influential in its drafting. Otherwise the inclusion of detailed allegations concerning the operation of Wolsey's legatine authority cannot be satisfactorily explained.[28]

Of the forty-four formal charges in the Articles, at least eleven concern purely ecclesiastical issues. Five concern the financial exactions imposed upon the regular religious by Wolsey, and the criticisms of monastic practice which he employed to secure his papal commission to reform

[26] Hall, pp. 758–9. The argument for redating the first draft of the Lords' Articles is advanced in E. W. Ives, 'Cardinal Wolsey's Fall', in S. J. Gunn and P. Lindley, eds., *Cardinal Wolsey: Church, State and Art* (Cambridge, 1991). For the question of the Bill of Attainder, see G. R. Elton, *Reform and Reformation* (London, 1977), p. 112. For an alternative view, see Pollard, pp. 256–63.

[27] The signatories were the Lord Chancellor, Sir Thomas More, the Dukes of Norfolk and Suffolk, the Marquises of Dorset and Exeter, the Earls of Shrewsbury, Sussex (elevated during this parliamentary session but still subscribing himself 'R. [Viscount] Fitzwa[l]ter' here, although listed among the earls), Oxford and Northumberland, Lords Darcy, Rochford, Mountjoy and Sandys, Sir William Fitzwilliam, Sir Henry Guildford and the judges Sir Anthony Fitzherbert and Sir John Fitzjames. Herbert, p. 274.

[28] Interestingly Hall's account of the drafting of these articles grants an equal role to the clergy and the lay lords. It is perhaps also significant that he, a member of the Reformation Parliament, does not describe the 1 December meeting as a parliamentary committee, but as a meeting of the Council. 'When the nobles and prelates perceived that the King's favour was from the cardinal sore minished, every man of the Kynges counsaill beganne to laye to hym such offences as they knewe by hym, and all their accusacions were written in a boke, and all their hands set to it'. Hall, p. 759.

them. Neither of these issues is likely to have greatly troubled the majority of the signatories to the indictments. A further three articles relate to legatine interference in the ordinaries' probate jurisdictions, and in promotions to livings in episcopal hands. All of these charges display so detailed a knowledge of the cases concerned that they can only have been compiled with the close cooperation of the interested parties.[29] This need not mean that the Lords Spiritual were all antagonized by Wolsey's use of his legacy, and consequently acted to voice their collective grievances in the Articles. But it does suggest that a group of such clerics, perhaps only small in number, was anxious to see that the type of central interference in their affairs represented by the legatine authority was roundly condemned, certainly by the Council, and perhaps even by Parliament.

This anxiety was partially the result of a history of friction between Wolsey and elements of the regular clergy which extended well beyond the small-scale suppressions of 1524–8. As early as August 1518 Wolsey, in joint commission with his fellow legate Cardinal Campeggio, received a bull empowering him to visit and reform all religious houses. This need not have caused the religious any serious concern. Such rights of visitation had traditionally rested with the Archbishops of Canterbury, whose prerogatives Wolsey's legacy superseded. But neither William Warham (Archbishop 1503–32), nor his predecessors Archbishops Dean and Morton, had conducted a general visitation of the southern province. What made Wolsey's authority different was, first the fact that it extended to those orders previously exempt from outside interference, and second his declared intention of employing his rights energetically in the interests of reform. The Cardinal is known to have ordered visitations of over sixty religious houses, in addition to cathedral chapters, colleges and the mendicant orders.[30] He also took determined steps towards initiating a more general reform of the religious orders. On 19 March 1519 he issued new statutes for the regular Augustinian Canons.[31] On 12 November 1521 he summoned the abbots and priors of the Benedictine order to York Place to

[29] Note the list of deceased clerics whose goods Wolsey is alleged to have seized in Article XXX, and the knowledge exhibited in Articles XXIX, XXVII and XIX, of the terms of Wolsey's petitions to Rome, of the acceptance of his legacy by the King, and of the conditional clauses in his bulls permitting the religious suppressions.
[30] M. Kelly, 'Canterbury Jurisdiction and Influence During the Episcopate of William Warham, 1503–1532', unpublished Cambridge University Ph.D. dissertation, 1963, p. 193. For evidence of Wolsey's earnest in the matter of reform, see the injunctions issued by his agent John Allen at Wenlock Priory in 1523. R. Graham, *English Ecclesiastical Studies* (London, 1929), pp. 132–6.
[31] D. Wilkins, *Concilia Magnae Britanniae et Hiberniae* (4 vols., London, 1737) III, p. 613. P. J. Gwyn, 'Wolsey and Church Reform', paper read to the Graduate History Seminar at the History Faculty Centre, the University of Oxford, 18 February 1985. I am grateful to Peter Gwyn for the chance to discuss and cite his views in the current chapter, although my interpretation of the evidence differs from his in several important respects.

discuss reform, and at their provincial chapter in February 1522 he formally criticized the order for its avarice and the irregular life of its members, concluding this warning of the need for change by signally descending upon the monks of Westminster for an admonitory visitation.[32] The book of statutes which he subsequently circulated to the Benedictines was sufficiently reformist to arouse a chorus of protest, on the revealing grounds that they asked too much of an order which did not profess to practise the strict discipline of the Observants.

Clearly, despite modern scholarly portraits of Wolsey as an all too erring man of the flesh, ready to wink at even the worst excesses of the late medieval Church,[33] the Cardinal took the need for reform seriously. And his insistence on the point aroused considerable protest from the religious: not only from those whose laxity he exposed, but also from those less culpable. When he proposed to visit the Franciscan Observants, an order with a reputation for strict adherence to their rule and exemplary living, he faced the concerted opposition of a community of Greenwich determined to defend its independence against his interference. At first the Observants used their influence in Rome to prevent the visitation. On 7 July 1521, both Pope Leo X and Cardinal Quinones, the General of the order, wrote at the Observant's request to Wolsey, asking that he abandon the proposed visit.[34] Later in the same month John Clerk, the English agent in Rome, informed the Cardinal that the Pope had personally requested him 'for God's sake to use mercy with these friars, saying that they be as desperate as beasts past shame, that can lose nothing by clamours'.[35] Such entreaties could only gain a stay of visitation until 1523, however, and the friars were left to declare their opposition to the intrusion, when it finally occurred, in a more direct form, nineteen of them pointedly walking from the building when Wolsey's commissioners arrived, forcing the adjournment of the proceedings. In the aftermath of this demonstration a number of the friars found themselves imprisoned in the porters' lodge at York Place on Wolsey's orders.[36]

There was, then, a history of tension between the more independently minded religious and Wolsey which partially explains the inclusion of religious grievances in the Lords' Articles of 1529. But this does not fully account for the inclusion of references to the monastic suppressions in these articles. Nor does it indicate why this particular issue, rather

[32] D. Hay, ed., *The Anglica Historia of Polydore Vergil* (Camden Soc., 1950), p. 259. Knowles, p. 159.

[33] See, for example, G. Mattingly, *Catherine of Aragon* (London, 1942), p. 174, or, most recently, W. J. Sheils, *The English Reformation, 1530–1570* (London, 1989), pp. 4–6.

[34] Knowles, p. 160.

[35] *L.P.* IV (i) 477–8.   [36] Hall, p. 691; Knowles, p. 160.

than any of the other projects conducted during the period of the legacy, should have been thought important enough to be taken up in a satirical play.

What made a retrospective defence of the suppressed houses so relevant in 1529, was the possibility that the government was intending to embark upon a second, far more significant, series of suppressions in the last years of the 1520s. For a number of years Wolsey had been considering a scheme for the creation of an unspecified number of new English bishoprics, to be financed, like Cardinal College, from the incomes of suppressed religious houses. This time, however, the wider scale of the project required more substantial financial provision, so it was the greater abbeys which were targeted for conversion into cathedral churches. On 12 November 1528 the Cardinal, again in conjunction with Campeggio, who had returned to England to examine the King's matrimonial problems, was granted a bull empowering him to investigate the viability of such a scheme, and to submit proposals for its implementation to Rome.[37] Then on 29 May 1529 a second bull authorized the execution of the plan, allowing the legates to dissolve the relevant monasteries and transform their occupants into secular canons.[38] Moreover, further bulls of 12 November 1528 and 31 April 1529 gave Wolsey still wider powers to dissolve religious houses with fewer than twelve inmates in order to eliminate those institutions unable to fulfil their proper functions. The powers created by these grants threatened a far more widespread attack upon the religious orders than had been undertaken in 1524–8.[39] Only Wolsey's fateful failure to obtain Henry his divorce, and Campeggio's subsequent departure, prevented the implementation of these schemes. The possibility that they might outlive their architect and be revived by the government in the future surely explains the anxiety of the Lords Spiritual to see the whole notion of suppressions identified as closely with the fallen minister as possible, and thus confined to the political wilderness with him.

There were, then, two periods during which a play like *Hester*, which contained both a defence of the religious and criticism of Wolsey would have been relevant. The first, between 1524 and 1528, was at the time of the suppressions themselves, when a considerable amount of heat seems to have been generated at a local level by the supporters and patrons of the houses concerned.[40] The second followed Wolsey's fall in 1529, when the

---

[37] Knowles, p. 160.   [38] *L.P.* IV (iii) 5667–8.

[39] I am further indebted to Peter Gwyn for the opportunity to read, in advance of publication, summaries of the chapters on religious reform in his forthcoming study of Wolsey which support the interpretations offered on these pages.

[40] In addition to the riot at Bayham Abbey and the petition at Tonbridge, the Duke of Suffolk was imposed upon to write in favour of Conished Priory, Lancashire, and the Duke of Norfolk in favour of Felixstowe, *L.P.*, III, 1253.

issue was revived at the political centre as part of a more general assertion of clerical independence. From those passages in *Hester* which treat monastic issues alone, it is impossible to decide which of the two dates is the more likely. But the inclusion of other political material in the text allows a more definite dating. For the allegations against Aman in the play correspond closely to the charges issued against Wolsey in 1529.

The criticisms of Wolsey's authority implicit in the figure of Aman are in fact far more specific than has been suggested by previous commentators. They do not constitute simply an attack upon the Cardinal's personal failings, but are a detailed critique of his legatine jurisdiction.

Ambitious clerks, it is claimed, cannot rise quickly to good livings, because Aman controls promotions.

> For yf yt be a good fee, Aman sayeth that longeth to me
> Be yt benefyce or parke,
>   Yf he espy to [that] ... promotion, he wyll streyt geve him a portion,
> A lappe of a thowsande markes.
> He shalbe purged cleane...
>
> (lines 440–4)

This is not simply a generalized allegation of avarice, it is a reference to a specific aspect of Wolsey's legatine jurisdiction. For Wolsey was able, as *legate à latere*, to intervene in the prerogatives of all bishops within their diocese, and appoint his nominees to the ecclesiastical livings in their hands through the process of prevention. Thus, in Ambition's opinon,

> my lorde Aman
> Handelles all thynge so,
> That every office and fee, what so ever it bee,
> That maye bee seene and fonnde;
> By his wit he wyl it featche, and or it fal he wil it catche
> That never commeth to the grounde.
>
> (lines 488–93)

Thus Aman's sycophantic nominees gain all the good benefices.

> They solde theyr woll, and purchased a bull,
> Wyth a pluralyte.[41]
>   And lefte predication, and toke adulation,
>   And what by mendation, and dyspensation,
> They gat the nomynation, of every good benefyce.
>   So better by flatterynge, then by preachynge,
> To wealthe they dyd aryse.
>
> (lines 430–6)

---

[41] Another of Wolsey's legatine prerogatives was the right to grant dispensations to clerics holding more than one living.

The same charge is made in the Lords' Articles, where the giving of benefices by prevention is cited as an example of Wolsey's interventionism,[42] as is the more general issue of exploitation of others' livings raised in the playwright's reference to the 'portion' demanded from each incumbent by Aman.[43]

Also, the said, Lord Cardinal constrained all Ordinaries in *England*, yearly to compound with him, or else he will usurp halfe or the whole of their Jurisdiction, by prevention, not for the good order of the Diocese, but to extort treasure: for there is never a poore Arch-Deacon in England, but that he paid yearly to him a portion of his living.

There is a similar precision to the lines in which Ambition criticizes Aman's arrogance, and his contempt for learning. For the examples of the Chancellor's behaviour which he cites to illustrate his contempt for learned men return us directly to those religious suppressions which are the central issue of the play. In claiming the right to reform the religious orders, those nominally exempt from external authority as well as those open to visitation, and in imposing his own regulations upon them, Aman/Wolsey was, the play suggests, vainly exalting his own wisdom above that of the founders of the houses and the creators of their rules.

> For all rewlers and lawes, were made by fooles and dawes
> He [Aman] sayeth nerely.
>   Ordynances and foundation, without consyderation,
> He sayeth, were devysed.
> Therefore hys Imagination, bringes all out of fashion
> And so all is dysguised.
>
> (lines 459–64)

Perhaps the most obvious indication that Wolsey's legatine authority was the true target of the satire is provided by the extended exchange between Pride and the other vices concerning the need to draw up their wills. As a criticism of Wolsey this scene seems curiously oblique, until it is placed in the context of the legatine prerogative. Pride begins the exchange with the observation

> I hearde once a Fryer, as trewe a lyer,
> As anye in the countray:
> Hee preached veramente, that our testamente
> Alwaye, readye shoulde bee.
>
> Adulation: For at our deathe, we shall lacke breathe,
> And than fare well wee.
>
> (lines 502–7)

---

[42] Herbert, p. 267, Article VII.   [43] Ibid., p. 269.

After the vices have each symbolically bequeathed their sinful qualities to Aman, they conclude their testaments.

> Pride: Now by Wades myll, I wene it be wysedome,
> For folke often chat, howe men dye in estate [intestate],
> But so shall not wee:
> Ambition: No by Sainct An, but yet my Lorde Aman,
> Never the better shalbe:
> Pride: No forse so god me save, yf we our wyll myght have
> We woulde he shoulde never thee [thrive]
> Nowe made is our Testament.

(lines 566–75)

The allegorical level to all this is quite clear. By bequeathing all their evil characteristics to Aman the vices do indeed ensure that he will never thrive. But there is a clear political meaning to the arguments too. For by ensuring that they do not die intestate, the vices are also ensuring that Aman/Wolsey does not benefit materially from their deaths. For under the terms of his legatine commission Wolsey had the right to appoint executors for the estates of those individuals who died intestate, or whose appointed executors would not undertake the task, regardless of the diocese in which the deceased resided. And the Cardinal's officers seem vigorously to have pursued this right, particularly after 1523, when a composition between Wolsey and Archbishop Warham led to their exercising a joint jurisdiction throughout the southern province.[44] Thus not only did Wolsey (and Warham) have the right to exact probate fees for the proving of wills worth over 100s. in their jurisdictions (a right which brought in the considerable sum of £630 4s. and 3d. in 1529 alone), they could also take over completely the disposition of estates *ad viam intestati*, and those with unwilling executors. And under the joint administration the suspiciously high proportion of one in ten wills fell into the Archbishops' hands through the latter means,[45] prompting allegations of intimidation which were formalized in Article XVII of the lords' indictment.[46]

Also, the Lord Cardinal, by his authority legatine, hath used, if any spirituall man having any riches or substance, deceased, he hath taken their goods as his own, by reason whereof their wills be not performed; And one mean he had, to put them in feare that were made Executors to refuse to meddle.

Again, like the appointments to benefices by prevention which undercut the ordinaries' rights of patronage, and the monastic visitations which intervened in hitherto exempt areas of religious self-regulation, this

---

[44] Kelly, pp. 60–1.   [45] Ibid.   [46] Herbert, p. 269.

prerogative was exercised at the expense of others. In this case Wolsey and Warham between them contrived to annex the probate rights of their suffragan bishops who had to compound with their metropolitans in order to retain some of their income.

Yet the text of *Hester* does not simply echo charges in the Lords' Articles. It seems likely that the Articles are themselves referred to in the play. At one point the author has Aman protest to Assewerus about attacks upon him circulating in the country. He bemoans

> The sclaunderous reportes, the lyes [that] ... be made
> The fained detractions and contumilious
> The rimes the railings, so farre sette abrode
> Both payntyd and printyd in moste shamefull wyse
> And God to recorde all is but leasinges and lyes.
> Was never made on man lyke as is on me
> Only for aplyment of law and equite.
>
> (lines 595–601)

Could this be an allusion to the Articles, and to such unofficial 'detractions' as the popular ballad, the *Impeachment of Wolsey*, circulated at the same time?[47] The Articles had been signed on 1 December, and were subsequently read out in the House of Commons.[48] Thus it is interesting that Aman protests that

> of late now in dede
> *Before all the commins* upon myne and me,
> Moste damnable reportes were sett a brode,
> To my dyshonour and shamefull villany,
> And all that were there of that cumpanye,
> As I myghte see by theyre countenaunce and voice,
> That same alowed and greatly dyd rejoyce.
>
> (lines 602–8, my italics)

The reference to 'that cumpanye' indicates that the author is referring to a single occasion in which 'the commins' were presented with 'moste damnable reportes', rather than any more general dissemination of allegations against Aman. Thus it would seem extremely likely that the event referred to was the reading of the Articles in the Commons House. This would certainly illuminate the otherwise curious reference by Aman to allegations 'upon myne and me' (line 604). For nowhere in the play is any reference made to relatives of the Chancellor. But in the Articles criticism was levelled at Wolsey's provision for his illegitimate son, Thomas Winter. Article XXVII objected that the Cardinal 'hath made his sonne *Winter* to

---

[47] 'The Impeachment of Wolsey' (dated 1528 by the editor), in F. J. Furnivall, ed., *Ballads from Manuscripts* (2 vols., London, 1868–72), pp. 340–63.
[48] Hall, p. 767; Elton, *Reform and Reformation*, p. 113; Pollard, p. 261.

spend twenty-seven hundred pounds by year, which he taketh to his own use'.[49]

The possibility that the reading of the Articles was the first stage in subsequently abandoned proceedings for a parliamentary Act of Attainder,[50] also helps to explain Aman's fear that

> ... for the same greate malice I do sustayne,
> Both of your nobles and communaltie
> To my greate grevaunce and merveylous payne,
> And eke further, I fear the jeopardye
> Of my lyfe, goodes, credence and honestie.
>
> (lines 588–92)

For, had attainder proceedings been intended, the penalty, had Wolsey been found guilty would have been precisely the loss of life and goods complained of.[51]

If the above is correct and these passages do allude to the presentation of the Lords' Articles to the Commons, then the dating of the text becomes clearer. For it can only have been after the completion of the Articles on 1 December 1529 that the play was written, and it must surely have been performed whilst the Articles were still a live political issue. Thus a performance during the Christmas period of 1529 would seem the most likely possibility. This would, of course, rule out Skelton as a possible author, for the poet died on 21 June 1529, well before Parliament met, and before the full extent of Wolsey's fall became apparent.

But if it is possible to identify the issues raised in the play by a comparison with the Lords' Articles, and with the political situation in late 1529, how are those issues treated, and to what end? Can the charges against Wolsey made directly in the Articles, and implied in *Hester*, be accepted as accurate indictments of his administration? The analysis offered thus far might well have given the impression of a rapacious legatine jurisdiction which aroused seemingly justified opposition from its victims. But to leave the discussion there would be to simplify the situation to the point of distortion. For there was rather more to the attacks of 1529 than merely heartfelt opposition to Wolsey himself.

It cannot be denied that there were groups and individuals with genuine or imagined grievances against the Cardinal who took the opportunity provided by his fall to gain a measure of personal revenge. Among these was Lord Darcy, who provided a series of charges of his own, independent

[49] Herbert, p. 270.
[50] Elton, *Reform and Reformation*, p. 113 and n. 7.
[51] The original allusion to attainder proceedings is in G. Cavendish, *The Life and Death of Cardinal Wolsey*, ed., R. S. Sylvester, E.E.T.S. 243 (Oxford, 1959 for 1957), pp. 112–13. The failure of the move is attributed there to a defence of Wolsey in the Commons by his former servant Thomas Cromwell.

of the formal Articles presented by his noble colleagues,[52] and who seems to have held Wolsey personally responsible for his own failure to obtain significant royal offices in the North. But beyond such isolated cases of real animosity, most of the apparent opposition to the Cardinal was more subtly motivated and more opportunist than it at first appears.

There is little to suggest that the legatine jurisdiction had been exercised illegally. Indeed what evidence there is demonstrates that it was employed only conservatively in many areas. Even Warham, whose correspondence with Wolsey in the early 1520s, full of protests of injustice, is a major source of evidence for the rigorous enforcement of the authority, was permitted to retain many lucrative rights of advocation to his Court of Audience which Wolsey could have denied him, had he insisted on the full enjoyment of his prerogative.[53] Moreover, the extensive rights of patronage by prevention complained of both in the Articles and in the text of *Hester*, were also employed modestly, and then generally in favour of Crown nominees rather than Wolsey's own. The legatine jurisdiction was not a corrupt dictatorship in the Church conducted for Wolsey's benefit at everyone else's expense. There was certainly a considerable element of venality involved in its implementation which may offend modern perceptions of the religious vocation. But in the context of sixteenth-century episcopal politics this was nothing new. Financial disputes were endemic among the Henrician bishops, as each sought to protect and expand jealously guarded rights and privileges. Thus a degree of opposition to Wolsey's attempt to reconcile the episcopate to the new and overarching authority represented by his legacy was inevitable. All such innovations and attempts to widen prerogatives, however legally valid, aroused opposition. In the period before Wolsey's rise to power Archbishop Warham had undertaken a determined attempt to enforce his archiepiscopal prerogative rights at the expense of his suffragans which had aroused such heated opposition, led by Bishop Fox of Winchester, that the King had had to intervene before it could be settled, and then with bad grace on both sides.[54] It would be entirely wrong to dismiss the attacks upon Wolsey at his fall as simply well justified grievances aroused by a novel and rapacious legatine authority. What prompted the opposition to the Cardinal was the opportunity provided by his fall to throw off a financial burden and an intrusive jurisdiction, and to establish a claim for future independence.

The clergy were under no illusions about where the real authority behind the jurisdiction lay. As M. Kelly observes, 'Wolsey's power in the Church was the Crown's, and the mastery he achieved over the English

---

[52] *L.P.* IV (iii) 5749. [53] Kelly, p. 177. [54] Ibid., pp. 45–92.

ecclesiastical system was a measure of royal power at home, and secular influence at the papal curia.'[55] It was Henry's influence which had secured Wolsey the legatine commission, and it was Henry's word which could remove it.[56] Hence the appeal to the King inherent in both the Lords' Articles and *Hester*.[57] But such an appeal had to be carefully worded, for the King who could appoint and dismiss Wolsey could always arrange for another to replace him, and removing Wolsey would be of no benefit to the English clergy if it simply meant his replacement as legate by another royal nominee, particularly if, as was rumoured in 1529, Henry was listening to those around him who argued for a general despoliation of the Church to reduce it to its 'primitive' state.[58] Nor would the lot of the bishops of the southern province be greatly improved if the removal of the legatine jurisdiction led simply to the restoration of Archbishop Warham's own burdensome metropolitan regime. What was needed was so to criticize Wolsey and the legacy that the one was irrevocably linked to the other, and so the political neutralization of the man would leave the unwanted aspects of his legatine prerogative too unpopular to be revived. In the long term, of course, this strategy was to prove fruitless. The Royal Supremacy in the Church, the creation of the Vicegerency and the dissolution of the monasteries, realized the clergy's worst fears of interventionism, and answered the appeals for personal royal government voiced in *Hester* in decisive and unwelcome manner. But in the short term it may have enjoyed more success. For no attempt was made to appoint a legate in Wolsey's stead, and Warham, albeit he quickly began to reassert the rights of his prerogative courts upon Wolsey's fall,[59] was not to attempt to enforce them with the same vigour as he had prior to the legacy.

'HESTER' IN PERFORMANCE: THE APPEAL TO ROYAL AUTHORITY

The arguments advanced earlier have stressed the close association between the case against Aman presented in *Hester* and the charges against Wolsey contained in the Lords' Articles. This association will become clearer as we turn to a closer examination of the play text, and its didactic and dramatic strategies. For both the interlude and the Articles, or at least

[55] Ibid., p. 150. P. J. Gwyn, 'Wolsey and Church Reform', reaches a similar conclusion.
[56] Hence the tacit acceptance on the part of both Wolsey and the Duke of Norfolk, whom the King had sent to the Cardinal with a message, that Henry had deprived Wolsey of his legacy after his dismissal from office, despite the fact that the legatine commission from Pope Clement in 1524 had been for life. Cavendish, p. 116.
[57] Aman, it must be noted, was both appointed and dismissed by King Assewerus. There is no attempt to portray his authority as a 'foreign' jurisdiction, as the legacy technically was.
[58] L.P. IV (iii) 5416–7 and 6011.
[59] Kelly, p. 202.

that portion of them which deals with clerical grievances, share a common strategy. Both disguise what are essentially pleas for greater clerical independence with a veneer of concern for royal authority. In order to make their protests politically acceptable to the Crown, both documents stress the damage done to the royal prerogative by the exercise of Wolsey's legatine jurisdiction, whilst at the same time presenting complaints which actually concern the infringement of clerical liberties. Always the damage done to the bishops and the regular clergy is portrayed as damage to the Crown.

In the first of the Articles, which is concerned with the alleged spoliation of the monasteries and bishops' prerogatives, it is the infringement of Henry's own 'prescription' which is stressed. Wolsey had, the lords alleged, obtained the legacy,[60]

by reason whereof he hath not only hurt your said prescription, but also ... hath spoiled and taken away from many houses of Religion in this your Realm, much substance of their goods. And also hath usurped upon all your ordinaries within this your Realm much part of their jurisdiction, in derogation of your Prerogative, and to the great hurt of the said Ordinaries, Prelates, and Religious.

Other clerical grievances are similarly presented as defences of the royal dignity. Wolsey's legatine visitations are described as 'to the great extortion of your subjects, and derogation of your laws'. The legacy itself is described as being exercised 'contrary to your gracious Prerogative or Regality', and the execution of the estates of a number of deceased clergymen is termed 'contrary to their wills and your lawes and Justice'.[61]

The author of *Hester* pursues an identical strategy. The play is written as an appeal to the King, figured in the character of Assewerus, to exert himself and dismiss his legate, ruling personally in his stead. But a closer reading of the text reveals that what the author is actually asking for is a greater degree of self-regulation for the clergy, free from interference of any kind, whether legatine or royal. The message is conveyed both in the arguments employed by the characters and, as in *Magnyfycence,* in the dramatic use of the acting area and the available properties.

The story of Esther drawn from the Old Testament is framed in the play by a discussion of the responsibilities of a monarch, which finally insists upon the need for the King to dispense with the services of favourites and lieutenants and take up the reins of government himself. Given that in the original story King Ahasuerus merely removed Haman and replaced him with a new 'lieutenant', Mordecai, this discussion would seem curiously incompatible with the tale it envelops, were that simply a moral drama.

[60] Herbert, p. 266.   [61] Ibid., pp. 270–1, Articles XXV, XXVII and XXX.

But in the context of the play's political intentions this 'framing debate' is clearly relevant to the main text.

The opening scene of the play has King Assewerus 'sittinge in a chaire' consulting his council regarding the best means of distributing honours among his subjects. The question arises, where should true honour be bestowed? It is quickly established that virtue should be honoured above all other qualities, and that among the virtues pertaining particularly to a prince, justice is the most admirable. But this moral is taken further by the 'Third Gentleman', who suggests that justice is of no value without the diligence required to implement it. And that diligence must, he argues, be found with the prince himself, 'in his owne person' (line 64). It is only through strong personal rule that a sovereign brings honour to his realm. For, without such a personal involvement and commitment to good government on the part of the one man who is above temptation, the machinery of justice will appear to be merely an instrument of advancement employed by self-interested courtiers. Even the renowned justice of Solomon, the Gentleman suggests, would have been less effective

> If by his lieutenante had been done the same,
> Hys honoure shoulde never have spronge so farre…
> Nor yet hys subjectes to suche awe and fear,
> He coulde have dryven by no meanes at all
> As he dyd by hys justice personall
>   And over thys many a noble man,
> At the prynces Wyll and commaundymente,
> To employe justice, dyd the best they can
> And yet the commons unneth coulde be content
> And why? for in their mynde they thyncke verament
> That either for riches and honour Justis will doe
> And he onely, for the Zeale that to Justis he hath to
> Wherfore noble prince, if in youre owne person will ye
> Employe Justis the more youre honour shallbe.
>   (lines 75–86)

What follows in the play proper is, in effect, the education of Assewerus in the wisdom of his advice. For although he seems to accept the Gentleman's counsel here, his actions immediately reveal that he has fundamentally misunderstood the nature of the advice. At first he adopts the assumption

> That Justis mainteneth ye common weale,
> And namely ye prince muste nedes him selfe applye,
> Unto the same, or els utterly
> Shall folowe decay by warre or els death,
> Quoqz, *si princeps malus populus corvet*
>   (lines 89–93)

But, whereas the Gentleman's assertion had been that a personal monarch must rule without the use of lieutenants, the King interprets his argument simply as a warning to select such lieutenants more wisely in the future. For he concludes this speech with the crucial qualification that

> ... if that his [the Prince's] lieutenant,
> Shal happen to square from trueth and Justice,
> Albeit his faire wordes and good semblaunt,
> The prince must nedes be circumspect and wise,
> That no ambicion nor covetise
> Through great welth and riches inordinat
> Do erect his corage, for to play checkmate
> For though it be as well as it may neede,
> It shall be thought nay, I assure you in dede.
>
> (lines 94–102)

Thus, despite the Gentleman's efforts, precisely the opposite conclusion ensues from the debate to the one he intended. Rather than deciding to govern without lieutenants, Assewerus immediately appoints one in the form of Aman, and does so on the most unpromising grounds: simply asking his 'name and progeny', declaring himself pleased with his 'learnyng and reason' (of which the audience has seen nothing), and instantly appointing him Chief Minister, with wide-ranging discretionary powers to administer justice, merely because he appears to be discrete and wise.

> ... ye seeme to be of discretion.
> We beare ye therefore our favour and zeale
> So that withoute meanes of intercession
> We make you our chaunceloure, take hede to this lesson.
> Or to your destruction, we shall you soon remove.
>
> (lines 107–12)

Whilst this final warning to Aman proves all too prophetic,[62] the King's

---

[62] In his stress upon the point (repeated at lines 621–5) that Aman's appointment was conditional upon his continuing to do justice and approving truth, the author is perhaps again echoing the Lords' Articles. For in Article XXVII it is stressed that Wolsey 'did first sue unto your Grace to have your assent to be *Legat de Latere*, Hee promised and solemnly protested befor your Majestie and before the Lords both Spirituall and Temporall, that he would nothing doe or attempt by vertue of his Legacy, that should be contrary to your gracious Prerogative or Regality, or to the dammage or prejudice of the Jurisdiction of any Ordinarie, and that by his legacy, no man should be hurt or offended; and upon that condition, and no other, he was admitted ... Which condition he hath broken' (Herbert, p. 270). Just as the article argued that the legacy was thus nullified as the result of Wolsey's oppressive actions, so *Hester* presents a minister who clearly nullifies his own commission by breaking its terms. Both texts suggested that to remove Wolsey's legatine authority from him would be no major constitutional step, as the terms of its acceptance in England had already been broken.

statement reveals both the depth of his own misunderstanding of his councillor's arguments, and the aptness of the Third Gentleman's strictures concerning the need for royal diligence. For without that quality in the Prince, the proposed solution to the problems of administering impartial justice proves no solution at all. Investing full executive powers in the Prince will only be effective if he can be trusted to use those powers. If his first act is to devolve responsibility upon a lieutenant, then all that is achieved is the redistribution of authority from King-in-Council to the person of the Chief Minister. Only after the misfortunes of Aman's ascendancy have been experienced is the lesson brought home to the King. Only then is he able to offer the audience the moral of the play.

> My Lordes by this fygure ye may well se,
> The multitude hurte by the heades necligence,
> If to his pleasure so geven is he,
> That he will no paine take nor dilligence,
> Who careth not for his cure ofte loseth credence.
> (lines 1162–6)

The relevance of this opening debate to the Hester story is kept in the audience's mind throughout the play, not only as the unfolding corruption of Aman's administration so clearly exemplifies the perils of Government by lieutenant identified by the Third Gentleman, but also as the author constructs the action around a powerful dramatic symbol which dominates his production.

From the opening lines it is clear that the author envisaged the use of a theatrical device perhaps unseen in English drama before this point. For in a number of places in the text the stage directions refer to a 'traverse' which the King is said to enter. As R. Southern has observed, this was probably a small booth fronted by curtains and placed against the screens at the lower end of the hall, between the two conventional entrances used by the players and hall servants alike, into which the King would disappear at times when he was not involved in the action, and from which he could emerge without the need for a formal entrance.[63] Professor Southern's interest in this structure is in its novelty as a staging device, but in the current context it is crucial to note the potent metaphor for lapsed royal authority which it provides. For the author to have introduced so novel an element into the play he must have had a strong idea of how to use it. And the implicit statement which the device makes about the state of Assewerus' government would seem to provide the stimulus necessary to mother this particular invention.

[63] R. Southern, *The Staging of Plays Before Shakespeare* (London, 1973), pp. 258–70.

It has been suggested that the traverse was used to conceal the 'chair' or throne upon which the King was seated at the start of the play, and that the curtains would be drawn across it to conceal both King and throne whenever Assewerus was assumed not to be present. But this assertion seems unconvincing in the light of the stage directions provided. More reasonable is the suggestion that the throne remained in the acting area immediately in front of the curtained booth throughout the drama, and the King left it to enter the traverse when he was not needed. This both helps to make sense of the otherwise confusing marginal directions, and adds greatly to the iconography of the production.

At the conclusion of the council meeting at line 140, the stage direction gives 'Here the/Kynge en/tryth the/travers &/aman go/eth out'. This does not seem compatible with the notion that Assewerus simply sat whilst the traverse curtains were closed in front of him. He is said to 'enter the traverse', thus he must move into it. As Professor Southern has argued, the text's marginal notes are so cramped and contracted that it must be assumed that they aim to be the most economical use of words possible.[64] Thus the fact that the King is said to enter the traverse must mean exactly that. Otherwise the author or printer would hardly have used three lines of tightly cramped marginal text to say so, when 'traverse closeth' would have served better. Thus the council meeting must have been closed by the King rising and striding from the area into the traverse: a far more satisfactory representation of such a meeting than the notion of the King being concealed and the group of councillors breaking up in desultory fashion.

But what, then, of the chair in which, we are told, Assewerus sat during the meeting? Professor Southern, both in his analysis of the play, and his speculative pictorial reconstruction of the staging, suggests that it did not remain onstage.[65] But are we then to assume that the King dragged it into the traverse with him, or that it was removed by the other players and returned later? The former seems too awkward to contemplate, and the latter an unnecessary and even counter-productive exercise. For the chair, if it remained in the place throughout the action, would recall the message of the opening debate, and suggest to the audience the continuing relevance of the Third Gentleman's arguments.

The throne was second only to the Crown itself as a visual symbol of royal authority. At the start of the play it is occupied by Assewerus as he performs one of his proper regal functions, taking counsel from his leading subjects. It must be assumed that he occupies it again at lines 211–337 as he exercises his authority in overseeing the arrival of the virgins from

[64] Ibid., pp. 267–8.   [65] Ibid., p. 273 and Plate 3.

among whom he will choose his queen. And he will return to it during the final banquet when he will hear Hester's plea for the dismissal of Aman and the pardon of the Jews. But in the interim, during the antics of the vices and the descriptions of the excesses of Aman's government, the throne will be unoccupied, pointedly remaining in the audience's view as a symbol of abdicated royal responsibility. The opening debate had stressed the need for the King to oversee the business of government himself. The fact that an empty throne oversees the misrule of the vices demonstrates in the clearest possible manner Assewerus' failure to heed the advice given to him, and suggests the causal link between that failure and the tyranny of Aman.

The symbol would be made all the more effective by the audience's awareness of Assewerus's presence, unseen, behind the traverse curtain. That he is there rather than outside the acting area, in the screens corridor with the other 'offstage' players, creates a dramatic tension otherwise impossible. It is always possible for him to re-enter the action, stepping forward from the traverse to reassert his authority. That he is always present throughout the play, but unseen and inactive, demonstrates Assewerus' latent authority, whilst the presence of the empty chair underlines his failure to realize that authority and fulfil his royal responsibilities.[66] The symbolic uses to which the traverse and the chair are put add a powerful visual dimension to the author's argument, and demonstrate the dramatic unity of the play and its prologue.

Thus on one level the moral debate complements the satiric theme of the Hester story. The drama whose covert intention was to criticize Wolsey's legatine authority was contained within a debate which demonstrated that kings ought not to trust such lieutenants as Wolsey with the exercise of authority, and which suggested the unnaturalness of rule by lieutenants by having an empty throne preside over the drama whilst the King hid behind curtains. But, just as the Lords' Articles carried the subtext that the best way to preserve the royal prerogative was to restore the traditional liberties of the bishops and the religious orders, so the play insists, despite its call for the King to govern personally, upon the right of the clergy to govern themselves. When Hester gains the removal of Aman, and pleads for the pardon of the Jews, she begs that

---

[66] Assewerus' withdrawal into the traverse contrasts markedly with that of Jupiter in Heywood's *A Play of the Weather*, considered in Chapter 5 below. The latter's retreat is presented as further evidence of his wisdom. He is aware that his presence might intimidate would-be suitors. Thus he declares, 'A whyle we woll wythdraw our godly presens/To enbold all such more playnely to dysclose' (lines 185–6). The identical act in *Hester* is invested with quite contrary significance, as it symbolizes the King's lack of wisdom in elevating Aman.

The precepte youre grace sent at Aman's desyre,
Againste me and all the Jewishe nation,
May be revoked and upon convocation
A new devised by them that can do best,
And that sente forthe to set the Jewes at reste.

(lines 1083–8)

The arguments advanced earlier by Hester concerning the divine origins of the religious orders and their immunity from all but divine suppression, are here taken to their logical conclusion in the plea that the churchmen should decide for themselves how they should be governed in future. Significantly Hester requests that 'them that can do best', evidently the clergy themselves, decide their fate, rather than that Assewerus simply contradict his 'precepte' with a new proclamation. In the biblical original the future of the Jews was settled rather more simply and directly. Esther begged Ahasuerus to write new letters to cancel those sent at Haman's request.[67]

Then the King Ahasuerus said unto Esther the queen and to Mordecai the Jew ... Write ye also for the Jews, as it liketh you, in the King's name, and seal it with the King's ring: for the writing which is written in the King's name, and sealed with the King's ring, may no man reverse.

At Mordecai's instructions the King's scribes then take down and despatch new directives, permitting the Jews to take revenge upon their enemies.

For all the play's rhetoric concerning the need for a vigorous personal monarchy, the author chooses to omit entirely this declaration of royal authority from his play. Instead of giving Assewerus the chance to reassert his authority over the Jews/Church at Aman's fall, he introduces the call for collective, and by definition independent, self-regulation by Convocation. This exposes his true intentions at their most obvious. It may well have been expedient to appeal to the King to act decisively in extinguishing the legatine authority, but it was certainly no part of the author's intention to encourage Henry to take over himself the intrusive regulation of religious affairs which the legacy entailed. To replace one overlord with another was not what was intended. Hence the need, not only for the attack upon the person of the Legate, designed to gain the removal of the legacy, but also the stress upon the benefits of a return to the traditional forms of clerical self-regulation.

[67] Esther, 8:7.

AUSPICES

The arguments advanced above suggest the viewpoint from which the play was written and indicate the strategies by which its arguments were conveyed. What remain to be considered are the more practical questions of performance. For what sort of audience was the play written, and where might it have been performed?

Clearly, as the play attempted to join the political debate arising from Wolsey's fall, a performance close to the political centre in London or Westminster would seem appropriate. The close links between the play and the Lords' Articles would add weight to this suggestion, as it indicates that the author was himself well informed about proceedings in Parliament and expected his audience to be similarly knowledgeable. But, as with *Magnyfycence*, no record of a performance at court survives.

Yet an author aiming to influence political opinion need not present his arguments directly to the Sovereign. Indirect influence might be exerted by counselling those who in turn were able to counsel the King. Thus a performance in a less august hall would be quite possible. It has been suggested that the play may have been performed in the household, or more specifically in the chapel, of Katherine of Aragon,[68] but despite the apparent compliment paid to Katherine in the text, this seems unlikely.

From a number of references in the play it is evident that the character of Hester is intended as a figure for Katherine. The association is implicit in the correspondence of Assewerus with Henry. But it is made more overt by Hester's statement concerning the 'virtues' and duties of a Queen, which stress the need to be able to administer the realm in the King's absence 'when warre doth call': a clear allusion to Katherine's role as regent during Henry's French campaign of 1513.[69] What is less clear is what the author expected this association to suggest to his audience. It is possible to read the play as a supplication to Katherine on behalf of the religious.[70] But it is unclear why the author should have expected the Queen to be either willing or able to emulate her biblical forebear in intervening with the King for their survival. In 1529 her position was hardly secure, as the proceedings for the annulment of her marriage to Henry were well underway, and her resistance to his initiatives in the matter had already roused his anger on more than one occasion. If the association of Katherine with Hester was intended simply as a flattering comparison and an indication of the author's support for her cause, then the strategy is explicable. But if a more specific reference to her championing the cause of the religious was

---

[68] D. Bevington, *Tudor Drama and Politics* (Cambridge, Mass., 1968), p. 94.
[69] *Hester*, lines 281–95.   [70] Bevington, pp. 89–94.

intended, then its significance is lost. Perhaps her unquestioned orthodoxy was seen as a bulwark against unwelcome initiatives in religion. Certainly the allusions to the charitable role of the religious houses might appeal to her, as she took a considerable interest in alms-giving and the fate of the poor.[71] But it is unlikely that the author could seriously have expected her intervention on behalf of the religious to have been effective. The implicit praise of Katherine in the text might well indicate that its author was associated with those conservative clergy who took her side in the divorce controversy, but it cannot be used to prove that her household provided the venue for the performance.

More plausible, given the saturation of the play with the views and grievances of the religious, would be the suggestion of a performance in an abbot or prior's hall, perhaps even that at Westminster Abbey where the political debates of 1529 would be most readily understood.[72] A number of references in the text suggest that, unlike *Magnyfycence*, *Hester* was intended for performance by a company with recourse to a large number of additional non-speaking 'extras'.[73] A hymn is also included in the play which, the directions indicate, was sung by 'the chappell' (line 861). A monastic house would provide both a large number of individuals able to perform the 'walk-on' roles and a choir well used to devotional singing. Similarly a hymn would seem more appropriate as an entertainment in a house of religion than in a secular household, where more profane interuptions to the dramatic proceedings were the norm. The possibility that the author was himself a regular cleric would also explain his familiarity with the operation of the legatine jurisdiction, and with the grievances against it which found their way into the Lord's Articles.

The above is, of course, speculative. But in the absence of hard evidence such speculation is all that is possible. If it is correct, and *Hester* was performed in an abbot's hall before his guests and his leading brethren, then the circumstances for indirectly influencing the Sovereign suggested above would be fulfilled. Certainly the allegorical message of the play would suit a religious host intending to reinforce the case for his house or order in the minds of his guests, who may have included both spiritual peers and lay councillors.

If this was the case, then the existence of the play suggests that at least some churchmen, and perhaps sympathetic laymen too, were acting with a degree of cohesion during 1529–30 in order to defend the religious

---

[71] G. Mattingly, *Catherine of Aragon* (London, 1942), p. 134.
[72] That plays were performed at Westminster in this period is revealed by the limited extant evidence. See Lancashire, *Dramatic Texts and Records*, p. 194.
[73] At line 130 Aman is said to enter 'with many men awaiting on hym', and at line 187 the Pursuivant enters 'with manye maydens'.

establishment against attack. This need not necessarily support the idea of an 'Aragonese faction' at work upholding both the Queen's side in the 'divorce' controversy and a conservative interpretation of the religious polity. But it does provide evidence that conservative religious opinion was not simply dormant during 1529. The following chapter will add further weight to this suggestion.

Chapter 5

CONSERVATIVE DRAMA II: JOHN HEYWOOD'S *A PLAY OF THE WEATHER*

THE AUTHOR

John Heywood's *A Play of the Weather* (first printed by William Rastell in 1533) is, like *Magnyfycence,* a play set in a royal household, which deals with the conduct of the Sovereign in a personal monarchy. Like *Hester,* however, it is evidently also part of a wider debate about religion and politics.

There is little direct external evidence which helps to date the play. But what biographical information exists would point to the period between 1519 and 1533, and most probably to the late 1520s. The earlier date marks the first payment of substantial wages (100s. quarterly) which the author received at Court, the second the date of the play's first printing. Between these years, and for many years thereafter, Heywood lived and worked at Court, as a 'singing man', a 'player of the virginals' and as a Sewer of the Chamber.[1] From this experience he gained the knowledge of the Household and its procedures which he displayed in *Weather.* In particular his appointment as Sewer of the Chamber in 1528 gave him the familiarity with Chamber procedures evident in the text. Thus it would seem most sensible to date the play after 1528, and probably, as what follows will suggest, in 1529–30, in that period immediately following the fall of Wolsey which also saw the writing of *Hester.*

Heywood's role as a provider of entertainment for the Court seems to have been a thoroughly varied one. In the 1530s he can be found not only presenting plays performed by 'his children' (evidently the boys of St Pauls' choir school) but also producing music and poetry for Court events and private royal entertainments.[2] The evidence of his dramatic works, including *The Play of the Weather,* which were published by William Rastell in 1533 and 1534, moreover, suggests that, even before that date, he was already writing plays for performance at Court. The manuscript version of his *Witty and Witless,* which on stylistic grounds seems to have been his

---

[1] R. W. Bolwell, *The Life and Works of John Heywood* (New York, 1921), pp. 1–3.
[2] Ibid. pp. 1, 8–12.

earliest play, confirms this suspicion. For it contains an epilogue to be performed only if the King was present at the performance.[3]

That *Weather* was intended for an evening performance in a dining hall is evident from a number of allusions in the text. When Merry Report, the chief comic character, enters the place, for example, he accosts a nearby spectator with 'Brother, holde up your torche a lytell hyer' (line 100), evidently a reference to one of the servants employed to illuminate the hall after nightfall. Similarly, much of the comic business performed by Merry Report involves, as what follows will demonstrate, his pushing through the throng of spectators which the author could guarantee would group about the screens doors at the lower end of any large dining hall. Most convincing of all on this point is the statement of the Boy, towards the end of the play, that Jupiter, the King of Heaven, has come

> ... by his owne accorde
> This nyght to suppe here wyth my lorde.
>
> (lines 1049–50)

This establishes both an evening performance and one in a dining hall.

The reference to 'my lorde' in the passage just cited further suggests, although it does not confirm, that the play was intended for the Court. 'My lorde' need not necessarily be the King, but given that Heywood did present other plays to a royal audience, and given the themes of the play, as outlined below, it would seem safe to assume that the King was present – or at very least that a Court audience was expected and that the King was the nominal host for the event.

The only other observation which can be made with any certainty concerning the audience for the first performance of the play is that ladies were present, and were the butts of some bawdy humour on the part of the players. For when the hunting Gentleman enters the place blowing his horn, Merry Report quips,

> A hunter he is and comyth to make you sporte
> He wolde hunte a sow or twayne out of this sorte.
>
> (lines 256–7)

---

[3] A marginal direction reads 'These three stave next following, in the King's absence are void'. J. Heywood, *Witty and Witless*, in J. S. Farmer ed., *The Dramatic Writings of John Heywood* (London, 1905), p. 216. William Rastell also published Heywood's *Johan, Johan* and *The Pardoner and the Friar* in 1533. *The Play of Love* followed in 1534. All these plays have been reprinted by the Malone Society. All references to *Weather* in what follows are to the Malone Society's edition, J. Heywood, *A Play of the Weather* (London, 1977).

A marginal note makes the allusion all too obvious. 'Here', it states, 'he poynteth/to the women'. That he pointed to the lower rather than the upper end of the hall when speaking these lines seems likely. But the remark, along with the bulk of the play, nonetheless serves to illustrate that bawdiness and courtliness, in dramatic terms the 'popular' and the 'coterie', should not be as readily separated as is often suggested.[4] The Court was, it seems, quite prepared to entertain sexual and scatological humour of the grossest kind. And playwrights were not averse to using such plays as vehicles for serious political purposes.

Who provided the actors for this first Court performance is also problematic. It is usually asserted that *Weather* was a play written for child actors.[5] But, as R. W. Bolwell has warned, further evidence is needed before this assertion can be proven.[6] It is certainly true that in 1538, and again in the 1550s, Heywood led troupes of child-actors, probably the St Paul's choirboys in both cases, in Court productions.[7] But the surviving evidence does not allow the origins of his association with the school to be dated. Internal evidence does provide hints of a juvenile, or perhaps more plausibly a partially juvenile, cast. The title page of Rastell's edition lists the part of the Boy as 'A boy the le[a]st that can play', implying freedom on the part of a director to choose the smallest from a number of potential child-actors. But this instruction to subsequent readers of the printed text need not necessarily, of course, have any direct bearing upon the company from which the original cast was drawn.

The play also requires the actors to play two female parts, one of whom, the Gentlewoman, must sing a two-part song with Merry Report. This would seem further to suggest that at least one choirboy was involved. Thus, assuming that a boy did take the Gentlewoman's part, and that the actor playing the Boy was too small convincingly to double in that role, then at least two boys would be required.[8] It has been suggested that the second female role, that of the Launderess, would also call for a child-actor,[9] but as this is an essentially comic part in the Noah's Wife tradition, this would seem unnecessary. Indeed, use of an adult male actor in the role would seem desirable to maximize the comic potential. The company need

---

[4] D. Bevington, *Mankind to Marlowe*, Chapters 1 to 3, see pp. 25–8, above.
[5] See the Malone Society edition, p. v; N. Sanders, *et al.*, eds., *The Revels History of Drama in English*, II (1980), p. 125; T. W. Craik, 'Experiment and Variety in John Heywood's Plays', in *Renaissance Drama*, New Series, VII (1964), p. 2.
[6] Bolwell, *Life*, p. 12.
[7] H. Ellis, ed., *Original Letters Illustrative of English History* (3 series in 11 vols., London, 1824–46), First series, I, p. 275. Bolwell, *Life*, pp. 52–3.
[8] That the tiny child playing the Boy could have doubled as the Launderess seems unlikely, that part being clearly suited to a larger actor.
[9] Bolwell, *Life*, p. 119.

not, therefore, have been exclusively juvenile. As Bolwell has observed, Heywood may just as easily have used connections with the Chapel Royal or with either of the companies of 'King's Players' to provide his cast, only borrowing choirboys for the one or two parts where this was desirable, and perhaps using a formal choir to provide the two songs which the text requires.[10] This possibility would also better suit the style of performance required by the text. For the play relies upon a considerable amount of innuendo and crude jests for its comic effects, material which would seem not only inappropriate for a cast of choirboys, but also less effective when delivered by such a cast, however competent they may have been.

POLITICAL THEMES

The plot of the play is loosely drawn from an episode in Lucian's *Icaromenippus*,[11] but concerns a dispute in the heavens between the gods concerning their respective prerogatives for influencing the weather. At a parliament specially convened to resolve their dispute, Saturn, we learn, had accused Phebus of over-using his sunshine to the detriment of Saturn's frosts. Phebus had then joined Saturn in decrying Phebe's rain which, they argued, destroyed both sun and frost. Finally all three turned upon Eolus, whom they accused of negating all their labours with his great windstorms. The dispute remained unresolved until, by mutual agreement, all four gods gave up their powers into the hands of their king, Jupiter, in order that he might settle the matter, and determine how the weather might be better organized in the future. So much the audience learns from Jupiter himself, who enters the acting place alone and formally introduces himself, announcing that he has descended to Earth in order to hear the views of his mortal subjects how he might best employ his new-found powers.

Like a Tudor sovereign on progress through his realm, Jupiter establishes his Court in the place, turning the Great Hall into his presence or audience chamber (an act laden with irony, as the hall is itself, of course, in the Court of the most distinguished spectator, Henry VIII). Establishing himself in what appears, from the acting directions, to be a curtained throne,[12] he decides to appoint a servant to proclaim throughout the realm his wish to hear suits concerning the weather, and to act as his usher once those suits begin to arrive. In response to this, a second character, Merry Report, listed in the *dramatis personae* as 'the vyce', steps forward from among the audience to apply for the post. As he cheerfully informs Jupiter,

10 Ibid., p. 12.
11 Lucian, *Works*, ed. and trans., A. M. Harmon (8 vols., London, 1915), II, pp. 310–13.
12 N. Sanders, *et al.*, eds., *The Revels History of Drama in English*, II (London, 1980), p. 91. The structure would seem to resemble the 'traverse' employed in *Hester*, see pp. 126–7, above.

he should be given the job at once, despite his uncouth manner. For not only is he good at making bad news seem good, a useful skill in a courtier, but he is also the only applicant. Faced with such relentless logic, Jupiter has little choice but to appoint him, and so the newcomer leaves to fulfil the first part of his task, whilst the King symbolically withdraws into his throne to hear a song performed by his courtiers.

On his return Merry Report takes up his post as Keeper, or Usher, of the King's Chamber, and prepares to receive the suitors. Once they enter, the action again demonstrates the political potential in the use of acting space which was utilized so effectively in *Magnyfycence*. In one part of the hall sits Jupiter in his elaborate throne. Around him is the privileged domain of the politically powerful. Admission to it is governed by Merry Report who, on the opposite side of the hall guards a notional Chamber door. Each of the suitors must first appeal to him before either being granted the freedom to cross the place to Jupiter or told to leave via the screens doors. Through this simple device the production demonstrates in kinetic and spatial terms the social and political rank of each character.

The first to arrive is the Gentleman, who is let through to plead personally with Jupiter for continuous mild weather suitable for hunting. Next comes the Merchant, who begs for steady regular winds to drive his ships. Then follows the Ranger, the first to be denied access, who begs for heavy winds to provide him with the windfalls which supplement his wages, and the Water Miller, who asks for rain to fill his mill-race and drive his stones. Following these comes the Wind Miller, who holds a lengthy disputation with the Water Miller over the respective merits of wind and rain; the Gentlewoman, intent upon mild weather to suit her delicate complexion; the Launderess, begging for long hours of drying, bleaching, sunshine, and a small boy, anxious for snow and frost, to provide him with the materials for snowballs and bird-pits. Merry Report promises to take each of their suits to Jupiter, and this he does, after much coarse and frequently obscene by-play both with the characters and with the audience.

Aware that each of the petitions he carries contradicts most of the others, Merry Report is confused as to how Jupiter will resolve them. But he gamely gathers the suitors together at the King's request, when the latter declares that he will give judgement. He then watches with admiration and amusement as Jupiter satisfies all concerned, by promising each character the weather which he or she desires, but only for some of the time. At this, Merry Report dismisses them all with the quip, 'Syrs, now shall ye have the wether evyn as yt was' (line 1266), and Jupiter returns into the heavens, resolved to maintain a balance in the weather thereafter.

Although the situation which the play presents is essentially comic, and its humorous potential is maximized by the irreverent badinage between Merry Report and the suitors, the play is not without political significance. For, through its two major characters, Merry Report and Jupiter, it raises a number of issues concerning access to and influence upon the monarch, themes which, as has been suggested, have considerable significance in a period when the monarch was the central engine of government. In its treatment of Merry Report the play examines the role and responsibilities of those officers of the royal household who control access to the Sovereign, and in Jupiter's responses to the various political challenges put to him, it explores the role of the King as judge and guardian of his people. Both themes carry a specific contemporary significance. But whereas the first is essentially satirical, in that the figure of Merry Report is used to illuminate a number of the more questionable aspects of household administration, the second theme goes beyond comedy and seems to offer a more radical assessment of the problems of royal government. And, as will be shown, it does so, like *Hester*, in order to plead a specific case in the guise of general advice.

In the character of Merry Report Heywood provides an almost farcical treatment of the responsibilities of, and the opportunities for abuse open to, servants of the Royal Household. In particular he offers a parody of the office of Yeoman Usher of the Chamber, a post about which he was well qualified to comment, being himself a regular courtier, and specifically a Sewer of the Chamber, a kind of Tudor head-waiter to the Crown, from 1528 to 1558. Thus Heywood would have witnessed at first hand the activities of the Chamber staff, and the protocol which governed access to the Presence or Audience Chamber, that part of the Court in which the action of *Weather* is set.[13]

The Yeomen Ushers of the Chamber were the officers charged, among other duties, with keeping the doors of the King's outer Chamber, and ensuring that only those individuals of gentle status and above, or those with legitimate business within, were permitted to pass into the Chamber beyond. As the Eltham Ordinances of 1526 stated,[14]

It is ordeyned that there be daily one yeoman usher at the said chamber doore, by eight of the clocke in the morning at the furthest, to attend and take charge thereof ... and that he permitt nor suffer any man to come in the same chamber, but lords, knights, gentlemen, officers of the King's house, and other honest personages, as by his wisdome and discretion shall be thought good.

[13] As a relatively lowly courtier, Heywood is likely to have fulfilled the duties of a Sewer personally, if only for a time, rather than immediately appoint a deputy in his stead, as was the practice with more august holders of household offices.

[14] Society of Antiquaries, *A Collection of Ordinances and Regulations for the Government of the Royal Household* (London, 1790), p. 152.

Such instructions, which gave considerable discretionary powers to the Ushers, are closely reflected in Jupiter's orders to Merry Report. The latter, like the Ushers, is given the responsibility of determining precisely whom should be granted the privilege of access. As Jupiter commands him, he must wait at the Chamber entrance,

> Here to receyve all sewters of eche degre
> And suche as to the[e] may seme moste metely
> We wyll thow brynge them before our majeste
> And for the reste that be not so worthy
> Make thou reporte to us effectually
> So that we may have eche maner sewte at large.
> (lines 170–5)

As the play progresses Merry Report performs the role of the Usher as outlined in the Eltham Ordinances quite faithfully, for he admits the Gentleman into the royal presence without demur, as the Ordinances enjoined, but is more circumspect in his responses to the other suitors. The Merchant, who is not of gentle birth but clearly of considerable wealth and standing, is allowed to pass through after a brief consultation with Jupiter. The others are told to leave their suits in Merry Report's hands. Only the arrival of the Gentlewoman, whose class might entitle her to access, but whose sex makes her problematic, prompts the usher to consult his master again, but on Jupiter's advice she too is refused admission.

In Merry Report, then, we see dramatically presented the Yeoman Usher's power to thwart or favour suits. But, more than this, Heywood also suggests the possibilities for corruption inherent in the post. On a number of separate occasions Merry Report seems to mingle personal profit with the pursuit of his duties. Never is the issue advanced beyond a suggestive line or an enigmatic quip, but in such ambivalent episodes lie the best opportunities for satire. Once the Gentleman has left the royal presence, for example, he returns to Merry Report, who promises to 'ease' his suit with Jupiter after his departure (line 329). In return the Gentleman promises that,

> ... yf for my sake any sewt thou do make
> I promyse thy payne to be requyted
> More largely then now shall be recyted.
> (lines 330–2)

Is this simply a reflection of the tips or fees which an Usher might ordinarily expect as a perquisite of his job, and which were one of the universal lubricants of the Tudor administrative system which chronically underpaid its officers? Or is it an attempt to buy Merry Report's services at the expense of his impartiality? The character's exchanges with subsequent visitors to the Court tend to support the latter possibility, and reveal that he is not unaware of the opportunities which his post provides.

Perhaps the most obvious example of this opportunistic trait in action is the Usher's encounter with the Gentlewoman. She, seeing the rout of suitors already surrounding the Chamber doors, requests that Merry Report use his influence to find her another route to the King and let her 'in at the backe side' (line 786). After he has taken up the obvious cue for a bawdy jest, he seems to suggest that he will grant her request, but only in return for sexual favours. 'Syns ye love to be alone', he quips, 'We twayne wyll into a corner anone' (lines 789–90). He then crosses the place to Jupiter's throne, offering to act as Pandar should the King wish to 'marry' her. But Jupiter's insistence that only those with legitimate suits concerning the weather should be admitted sends the Usher back to his post to 'heare her and make ... report' (line 806) whether she has any such suit. On his return the Gentlewoman makes her request about the need for mild weather, but this initially fails to impress the usher. Only after she expresses her willingness to sing 'lustly' (line 873) a romantic song with him – surely in this context a metaphor for a sexual encounter – does he promise to forward her suit with the King.

In these two encounters, then, first with the Gentleman, then with the Gentlewoman, Heywood suggests the potential for financial and moral corruption inherent in the Usher's office. As the play was almost certainly performed at Court, he was perhaps wise to make this institutional aspect of his satire no more firmly. But he does go further with his ridicule of the usher in what seem initially to be less politically contentious areas.

As our examination of *Manyfycence* suggested, those officers of the Household who enjoyed proximity to the person of the Sovereign, and who controlled access to him, gained considerable influence as a result.[15] Their positions of trust acted as signal tokens of royal favour – tokens which they might attempt to convert into the hard currency of political power or social elevation. It has even been suggested that the very closest royal attendants, the officers of the Privy Chamber, acquired an almost mystical distinction through their body service, gaining thereby some aspect of the grace with which the Sovereign was endowed at his coronation by the application of the sacred chrysm.[16] This is surely excessive. But it is undoubtedly the case that the most intimate and trusted servants

---

[15] The influence exerted by, and the deference expected by such men, can be gleaned from the advice given to Sir Thomas Cheyney, concerning Sir Anthony Denny, Henry VIII's Groom of the Stool, in 1546. Denny, it was said, was 'near about the King, and so unmeet to be trifled or mocked with in any cause'. P.R.O. SP 1/245/160 (*L.P. Addenda*, I (ii) 1794), see also *L.P.* XIX (i) 293.

[16] D. R. Starkey, 'Representation Through Intimacy', in I. M. Lewis, ed., *Symbols and Sentiment* (London, 1977), p. 208.

of the King expected a degree of deference to accrue to them owing to their close service. And this social pretension is held up to ridicule by Heywood in *Weather*, both to further the comic treatment of the Usher, and, as the second part of this chapter will suggest, to make a serious political point concerning the nature of sovereignty and the powers of the Sovereign.

Having been appointed Usher by Jupiter, Merry Report quickly goes about his duties, announcing Jupiter's wish to hear the views of his subjects. But, despite his diligence, he is not slow in attempting to make social capital out of his new-found promotion either. On his return to Court he finds his way back into the place blocked by the throng of spectators about the screens doors. As his lines indicate, he is forced to push through, at the same time attempting to berate the audience into a sense of respect for his office, and the dignity which it ought to bestow upon him.

> Now syrs take hede for here cometh goddes servaunt
> Avaunt cartely keytyfs avaunt
> Why ye dronken horesons wyll yt not be
> By your fayth have ye nother cap nor kne
> Not one of you that wyll make curtsy
> To me that am squayre for goddes precyous body
> Regarde ye nothynge myne authoryte [?]
>
> (lines 191–6)

Despite his stress upon the intimate nature of his service, however, the audience is made to appear singularly unimpressed, as his increasing frustration indicates.

In this treatment of Merry Report, then, Heywood ridicules the pretensions to personal authority and power of the King's closest servants. Merry Report claims a status above himself due to his body service (or rather, his claim to body service. His own duties are rather less personal, but he exaggerates their intimacy, claiming to be an Esquire for the Body, in an attempt to gain respect). He expects others to appreciate his newly elevated position. But Heywood continually deflates such grand expectations. He has Merry Report push through the crowd in an undignified manner, loudly drawing attention to his own discomforture, and has him snubbed by even the most humble of characters. Neither the Gentleman nor the Merchant recognize him at first as a royal servant. The Water Miller addresses him as a 'fellow knave' (line 493), and the Launderess calls him 'an olde baudy knave' (line 897). By such signal slights and practical demonstrations of his lack of an air of authority the play demonstrates that Merry Report gains nothing tangible from his elevation to Court office. His authority exists only so far as the exercise of his office extends. Beyond that he is nothing. On his first entrance into the place, prior to his promotion, he was forced to push through the crowd, asking one of the hall servants to 'holde up . . . [his] torche a lytell hyer' (line 100) as he passed, to light his way through and draw attention to him.[17] At his first exit after his promotion he has a more obvious struggle before he can leave. 'Frendes a fellyshyppe', he is forced to plead,

> . . . let me go by ye.
> Thynke ye I may stand thrustyng amonge you there [?]
> Nay by god I muste thrust about other gere.
>
> (lines 178–80)

And on his return to the place the struggle is more pronounced still. As the text thus makes clear, despite his office, Merry Report remains a knave. And this frustration of his aspirations casts into comic relief the pretensions of all his class of household servants.

But the character of Merry Report is more than just a lampoon of Tudor Yeomen Ushers and their colleagues. His role is crucial to both the tone and the outcome of the play. Yet he is an initially ambivalent character. As we have seen, the *dramatis personae* on the title page of the text declare him to be 'Merry Reporte, the vyce'. But how was this quality supposed to be interpreted, and how would the audience have read the character? By having access to Jupiter controlled by a figure who is formally referred to as 'the vyce', Heywood might seem to be suggesting that the Court which he is dramatizing, and by analogy the Tudor Court in which the play was performed, was dominated by corruption. And the morally suspect behaviour which Merry Report exhibits might lend weight to this suggestion. Yet Merry Report is a far from clear-cut exemplar of viciousness. He has little in common with the overtly evil courtiers of *Magnyfycence* or the sinful vices of the morality tradition, Titivillus, Newguise, Freewill or Hickscorner. In his case the term 'vice' seems to refer more to the style of acting required by the role than to the character's moral function within the play. For Merry Report evidently shares the capacity for comic interaction with the audience, for bawdy jest and physical comedy that is part of

17 Heywood's use of the character's entrances and exits provides a further useful example of how a literary convention may be utilized for specific contemporary ends. Merry Report's entrance is, on one level, clearly an exaggerated adaptation of the 'make room' tradition to be found in the folk plays and medieval drama of all kinds (see, for example, Satan's opening lines in the Smith's play of *The Temptation of Christ* in the York cycle). Yet it is put to a number of specific moral and political uses by Heywood. It demonstrates Merry Report's lack of authority and so signally frustrates his pretensions. The fact that he enters the action from among the audience, and draws attention to the fact, also makes a moral point, implying, as in the Corpus Christi cycles, a complicity on the part of the audience in the Vice's shortcomings. Furthermore, that he enters from the crowd of servants at the lower end of the Hall serves further to indicate his lowly origins, and thus undercut his claims to respectability.

the Vice's stock-in-trade, without partaking of the figure's unambiguously degenerate moral stance.[18]

At the start of the play Jupiter seems to identify Merry Report as a vice in the traditional mould when he chastises him,

> Thou arte no mete man in our bysynes
> For thyne apparence ys of to myche lyghtnes.
>
> (lines 115–16)

The comparison with Fansy, the first vice to appear in *Magnyfycence*, would seem damning. Both enter the place irreverently, revealing their unsuitability for employment by rudely breaking into the King's presence and speaking without permission. Both are rebuked by their respective Sovereigns for approaching without formal introduction, and both proceed to gain employment at Court through less than honourable means: Fansy through the use of a forged letter of recommendation, Merry Report by default, as there are no other candidates for the job. Yet, once in employment, Merry Report fails to fulfil the expectations of villainy aroused by his inauspicious entrance. Not only does he not bring about Jupiter's corruption and downfall, he does not even attempt to do so. His bawdy treatment of the various suitors is undoubtedly unbecoming in a Court servant, and his acceptance of bribes, whether financial or sexual, is less than exemplary, but he is nonetheless essentially honest in passing on each of the requests put to him. Moreover, his employment of discretion in permitting access to the Gentleman and Merchant, but barring the way of the less august suitors is, as we have seen, entirely in accord with conventional wisdom concerning his responsibilities. At no point does he use the powers devolved upon him to the detriment of a suitor. Even those who, like the Launderess, personally abuse him and seem unworthy of advancement, have their wishes faithfully conveyed to the King. Thus Jupiter seems justified in praising him for his diligence at the conclusion of the play (lines 1147–8).

For all this, however, the character remains morally, and thus dramatically, awkward. He performs his allotted task well, but occasionally gives the impression that he does so only despite his natural inclinations. Always there is the suggestion that the rogue lies imperfectly submerged beneath the honest exterior. When, for example, he declares that he has no interest in which, if any, of the suitors succeed with their claims ('In fayth I care not who wynne or lose' (line 221)) it is unclear whether he is revealing the impartiality desirable for the perfect execution of his office, or the

---

18 B. Spivack, *Shakespeare and the Allegory of Evil* (London, 1958); F. H. Mares, 'The Origin of the Figure called "The Vice" in Tudor Drama', *Huntington Library Quarterly*, V (1958), pp. 11–29. The other character formally described as a 'Vice' in Heywood's plays, Neither Lover Nor Beloved in *The Play of Love*, is more obviously morally vicious.

reckless indifference of the vice.[19] The implications of this ambiguity will be further considered in the second half of this chapter. It is important at this point to turn to the other major character in the play, Jupiter.

In the figure of Jupiter *Weather* presents a surprisingly consistent and entirely serious view of monarchy and its responsibilities. Far from offering Henry VIII simply a light-hearted dramatic entertainment, the play actually presents a model Sovereign in whom the King would have seen many of his own preoccupations reflected. The ideal is expressed most obviously in the final judgement scene of the play, a scene which has prompted a number of contradictory readings.

It has been suggested that Jupiter's solution to the problems set him is nothing more than a confidence trick.[20] By offering each suitor the weather which he or she sought, but only for some of the time, it is claimed, Jupiter has in fact changed nothing. Yet his subjects leave the Court satisfied, apparently dazzled by his rhetoric. Hence Merry Report's seemingly contemptuous aside,

> Syrs now shall ye have the wether even as yt was.
>
> (line 1265)

Read in this light, Jupiter's final declaration is given an unconsciously self-deflating ironic edge.

> We nede no whyte our selfe any farther to bost
> For our dedes declare us apparauntly
>
> (lines 1267–8)

And indeed the character has been read as a pompous, essentially comic, figure.[21] Yet, far from betraying any pomposity or even cynicism on the part of Jupiter, his judgement does indeed, as he claims, make 'peace unyversally' (line 1271) from very unpromising materials. No other action he might have taken could have resulted in greater good for the commonwealth. As the text makes readily apparent at a number of points, the contradictory suits are irreconcilable. Each suitor requests privileges at the expense of the others. Thus Jupiter cannot satisfy all or any of them completely, as this will result only in greater distress for the majority. But, more fundamentally, the problem arises not simply from contradictory desires, but from contradictory perceptions of the world on the part of the petitioners. Their partial suits are born out of their partial readings of the world they inhabit. Each feels that he or she is unfairly treated by the

---

[19] For the Vice's traditional recklessness, note, for example, Skelton, *Magnyfycence*, lines 1005–42, 1492–3, and *Youth* lines 55–9.
[20] See, for example, Sanders, *Revels History*, II, p. 169, and P. Hogrefe, *The Sir Thomas More Circle* (Urbana, Illinois, 1959), p. 308.
[21] As above.

elements. The Ranger, reliant upon windfalls for his prosperity, feels that 'there blowyth no wynde at all' (line 432), as does the Wind Miller, who declares more colourfully that

> The wynde ys so weyke it sturryth not our stonys
> Nor skantely can shatter the shyttyn sayle
> That hangeth shatterynge at a womans tayle.
>
> (lines 525–7)

Yet the Water Miller, who relies upon a steady supply of rain, disagrees with the Wind Miller's claim that 'The rayne never resteth so longe be the showres' (line 528) and believes that

> We crye out for rayne...
> The wynde is so stronge the rayne can not fall
> Whyche kepeth our myldams as drye as a flynt.
>
> (lines 158 and 160–1)

Each suitor has an unreasonable view of his or her own lot, thinking themselves unfairly oppressed whilst their neighbours prosper, and so are led to make unreasonable demands in an attempt to reverse the perceived imbalance. Thus the Ranger pleads for terrible winds 'the rootes to turne up, the toppes to brynge under / A myschyefe upon them and a wylde thunder' (lines 439–40), which will cause havoc to all the other estates, but give him ample, if short-term, windfalls. Similarly the Wind Miller requests

> That in this world were no drope of water
> Nor never rayne but wynde contynuall
> Then should we wynde myllers be lordes over all.
>
> (lines 557–9)

With such unreasonable demands before him, Jupiter is faced with a seemingly insoluble dilemma. As the Millers acknowledge, they cannot both be completely accommodated.

> For ye must lacke wynde or I must lacke rayne.
>
> (line 755)

Yet their irreconcilability is entirely a product of their false views of society. The success of Jupiter's judgement is that it alters these mistaken perceptions and so removes the problem. Only Jupiter can see beyond the suitors' self-centred views and reveal to them the wider logic of the essentially beneficial system of which they each form merely a part. He brings them to understand that the various estates are not competitors for limited resources, but part of an interdependent social body. As he tells them,

> yf we had graunted
> The full of some one sewt and no mo
> And from all the rest the wether had forbyd
> Yet who so hadde obtayned had wonne his owne wo
> There is no one craft can preserve man so
> But by other craftes of necessyte
> He muste have myche parte of his commodyte.
>   (lines 1216–22)

This argument may well be conventional. But Jupiter is not simply pointing out the obvious here. Certainly it is not obvious to the suitors. Only the royal estate, the play suggests, grants the perspective from which such observations may be made. All other viewpoints are tainted with self-interest. The King, as Jupiter tells the Gentleman, must order things 'unyversally',

> As best may stand to our honour infynyte,
> For welth in comune and eche manys synguler profyte.
>   (lines 291–2)

His honour, his interest, lies in catering justly for the prosperity of all the other members of the commonweal.

Thus Heywood presents in Jupiter, not a pompous and foolish figure, but a sovereign who exemplifies royal wisdom and who demonstrates the special responsibilities, and the special powers, of the monarch. Yet, as with the other apparently encomiastic treatments of monarchy examined in this book, *Weather* carries a specific political lesson beneath the obvious flattery. The play does not simply reflect the difficulties of reconciling contrary petitions. It attempts to offer a deeper political insight and encourages the King to fulfil the obligations inherent in his vocation as a personal monarch. And here the contrasts with the plays considered above, most notably with Skelton's approach in *Magnyfycence*, are as instructive as the similarities.

Both *Magnyfycence* and *Weather* present ideal Kings in action. But the Sovereigns which they portray are fundamentally distinct. For all his wisdom in ordering his affairs, Magnyfycence is always a mortal man, prone to the flaws of humanity, a human being performing a role among other humans. In *Weather* Heywood presents a King who is also a god, a being who transcends the nature of his subjects, who is not merely *primus inter pares*, but of a quality apart from them. The full implications of this distinction are drawn out and manipulated by Heywood to suggest aspects of the royal estate far more radical than those which interested Skelton.

Skelton had built his model King upon Aristotelian principles, producing a Sovereign whom his audience could recognize as the exemplar of a rational ideal. His essence was demonstrably virtuous, accessible to reason and, above all, knowable. Heywood's Sovereign is precisely the reverse. For Heywood here majesty is a mystery, beyond human reason. The point is forced home in the opening lines, then returned to at the conclusion to ensure that it is appreciated.

Jupiter's first speech declares that his sovereignty is immutable, not conditional upon virtue and wisdom like that of Magnyfycence ('What honour, what laude [is] gyven us of *very ryght*', he announces (line 3, my italics)). His nature is inaccessible to reason.

> If we so have ben as treuth yt is in dede
> Beyond the compas of all comparyson
> Who coulde presume to shew for any mede
> So that yt myght appere to humayne reason
> The hye renowme we stande in at this season.
>
> (lines 9–13)

This mysterious qualitative difference between the God-King and his mortal subjects is restated in the judgement scene. Stressing that the disharmony in Heaven is the ultimate cause of the dissension on Earth, Jupiter announces that,

> As longe as heddes from temperaunce be deferd
> So longe the bodyes in dystemperaunce be
> This perceyve ye all but none can helpe save we
> But as we there [in Heaven] have made peace concordantly
> So woll we here now gyve you remedy.
>
> (lines 1159–63)

> Myche better have we now devysed for ye all
> Then ye all can perceyve or coude desyre.
>
> (lines 1209–10)

It might be suggested that this rhetoric of mystery, transcendent insight and power was forced upon Heywood by his subject matter, and so need not have any specific political significance. The scenario, taken directly from Lucian, forced upon him the character of Jupiter the judge, thus necessitating the portrayal of divinity in the play. And this portrayal required a language distinct from that employed to address merely mortal Kingship. The Corpus-Christi cycle tradition provided the most readily available model for this portrayal, in the form of God the Father, whose transcendent status was portrayed as mysterious.[22] Hence there is no need to see Jupiter as a model for Tudor sovereignty. He is set in the divine rather than the royal tradition.

[22] For a helpful exposition of the language of God the Father in the Chester Cycle, see M. Stevens, *Four Middle English Mystery Cycles* (Princeton, 1987), pp. 274–6.

Yet Heywood does not adopt the cyclic portrayals of God the Father for his characterization of Jupiter. Had he wished to convey the mystery of divinity, Heywood would have done so in the same way that the miracle plays had done. But he did not. Jupiter is far more a Tudor monarch than either a biblical or classical patriarch. In his actions, and in the whole setting of the play, the connection between the dramatized monarchy and its contemporary counterpart are stressed. Jupiter is not encountered in some Olympian or neutral *mise en scène*, but in the Great Hall of a Tudor palace, where in the style of the monarch on progress he establishes a temporary Presence Chamber clearly based upon the Tudor model.

In this way Heywood ensured that analogies would be drawn between Henry VIII and Jupiter. Indeed Henry had already been compared to Jupiter in encomiastic literature prior to this performance. Thus the association was a natural as well as an obvious one.[23] But Heywood does not leave the association there. Jupiter is not presented as an ideal figural type of Henry VIII simply to flatter the royal spectator. By examining the god-like aspects of English monarchy the play actually implies a fundamental critique of recent governmental practice.

The crucial fact about Jupiter is, as we have seen, that he is divine and thus different from his subjects. He is unreachably far above them in his nature, and his role is far beyond the grasp of their intellects. Heywood reiterates this point at signal moments in the action because it is the basis of the theory of monarchy which the play will expound.

The political implications of this assertion of monarchical transcendence of the mortal are explored in the two major corresponding events in the play, the parliament of the gods, as narrated by Jupiter himself, and the consultation of his mortal subjects which forms the substance of the play. From these two political events an identical pattern emerges. Power begins in the hands of the many, where it is misused. Consequently dissension breaks out and the community is riven with seemingly insoluble disputes. Only once all power is placed in the hands of the Sovereign are the problems resolved and harmony restored.

In the account of the turbulent parliamentary session which Jupiter provides in his opening soliloquy, the audience is told that the arguments between the gods had been resolved only by their voluntary surrender of executive power over the weather to Jupiter. The latter thus begins the play in full command of the elements. Yet he is unsure how to use his power. Hence his decision partially to devolve his responsibilities onto his subjects by asking for their counsel. In so doing he reverses the logic which had governed the solution of the earlier dispute. Power is again offered into the

---

[23] See John Skelton's *Speke, Parott*, lines 405–10, in V. J. Scattergood, ed., *John Skelton, the Complete English Poems* (London, 1982).

hands of the multitude, this time not the politically influential class, the gods, but the mortal populace. Only through the wearing experience of hearing all the petty, self-interested and contradictory suits of his subjects is Jupiter once more convinced to resume sole responsibility himself and settle the matter by *fiat*.

Thus the political message is first offered in narrative form, then reiterated in dramatic action. Only the King himself can properly exercise the sovereign governmental function. He ought to rely upon neither representative assemblies nor private petition, but should trust his own wisdom and insight. Perhaps in order that this message should not be misunderstood and its contemporary application missed, Heywood portrays Jupiter as convinced of the wisdom of his actions by his experience both of his mortal subjects and his fellow gods. It is not simply his superiority as a god among mortals that entitles, indeed obliges, him to exercise sole authority, it is his function as a King – among both gods and men. It is sovereignty that the play examines, not divinity.

In order to substantiate what might seem rather a grand claim to make about what is essentially a comic interlude, it is perhaps wise, before proceeding further, to examine each of these two major incidents in the play in some detail. First to establish that questions of political philosophy and practice are actually addressed in the play, second to demonstrate that a play which at first glance seems to be all about political consultation (it begins, after all, with a parliament, and proceeds to present a god taking the unusually liberal step of asking his subjects how they would like him to run the world) is in fact an apology for, and an education in, royal absolutism.

In the first eighty-five lines of the play Jupiter offers the audience a brief narrative account of the parliament of the gods. Much of the rhetoric he employs is that normally associated with ideas of government by consent. But the reality it describes is a monarch ultimately liberated to govern his domain at will. The parliament had met, as we have seen, to settle a dispute between the most powerful of the weather-gods.

> Before our presens in our hye parlyament
> Both goddes and goddeses of all degrees
> Hath late assembled by comen assent
> For the redres of certayne enormytees
> Bred amonge them thorow extremytees
> Abusyd in eche to other of them all.
>
> (lines 23–8)

Four gods in particular, Saturn, Phebus, Eolus and Phebe, were threatening the stability of the realm with their strife. These four,

Whose natures not onely so farre contraryous
But also of malyce eche other to defame
Have longe tyme abusyd ryght farre out of frame
The dew course of all theyr constellacyons
To the great damage of all yerthly nacyons.
(lines 32–6)

Each god offered his or her own complaint. But none would answer the accusations made against them by the others (lines 51–6).

They eche agaynste other and he agaynste all thre
Thus can these iiii in no maner agre.
(lines 63–4)

The only solution seemed to be to submit their dispute to the judgement of Jupiter. This they all agreed upon. But it is important to note precisely how the parliament concluded. It did not ask Jupiter merely to act as an arbiter of their dispute. The gods surrendered all their powers to their King, asking him to exercise them in future in their stead, in such ways as his wisdom dictated.

They have in conclusyon holly surrendyd
Into our handes as mych as concernynge
All maner wethers by them engendryd
The full of theyr powrs *for terme everlastynge*
To let suche order as standyth wyth our pleasynge.
(lines 72–6, my italics)

The ostensible subject of this dispute, the weather, the perennial topic of inconsequential chatter, gives it a comic aspect, but the context, and the language of commonweal, royal honour, 'enormytees' and 'great damage of all yerthly nacyons' employed to describe it, demonstrates that the debate is metaphorical, and the play's true concerns are political. The crucial point to note is that it is power which parliament has granted to the King, regardless of the exact form which that power takes in the context of the play.

That Jupiter did not seek this solution to the problem is made clear at once. 'Whyche thynge', he stressed,

... as of our parte no parte requyred
But of all theyr partys ryght humbly desyred.
(lines 77–8)

But he accepted his new-found executive strength, and the parliament was dissolved with a declaration of the new supreme authority of the monarch.

To take uppon us wherto we dyd assente
And so in all thynges wyth one voyce agreable
We have clerely fynyshed our foresayd parlement
To your great welth whyche shall be fyrme and stable
And to our honour farre inestymable
For syns theyr powers as ours addyd to our owne
Who can we say know us as we shulde be knowne.

(lines 79–85)

Now it might be possible, despite the restatement of the awesome mystery of monarchy in the final line, to read the text thus far as sympathetic to parliamentary sovereignty, and for the need for Kings to take counsel. The passage does vaunt what was originally the power of a parliament 'assembled by comen assent' (line 25), now devolved onto the King by conscious act 'of all theyr partys ryght humbly desyred' (line 78). Might it not be argued, then, that the play advances the singularly radical assertion that royal authority is granted the King by the people, as represented by parliament, an assertion which carries the unspoken corollary that authority so granted may in future be withdrawn should circumstances change? What follows demonstrates that this is not the case.

It must be noted that the parliament's surrender of its authority over the weather is not conditional, despite the references to Jupiter's wisdom and 'puysaunt power' cited by the gods as the reason for their decision. The grant is absolute and irrevocable, 'for terme everlastynge' (line 75). And it leads not to a contractual, rational, theory of Kingship, based upon consent and utility, but a further restatement of the mysterious, mystical, nature of Sovereignty, of the sort that began the play ('Who can we say know us as we shulde be knowne' (line 85)). Thus, although Jupiter leaves the assembly with the liberal intention of consulting his subjects before employing his authority, he has already taken the first steps towards an autocratic, unaccountable, rule – a rule which, from his opening lines, seems to accord with his own conception of his estate. The bulk of the play to follow is, in essence, a repetition of this process, and a re-education in the wisdom of his earlier course of action. The submission of his subjects only confirms the lesson learnt in parliament. Only the Sovereign can solve the political problems which face the commonweal. He thus needs no counsel beyond his own wisdom. Hence his abrupt statement to Merry Report,

... be thou suer we nede no whyt thy councell
For in our selfe we have forsene remedy.

(lines 1148–9)

The entire exercise of consulting his subjects has merely determined him to proceed henceforth without consultation.

Whilst the foolish and self-centred petitions which the suitors present, and their bawdy banter with Merry Report outside the Chamber door, no doubt entertain and amuse the audience, their manifest folly also serves a more serious purpose. By reducing the pleas of his subjects to facile and contradictory special pleading, Heywood makes Jupiter's decision to grant none of them outright seem not only logical but also morally fitting. Had any of the suitors brought forward a tale of genuine hardship, Jupiter's autocratic declaration would have been difficult to justify. But as the play makes the representatives of the populace entirely unsympathetic, we are forced to conclude with Merry Report that there are

> No sewters now but women, knavys, and boys
> And all theyr sewtys are in fansyes and toys.
> (lines 1076–7)

Just as we were led to see that the 'malyce' (line 33) and stubbornness of the gods rendered them incapable of settling their own dispute in a representative assembly, so we are now shown a group of subjects too foolish to exercise influence. Hence we connive quite naturally in Jupiter's solution. Power, we feel, ought not to be left in such immature hands.

What Jupiter actually proposes is not, as Merry Report suggests, to leave the weather as it was, but to determine it at his own discretion. He will give to each estate at various times, the rewards he feels they deserve, helping

> ... as many or as few as we thynke best
> And where or what tyme to serve moste or lest
> The dysseccyon of that doutles shall stande
> Perpetually in the power of our hande.
>
> Wherefore we wyll the hole worlde to attende
> Eche sorte on suche wether as for them doth fall
> Now one now other as lyketh us to stande
> Who that hath yt ply yt and suer we shall
> So gyde the wether in course to you all
> That eche wyth other ye shall hole remayne
> In pleasure and plentyfull welth certayne.
> (lines 1226–36)

Having begun with the parliament's surrender of its powers into royal hands, the play ends with Jupiter taking into those hands his subjects' welfare – again, freely conceded, as the concluding lines demonstrate. The moral wisdom of this resolution is suggested by the happy conclusion to the proceedings, Jupiter's exit being accompanied by that most effective dramatic symbol of harmony, a song. The political wisdom behind it is asserted in the final stanzas.

The value to the Crown in keeping all executive powers in the King's hands, in making no binding promises of redress, and in making future rewards contingent upon good behaviour, is emphasized as each suitor is made to offer in turn his or her pledge of allegiance to the Sovereign. The King binds every class to him, and to him alone, by subordinating their prosperity to his will. But he does so only by taking all power into his own hands. The Gentleman begins the list of supplicants, assuring Jupiter that, as he 'hath so bountyfully',

> Dystrybuted my parte that your grace shall know
> Your selfe sool possessed of hertes of all chyvalry.
> (lines 1242–4)

The personal nature of the loyalty so obtained is again stressed by the Merchant, who promises

> Lyke wyse we marchauntes shall yeld us holy
>   Onely to laude the name of Jupyter
> As god of all goddes you to serve soolly
> For of every thynge I se you are norysher.
> (lines 1245–8)

Similarly the Ranger pledges 'we shall gyve you our hertes with one accorde / For knowledge to know you as our onely lorde' (lines 1251–2), whilst the Millers, the Gentlewoman and the Launderess all offer not only their obedience, but also their hearts to him. Even the Boy offers him a share of his snowballs. To drive the point home, Jupiter then ascends into Heaven, enjoining the suitors to join in the song of praise,

> Syns cause gyveth cause to know us your lord
> onely'
> (line 1278)

Even the most obtuse of royal spectators – and Henry VIII was far from that – could hardly have failed to notice the lesson in *realpolitik* being offered.

In the light of the play's assertions of royal independence, the ambivalent characterization of Merry Report remarked upon earlier becomes more obviously dramatically effective. If the political message of the play suggests that the Sovereign ought to rely upon neither a divided parliament, nor individual special pleading, then the representation of his closest and most influential attendant as a bawdy and potentially corrupt rogue confirms and extends that message. Not even the King's most intimate household servants, the text suggests, can be relied upon for sound, impartial, advice. Hence reliance upon them would be foolish, a display of dangerous weakness.

Jupiter's statement that he does not need Merry Report's advice ('be thou suer we nede no whyt thy counsell / For in our selfe we have forsene remedy' (lines 1149–50)) is thus a further statement of the play's central theme. Moreover it has both a general and a specific significance. It both forwards the assertion of the need for monarchical independence, and offers advice concerning a key question of household administration.

In a Court in which proximity to the Sovereign provided unparalleled opportunities to exert influence, the question arose, where should the limits of that influence be drawn in the best interests of the commonwealth? It was one thing for royal attendants to use the advantages of their offices to suggest suitable recipients for royal grants or to accrue personal wealth and status (the aspects of household influence considered in *Magnyfycence*). But if they were to attempt to exert their influence in other areas, particularly in matters of government policy which were the responsibility of the King and his Council, then this would have serious political consequences. In theory a strict distinction ought to have been maintained between personal and political influence. And it seems, from the example of a man like Sir William Compton, the Groom of the Stool from 1510 until 1526, who performed the most intimate services for Henry VIII, but did not wield any political influence as a result, that Henry largely succeeded in upholding that distinction in practice.[24] But the balance could never have been easily achieved. In having Jupiter so signally deny his Usher a role in the determination of policy, Heywood encouraged Henry to continue his diligence. That the Usher concerned is not unequivocally vicious, and indeed seems worthy of some praise for the performance of his duties, widens the significance of the lesson. It is not simply corrupt or incompetent household servants who should be excluded from the political process, but all household servants. The point being made is institutional and political, not personal and moral.

POLITICAL EVENTS

If *Weather* does indeed carry the political message suggested above, however, more questions are raised than are answered. The absolutist theme of the play seems strangely at odds with the prevailing theories of government in the early sixteenth century,[25] and markedly out of place in

---

[24] G. W. Bernard, 'The Rise of Sir William Compton, early Tudor Courtier', *E. H. R.*, XCVI (1981), pp. 754–77.

[25] The development of what may be called an 'absolutist' conception of English monarchy is usually dated by scholars to much later in the sixteenth century or even the seventeenth. See, for example, R. Eccleshall, *Order and Reason in Politics* (Oxford, 1978), pp. 71–7.

the work of Heywood, a man usually associated with the humanist group centred around Sir Thomas More, a circle known more for its approval of contractual notions of sovereignty than for flirting with tyranny.[26] How can the appearance of such ideas in the specific context of the Henrician Court in 1529–30 be explained? And why might Heywood have been moved to expound them? The first question involves an examination of Henry VIII's position after the fall of Wolsey and will be considered below. The second may be approached more directly.

It is possible, of course, that John Heywood was far more of a maverick thinker than has hitherto been allowed, and so shared few of the political views which More or Erasmus expressed. Certainly the degree of homogeneity of thought suggested in some discussions of the More circle is overstated. But it is not necessary to dismiss Heywood to the political margins in order to make *Weather* explicable. What is known about the author's attitudes, particularly his religious attitudes, provides interesting clues as to why he should have tried to appeal to Henry VIII in such terms as *Weather* employs.

If Heywood was anything he was a catholic, and a defender of catholicism in England. His close association with the household of Princess Mary continued throughout her long period of disfavour with the King, and Heywood may well have dedicated a laudatory poem to her in 1534 at a time when any overt support for the Princess would have been seen as a tacit statement of opposition to the Crown's religious policies. A far more obvious act of opposition to the course of the Reformation was his involvement in 1543 in the abortive 'Prebendaries' plot' to overthrow Archbishop Cranmer, the discovery of which led to the execution of Germain Gardiner. Only a timely confession and abjuration at St Paul's on 6 July 1544 obtained Heywood a pardon and saved his life. But the sincerity and long-term significance of this gesture may be judged by his decision to leave England, after the accession of Elizabeth, for exile in the catholic Netherlands and France.[27]

From the evidence of his other plays, however, it is clear that Heywood

---

[26] More's own anxiety at the prospect of an unchecked and thus potentially tyrannous sovereignty is expressed, not only in his *History of King Richard III*, but also in his *Epigrams*. Note Epigrams 102 and 182, which laud senatorial government above monarchy, and suggest that Kings 'rule on suffrance'. L. Bradner and C. A. Lynch, eds., *The Latin Epigrams of Thomas More* (Chicago, 1953). Note also the advice supposedly given by More to Thomas Cromwell in late 1530, on the specific issue of how best to advise Henry VIII in the interests of the commonweal: 'ever tell him what he owght to doe, but never what he is able to doe . . . For if [a] Lion knewe his owne strength, harde were it for any man to rule him.' W. Roper, *The Lyfe of Sir Thomas More, Knighte*, ed., E. Vaughan Hitchcock (London, 1935), pp. 56–7.

[27] Bolwell, *Heywood*, pp. 1–18; Foxe, *Acts and Monuments*, VIII, pp. 24–6.

was no reactionary catholic, willing to defend the Roman Church without qualification. Like many humanists he shared Erasmus' contempt for the more obvious abuses of the orthodox Church, and argued for limited reforms to cleanse it of venality and ignorance, and promote a more spiritual, personal, faith, without ever criticizing the institution itself. Thus in *The Pardoner and the Friar* and *The Four PP* (printed in 1533 and 1534 respectively) he satirized the stupidity and greed of some friars and the chicanery involved in the exhibition of fraudulent relics, whilst insisting upon the value of both virtuous friars and piously undertaken pilgrimages in the quest for salvation.[28] As the Pedlar, the figure of moral authority in *The Four PP*, tells the 'Potycary', it is for the Church to determine the authenticity of relics, not the layman.

> ... beste in these thynges it semeth to me
> To make no judgement upon ye
> But as the Churche doth judge or take them
> So do ye receyve or forsake them
> And so be sure ye can nat erre
> But may be a frutfull folower.
>
> (lines 1355–60)

The play concludes with a clear submission to the authority of the Roman Church.

> Then to our reason god gyve us his grace
> That we may folowe with fayth so fermely
> His commandementes, that we may purchace
> Hys love, and so consequently
> To byleve hys churche faste and faythfully
> So that we may accordynge to his promyse
> Be kepte out of errour in any wyse.
>
> (lines 1368–74)

> Besechynge our lorde to prosper you all
> In the fayth of hys churche universall.
>
> (lines 1380–1)

The reiteration of orthodox sentiments here and elsewhere in the plays makes clear that Heywood had no intention of their being read as anti-clerical, evangelical, works. His conception of reform was essentially that of More, Erasmus and Colet, not that of Tyndale, Fish or Jerome Barlowe.

[28] John Heywood, *The Pardoner and the Friar and the Four PPs*, Malone Society (Oxford, 1984), *Four PP*, lines 1277–328.

It might seem curious, then, to suggest that Heywood's conservative religious position led him to advance an absolutist view of monarchy in *Weather*. The historian, aware of the events of the 1530s, is likely to see developments suggestive of the Royal Supremacy and the coming of the Reformation as insolubly linked, and to read arguments for one as tacit support for the other. But in 1529–30 no such association would have seemed obvious. Indeed a strong monarchical role in the determination of matters both temporal and spiritual (although stopping well short of a repudiation of the Papal Primacy) may have seemed to conservative reformers the surest means of defending the Church against heresy and spoliation.

Henry himself, whilst covertly encouraging anti-clerical initiatives at Court, and subsequently in Parliament, as a means of exerting pressure upon Rome and the English Church over the 'divorce' issue, simultaneously appeared in public as a friend of the Church, reluctant to succumb to the blandishments of its radical critics. Thus he was able to use the threat of anti-clerical legislation and schism to drive on a reluctant Pope, whilst also professing conspicuous loyalty to the Holy See and craving his just rewards.

Henry was no radical in religion. But he saw the tactical advantages in countenancing, even exaggerating, the influence of radical opinion at times in pursuit of his own ends. But his public persona remained that of the father of his people, concerned for their welfare in the face of increasing dissension between laymen and the clergy. He stayed aloof, as will be shown, from the debates in Parliament, acting as the arbiter of disputes rather than as a participant, always advocating moderate, necessary, reforms to remove the grosser abuses in the Church, but with a view to improving the institution, not destroying it.[29] This stance gradually gave way, in the face of papal intransigence and the refusal of leading English clerics to countenance a domestic settlement of the marriage issue, to increased bellicosity and more open hostility, leading to the Submission of the Clergy in 1532. But even here the fiction of impartiality was

---

[29] The opening address to Parliament, given by More, stressed the need for new laws to cope with 'divers new enormities ... sprong up amongst the people' (Hall, p. 764), a carefully worded declaration suggesting all things to all hearers, capable of being read as identifying either the need to reform the Church, to suppress heresy, or both. On 6 December 1529 Henry was arguing for moderate reforms, telling Chapuys that, as to the Church in his dominions, 'he hoped little by little, to introduce reforms and put an end to scandal' (*C.S.P.Sp.* IV (i) 224). His offer to sponsor an orthodox translation of the New Testament suggested evidence of the practical implementation of that wish. Yet on 15 October 1530 he was still promising 'a much stricter rule' to punish and suppress heresy (ibid., 460).

maintained, the claim being that only by heeding the complaints of his Commons did the King 'discover' the iniquitous dual-loyalty of his clergy. Henry retained the mantle of the judge of the Church long after he had in practice become its chief prosecutor.

Yet in 1529–30, and even in 1531, the King's position would have appeared far less duplicitous. His advocacy of moderate reforms within an orthodox framework ideally suited the aims of the humanist reformers among whom Heywood may be numbered. Certainly Thomas More did not at this stage see anti-clericalism and heresy as connived at by the Crown, for he accepted the Chancellorship from Henry and retained it until 1532, evidently believing that his harsh repression of heresy met with royal approval.[30] And Henry's proclamations against heretical books issued in 1529 and 1530 would only have furthered that impression.[31]

What made a strong monarch attractive to conservative reformers in general, and seemingly to Heywood in particular, at this time was not, however, purely Henry's public support for reform, but also the fact that the Church seemed in urgent need of a champion. It may well be that the strength of anti-clerical and heretical opinion in England has been exaggerated. Certainly, as Christopher Haigh has argued, the actual output in terms of acts directly hostile to the Church passed by the first session of the Reformation Parliament (3 November to 17 December 1529) was so limited as to call into question its reputation as the 'Anti-clerical Parliament'.[32] But it is the impression created by the debates and fostered at the time that is significant here, not the resulting legislation. And contemporaries were as convinced as modern historians that the Church was under severe attack in 1529, both from within and beyond Parliament.

As we have seen, the initial target of this attack was Thomas Wolsey. His failure to secure an annulment of Henry's marriage to Katherine of Aragon at the Legatine court at Blackfriars caused the King to unleash upon him a barrage of criticism which inevitably carried implications for both the Church in England and the Roman authority. The Duke of Suffolk's famous declaration at Blackfriars, accompanied by a loud bang upon the table with his fist, that 'it was never merry in England whilst we had Cardinals among us', was the first of many initiatives stage-managed

---

[30] See J. A. Guy, *The Public Career of Thomas More* (Brighton, 1980), pp. 50–64; R. Marius, *Thomas More* (London, 1986), pp. 325–70.

[31] Hughes and Larkin, *Tudor Royal Proclamations* (3 vols., London, 1964–69), nos. 122 and 129. Wilkins, *Concilia*, III, fols. 727ff. Both proclamations stressed Henry's personal concern for the welfare of the souls of his subjects, and his personal role in the suppression of heresy.

[32] C. Haigh, 'Anticlericalism and the English Reformation', in C. Haigh, ed., *The English Reformation Revised* (Cambridge, 1987), pp. 56–74, esp. pp. 60–2.

by Henry VIII, and designed to cow Church leaders into conceding an annulment, either in Rome or in England.[33] Thereafter threats and allegations concerning the wealth, power and abuses of the clergy became common currency at Court and in the City. In September 1529, Eustace Chapuys, himself a passionate defender of Queen Katherine's case and of the liberties of the Church, reported that Suffolk's words had found widespread agreement in London.[34] On 17 October the French ambassador du Bellay reported a general hostility towards the Church evident among the noblemen at Court.[35]

These lords intend, after he [Wolsey] is dead or ruined, to impeach the state of the Church and take all their goods, which it is hardly needful for me to write in cypher, for they proclaim it openly.

Moreover, according to Chapuys, Protestant literature was openly circulating at Court.[36] By 13 December the Imperial ambassador was claiming, in evident desperation, that 'nearly all the people here hate the priests'.[37]

This atmosphere of tension between the temporal and spiritual spheres was not, however, simply the product of covert royal propaganda. The first session of the Reformation Parliament, despite its limited yield of anti-clerical legislation, created a mood of anxiety and dissension which left Church leaders isolated and embattled. As Henry himself had signalled open season upon Wolsey and had created an atmosphere at Court in which criticism of the Church was tolerated, even encouraged, it became far easier for genuine grievances and opportunist claims alike to be advanced in Parliament. As Hall notes,[38]

These thynges [criticisms of the Church] before this time might in nowise be towched nor yet talked of by no man except he would be made an heretike, or lese al that he had ... [as the clergy had dominated the King]. But now when God had illumined the eies of the Kynge, and that ther subtell doynges was once espied: then man began charitably to desyre a reformation, and so at this Parliament menne began to shewe there grudges.'

---

[33] Cavendish, *Life of Wolsey*, p. 90. The fact that the Duke made this intemperate interjection has led to the suggestion that he was a confirmed anti-clerical, or even a Lutheran (J. A. Guy, *Public Career*, pp. 30, 107–9). But the context of the passage makes clear that he was simply acting on Henry's instructions. Cavendish describes how the adjournment was announced and then 'with that / stept forthe the Duke of Suffolk frome the Kyng And by his commaundement spake thes wordes with a stought and hault countenaunce / Yt was never (quod he) mery in Englond whilest we had Cardynalles among us'. Having made his speech, Suffolk then hurried out after Henry, who had left his gallery as soon as Suffolk had stepped forward. The incident thus says little about Suffolk's own theological position, even less about his supposed enmity towards Wolsey, but much for his loyalty to Henry VIII.

[34] *C.S.P.Sp.* IV (i) 160.   [35] *L.P.* IV (iii) 6011.   [36] *C.S.P.Sp.* IV (i) 228.

[37] Ibid., 232.   [38] Hall, p. 765.

Before Parliament assembled, the London Mercer's company had drawn up its own list of five articles for discussion there, one of which begged Henry to remember the plight of his poor subjects,[39]

pryncipally of London [who] have been polled and robbed without reason or conscience by th'ordenarys in probatyng of testamentes and takyng of mortuarys, and also vexed and trobled by citacions with cursyng oon day and absoilyng the next day, *et hec omnio pro pecuniis*

As Hall made clear, such overt criticism of traditional clerical practices would not have been tolerated in previous Parliaments. But as Henry had tacitly encouraged criticism, and openly declared that he wished 'abuses' to be discussed, precisely these issues were debated, when members of the Lower House[40]

began to comon of their grefes wherwith the spiritualtie had before tyme grevously oppressed them, both contrarie to ye lawe of the realme, and contrarie to all righte.

A debate upon probate fees, always a contentious issue (and one in which the common lawyers who were strongly represented in the Commons' House had a vested interest[41]) came to life once Sir Henry Guildford, the Controller of the Royal Household, had spoken up, criticizing the excessive fees allegedly charged under Archbishop Warham and Cardinal Wolsey's joint jurisdiction for the probate of the will of Sir William Compton.[42] Once a man so obviously connected with the Crown had set the tone of the debate, the other members lost their inhibitions and, as Hall records,[43]

After this declaracion were shewed so many axtorcions done by ordinaries for probates of willes that it were to muche to rehearse.

In order to coordinate and cope with the volume of material concerning the Church both submitted to members and generated by them, the Speaker of the Commons, Thomas Audley, established a committee to devise and present bills on clerical matters. This body, which may have included, among others, both Thomas Cromwell and John Petyt the evangelical London burgess,[44] began to receive, discuss and compile submissions for incorporation into bills. It may well have received or com-

---

[39] H. Miller, 'London and Parliament in the Reign of Henry VIII', *B.I.H.R.*, XXXV (1962), p. 144.
[40] Hall, p. 765.
[41] Haigh, 'Anticlericalism', p. 60; S. E. Lehmberg, *The Reformation Parliament* (Cambridge, 1970), pp. 81–3. A contemporary petition to the King complained that the common lawyers were 'rulers in [the] commen howse'. P.R.O. SP 2/Q fols., 138–40 (*L.P.* VII 1611 (3)).
[42] Hall, p. 765.   [43] As above.   [44] Lehmberg, p. 83.

piled, among other material, a number of undated petitions concerning heresy trials, the administration of Warham's archiepiscopal Court of Arches, clerical venality, exaction, and nepotism.[45] Certainly it presented in due course bills concerning mortuary and probate fees, the taking of secular employment by clerics, pluralism and non-residence. Rumours also abounded concerning other issues which Parliament was said to be going to discuss, but which seem not to have reached the stage of formal incorporation. In September Chapuys had reported that the Houses would debate a ban on the reception of Papal legates into England, but this seems not to have been actually discussed.[46] John Fisher's earliest biographer also thought that the Lords considered the suggestion that all the smaller abbeys, worth £200 or less yearly, should be suppressed in order to recompense Henry for the cost of the 'divorce' proceedings. But, again, no formal record of such a debate survives.[47] Yet the existence of such rumours illustrates the prevailing mood of criticism of the Church and anxiety for its future.

More tangible evidence of anti-clerical sentiments was provided once the House of Commons began to receive the bills drawn up by its committee on Church affairs. The first, that concerning mortuary fees, passed both houses with little opposition. But the second, on probate fees, aroused considerable controversy once it arrived in the Lords.[48]

at the which the Archbishop of Caunterburie, in especiall, and all other bishoppes in generall both frowned and grunted, for that touched ther profite, in so much as Dr Jhon Fisher, saied openlie in the parliament chambre... my lordes, you se daily what billes come hither from the comon house and all is to the distruction of the churche, for Godes sake se what a Realme Boheme was, and when the Churche went downe, then fell the glory of the Kyngdome, now with the Commons is nothing but doune with the Church, and all this me semeth is for lacke of faith only.

Hearing reports of Fisher's speech, the Commons took exception to the analogy to Hussite Bohemia, and to the implied accusation of faithlessness aimed at them and, 'after long debate', voted to petition Henry, through the Speaker to discipline the Bishop.[49] A hasty qualification of his original assertion, corroborated by Warham, seemed to satisfy Henry, but left the Commons frustrated. This frustration was voiced in the joint committees convened to discuss the 'anti-clerical' bills, where accusations of theft and

---

45 As above. For the details of the petitions and the problems involved in their dating, see G. R. Elton, 'Parliamentary Drafts, 1529–1540', *B.I.H.R.*, XXV (1952), p. 122.
46 *C.S.P.Sp.* IV (i) 168.
47 P. Hughes, ed., *Saint John Fisher: The Earliest English Life* (London, 1935), pp. 109–11. See also *C.S.P.Sp.* IV (i) 232.
48 Hall, p. 766.   49 As above.

exaction were made against the clergy by the Commons' representatives.[50] And when the Lower House sent up a third bill on clerical matters to the Lords, this time concerning pluralism, non-residence and secular employment, angry dissension broke out again. This bill, notes Hall, who himself sat as Member for Wenlock (Shropshire),[51]

so displeased ye spiritualitie that the prestes railed on the commons of the common house, and called them heretikes and scismatikes, for whych diverse prests were punished.

After a lengthy debate the proceedings reached deadlock, as 'the Lordes spirituall woulde in no wise consent' to pass the Bill. Again the Commons petitioned Henry for aid, and again he responded with a judicious, moderate proposal, convening a joint committee of both Houses to discuss the matter. Only timely concessions by the Commons' representatives and pressure by the Lords Temporal upon their clerical colleagues achieved a compromise document and a partial victory for the Commons.

With the prorogation of Parliament on 17 December, then, there ended a session which, although limited in its legislative impact upon the Church, had been characterized by dissension and temperamental outbursts between laymen and clerics. The eventual compromises reached over the various bills concerning the Church should not conceal the genuine fears for the future entertained by the religious conservatives. Behind the Commons' aggressive assertion of their grievances, both Fisher and More saw attempts by heretics to destroy rather than reform the Church. As Fisher warned the Lords,[52]

These men now amonge us seeke to reprove the life and doings of the clergie, but after such a sort as they indevour to bring them into contempt and hatred of the layetie, and so finding falte with other men's manners whom they have no authoritie to correct, emitt and forget their owne, which is far worse and much more out of order than the other.

Evidently at this stage the conservatives saw Henry as a potential protector rather than their chief critic.[53] The danger seemed to come rather from the

---

50 Ibid., p. 767.		51 As above.
52 R. Hall, *Life of Fisher* (London, 1921), pp. 69–70.
53 On 15 October 1530 Henry was still claiming that only he protected the Church from the hatred of the nobles and Commons (*C.S.P.Sp.* IV (i) 460). Indeed, as late as January 1531 the clergy seem to have been petitioning the King for redress in terms which suggest that they expected him to respond sympathetically. P.R.O. SP 1/56 fols., 84–7. See G. W. Bernard, 'The Pardon of the Clergy Reconsidered', *Journal of Ecclesiastical History*, XXXVII (1986), pp. 278–9. (For the suggestion that this document originated with the government rather than the Church, see J. A. Guy, 'Henry VIII and the *Praemunire* manoeuvres of 1530–1', *E.H.R.*, XCVII (1982), p. 491.) Certainly on 13 May 1532 Convocation was still attempting to distinguish between Henry's position and that of

House of Commons and elements at Court who were trying to persuade a reluctant Sovereign to countenance their ambitions.

Against this background Heywood's stance in *Weather* becomes more readily explicable. By suggesting to Henry that the ideal sovereign should take power out of the hands of a divided parliament, and refuse both the partial suits of his subjects and the advice of his household men, the play appeals to a King who seemed to share the author's religious position, to act according to his own wisdom, not the advice of others. The play's terms of reference also seem more significant once read in association with the events of 1529–30. The parliament of the gods, riven by malice and mutual accusations, and the self-interested appeals of Jupiter's subjects now appear to be, not abstract political devices, but direct allusions to contemporary events. If, as seems likely, *Weather* was performed at Court over the Christmas period 1529–30,[54] then the audience would have required little explanation of such allusions.

Such a background to the play would also explain its curious lack of any of the clerical figures normally so well represented in social satires. If Heywood's aim was to protect the Church and ridicule anti-clerical or reforming elements in Parliament and at Court, the absence of such stock clerical characters as litter his other works from this particular play is readily understandable.

The religious dissension of late 1529 can, then, partially explain the strategies adopted by Heywood in *Weather*. Some further explanation is required, however, to make clear the circumstances under which he felt able to portray an absolute monarch in his drama, and to connect that figure with Henry VIII.

It has been argued above that Henry himself, rather than a hostile faction or an aristocratic reaction, was the prime mover in Wolsey's fall from authority. Having decided that the Cardinal had let him down over the crucial issue of the 'divorce', Henry evidently had one of his not infrequent crises of conscience concerning his role in government. A combination of feelings of betrayal and self-confidence seem to have led him to assert himself once more in the administration of the realm, and particularly in the pursuit of his 'Great Matter', the annulment of his

Parliament when it offered to surrender the canons of the Church for scrutiny by the King alone, not by Parliament. Evidently the bishops still hoped for a more favourable response from Henry. M. Kelly, 'Canterbury Jurisdiction and Influence during the Episcopate of William Warham', Cambridge University Ph.D. dissertation, 1963, p. 266.

54 In 1529, as Hall notes (p. 768) 'After the parliament was thus ended, the Kyng removed to Grenewiche and ther kept his Christemas with the quene in great triumph: with great plentie of viaundes, and diverse disguisynges and Enterludes, to the greate rejoisynge of his people.'

marriage.[55] Henceforward, he seems to have decided, there would be no more favourites, but a correctly appointed personal monarchy conducted through the proper instrument of government, the Council. As Hall, usually an accurate reflector of royal policy, declared,[56]

The Kinge which after twentie yere past, had bene ruled by other, and in especial by the Cardinal of Yorke, began now to be a ruler, and a Kynge, yea a kyng of suche wytte, wisedome and pollicie, that the lyke hath not reygned over this realme.

Hereafter Henry not only took personal control over the direction of affairs, but, typically, made sure that everyone knew that he was doing so. On 1 October 1529, the Bishop of Bayonne informed his master, Francis I, that 'I do not see that I can for a long time speak with the King, who at present takes the management of everything'.[57] In January 1530 Henry confidently assured Chapuys that the errors of the Wolsey years were over.[58]

At that time ... those who had the reins of government in their hands deceived me, many things were done then without my knowledge, but such proceedings will be stopped in future.

Time was to demonstrate that this, like many of Henry's enthusiasms, was a temporary phenomenon, but as late as August 1530, it was still being reported that Henry was choosing 'to know and superintend everything himself'.[59]

It is, then, misleading to see the reassertion of aristocratic counsel which followed Wolsey's fall as either instrumental in that process, or evidence of a forceful re-emergence of a conciliarist approach to government which had hitherto been suppressed by Wolsey. That the Court aristocrats, Norfolk, Suffolk and Thomas Boleyn, Viscount Rochford (subsequently Earl of Wiltshire) emerged as the leading councillors in the wake of

---

[55] See G. R. Elton, *The Tudor Revolution in Government* (Cambridge, 1959), p. 113 and *Reform and Reformation* (Cambridge, 1977), p. 118; J. A. Guy, 'Privy Council: Revolution or Evolution', in C. Coleman and D. R. Starkey, eds., *Revolution Reassessed* (Oxford, 1986), p. 69.

[56] Hall, p. 759. That Hall makes the concession that Henry had been less than ideal hitherto suggests that (as with his account of the 'purge' of 1519) he is following an official explanation of events. In a work which is otherwise unstinting in its eulogy of the King, one does not expect to find such implied criticism offered, unless the author had reason to think that it would be accepted. That More's account to Parliament of Wolsey's fall also suggested that the latter had for a time 'juggeled with the Kyng' (Hall, p. 764) seems to confirm that the Crown, as in 1519, was tactically conceding that Henry had emerged from a period of subservience to reassert himself and restore order. Henry's comments to Chapuys in January 1530, quoted below, further support this suggestion.

[57] *L.P.* IV (iii) 5982. [58] *C.S.P.Sp.* V 250. [59] *C.S.P.V.* IV 601.

Wolsey's disgrace, and were to be found lauding the virtues of government by an aristocrat-dominated Council, was a consequence, not a cause, of the Cardinal's removal.[60] Once Henry had resolved that there should be no more favourites, and that government should be conducted by the traditional political virtues, it was inevitable that men such as Norfolk and Suffolk would be thrust into the foreground. In a reaction against an allegedly over-powerful individual, particularly an upstart commoner, an aristocratic group is always the most likely beneficiary. That the Dukes were convinced that this move was only right and proper, is not to be doubted. But that they had any say in the matter is less clear.

Nor is it clear that only Suffolk, Norfolk and Rochford gained as a result of Wolsey's fall. Indeed, what evidence there is suggests that they were not alone. As has already been noted, More gained the Chancellorship, despite Suffolk's having briefly entertained a desire for the post, and others were formally taken into Henry's favour through adoption onto the Council. What seems to have happened, as royal secretary Brian Tuke explained to Chapuys, is that Henry, having brought the Dukes and Rochford into his confidence, intended to ensure that he always retained the counsel necessary for him to act as an effective working monarch by widening still further the inner circle of those from whom he took advice. This had the added value of reducing the influence of any one individual, leaving the King as sole director of a board of governors. Tuke had, Chapuys reported,[61]

said that the King was resolved to manage his own affairs, and had nominated several councillors that he might not be without assistance when Norfolk and the Chancellor are detained here. Suffolk has been appointed president of the Council for this purpose, with the same authority as the Chancellor.

The significance of this change in governmental style for an understanding of Heywood's play is clear. From the time of Wolsey's publicly signalled disgrace at Blackfriars onwards, the King increasingly took over the reins of government himself, signalling to all who would listen that he was doing so. His actions had a profound effect upon the mood of the

---

[60] On 25 October Norfolk told Chapuys that 'Now the management of affairs will fall into the hands of men better qualified by their birth and nobility to promote the welfare and honour of the King and kingdom.' The Duke also observed 'that state affairs in England were not now as I [Chapuys] thought, conducted by a single individual, but by the Privy Council in general', *C.S.P.Sp.* IV (i) 194. For a more general account of aristocratic theories of counsel in the period, see D. R. Starkey, 'Privy Secrets: Henry VIII and the Lords of the Council', *History Today*, XXXVII (1987), pp. 23–31.

[61] *C.S.P.Sp.* IV (i) 257. As J. A. Guy notes ('Privy Council', pp. 59 and 73) the Council remained 'small but vibrant' in this period. There was no increase in absolute numbers, indeed there was an overall decrease from Wolsey's large Council to Henry's Council of late 1529–30. What increased was the number of councillors attendant. All the inner councillors now regularly met with Henry, which had not been the case hitherto.

Court. Suddenly it became necessary to adopt a different vocabulary when describing the processes of government. Henry set an agenda in which there was no further place for favourites or special relationships with the Crown – a point reflected in both Norfolk's conciliarist modesty and the Lords' Articles of 1529, with their condemnation of Wolsey's having 'used himself more like a fellow to your Highnesse than like a subject'.[62] Henceforth government would be conducted by the King himself, assisted by a broader group of councillors.

What Heywood seems to have done in *Weather*, then, is take up and extrapolate to its absolutist extreme this rhetoric of royal independence fostered by Henry himself. By stressing the absolutist possibilities, even the absolutist obligations, inherent in such an active, personal, sovereignty, Heywood reminded the King of his own resolution, and suggested that he pursue it to its logical conclusion. If he intended to rule personally, then he did not need to countenance either a fractious Parliament or anti-clerical advisers. The truly responsible sovereign ruled without partisan counsel of any kind.

Evidently the author's hope was that the King would dissolve Parliament and pursue the sort of Erasmian reforms in the Church that Heywood approved of and thought the King desired. Such a course of action might have seemed, to a writer unaware of Henry's private motives, likely to appeal to the King, particularly as the House of Commons had hardly endeared itself to him by resisting the government bill cancelling the Crown's debts.[63] That business now complete, there might seem little reason to reconvene so contentious an assembly.[64] If this were so, then the potent weapon of parliamentary legislation would be denied to the Church's enemies. Hence Heywood's artful appeal to Henry in *Weather*.

---

[62] Lord Herbert of Cherbury, *The Life and Reigne of Henry the Eighth* (London, 1649), Article IIII, p. 267. Note also articles IX and XV which charge Wolsey with stifling debate within the Council and preventing that body from performing its true advisory function. Wolsey, it was claimed, 'used himself that if any man would shew his mind according to his duty, contrary to the opinion of the said Cardinall, he would so take him up with his accustomable words, that they were better to hold their peace than to speak, so that he would hear no man speak but one, or two great Personages, so that he would have all the words himself'. Significantly, it is not suppression of aristocratic contributions to Council debates that is objected to here, but a lack of open consultation across the whole Council. It is specifically stated that Wolsey did consult 'one or two great personages' (most plausibly Norfolk, and perhaps also Suffolk), but this is not felt to be enough (Herbert, pp. 268–9). That Norfolk in particular was less interested in aristocratic government *per se* than his words to Chapuys suggest, is demonstrated by his opposition to Suffolk's claim to the Chancellorship. Norfolk did not, Chapuys reported, wish to see the Great Seal 'in such high hands': an unlikely sentiment in one genuinely interested in the advancement of government by magnates, *C.S.P.Sp.* IV (i) 211.

[63] Hall, p. 767.

[64] Indeed, after two further extensions of the prorogation, the second session was not convened until January 1531.

By allegorizing the need to dispense with such unwelcome and contradictory counsel, and by setting that allegory in terms which adopted and extended the King's own current preoccupation with personal government, the author subtly made his own partisan point through a vehicle so crafted as to delight as well as instruct its royal audience.

Far from being the purely farcical comedy which it initially seems, then, *Weather* is actually an extremely subtle mixture of political and apolitical material. Unlike *Magnyfycence* it does not seem to subordinate its comic effects to political ends. It does not stress its political implications through signal debates inserted at key points in the action. What it does is underpin an essentially farcical series of encounters with a political message which at times is made clear to the audience and at other times is consciously concealed behind the raucous badinage. Its political function consequently appears subordinate to its role as entertainment, and is delivered almost subliminally. In this it is, despite initial appearances, probably the most subtle of the political plays discussed in this study.

Beyond this, the play also provides further evidence of the diversity of opinions held and indeed expressed at the Henrician Court during the turbulent last years of the 1520s. In the interludes of *Godly Queene Hester* and *Weather* there exists clear evidence of educated and articulate conservative opinion which was unafraid to voice itself even in the centre of the Court, before the King.

Doubtless the boldness implied in these plays was in part the product of Henry's own deliberately ambivalent stance on the issue of religious innovation in these years. By posing as the concerned but impartial judge of his subjects' suits he clearly encouraged both conservatives and radicals alike to put forward their views. But the existence of such plays also has wider implications for our understanding of debate at the Henrician Court, and of the role of drama in the political culture of this period.

It is often assumed that the pervading political atmosphere during the early years of the English Reformation was oppressive and that the expression and discussion of radical opinion was largely suppressed by an ecclesiastical establishment which was essentially intellectually moribund and incapable of joining such discussions on equal terms. Thus one hears much about the surreptitious, underground, activities of religious radicals at home and abroad, who used covert means to infiltrate their ideas into the minds of Henry VIII and his leading ministers,[65] but little about the

---

[65] Note, for example, John Foxe's account of how Simon Fish's *Supplication of Beggars* was smuggled into Court and found its way, through the good offices of Anne Boleyn, into the hands of the King. Foxe, *Acts and Monuments*, IV, p. 657. See also the similar account of how William Tyndale's *Obedience of a Christian Man* was shown to the King, J. Strype, *Ecclesiastical Memorials* (3 vols., Oxford, 1820–40), I (i) 172.

intellectual responses of the conservatives. With the celebrated exception of Thomas More, the conservatives have been seen as employing only judicial weapons against their radical opponents as they had little else to hand. The work of Maria Dowling on the scholars surrounding Katherine of Aragon and her circle has begun to redress this imbalance, but the realization that plays such as *Weather* also formed a part of this religious debate can take the process further.[66]

Whilst it is evident that repressive measures were taken to restrict the importation of heretical books and to suppress the spread of unorthodox ideas through the 'unprotected' laity at large, it is far less clear that rigid censorship of discussions was practised, or was possible, among the political and clerical elite at Court and in the universities. That Henry VIII could have been presented with *Hester* and *Weather* at the same time as he was being shown Simon Fish's *Supplication of Beggars* suggests that, at Court at least, the pervading atmosphere in these years was more open and heterodox, and more riven by genuine debate than is usually assumed.

Henry's decision to 'consult' individual eminent scholars and subsequently the universities, both domestic and Continental, over the merits of his case for an annulment of his marriage; his willingness to be tried in open court by Wolsey and Campeggio on the issue and the call for grievances against Wolsey and the Church generally to be aired after the Cardinal's fall, all contributed to an atmosphere in which views were expressed openly in high places on the most contentious of political and religious issues. Clearly Henry had no real desire for a genuinely open debate. Each period of 'consultation' was entered into with the intention of producing predetermined answers. But, having employed the rhetoric of free discussion, the Crown could not easily revert to a rigid censorship of ideas. Once the debate had begun there would necessarily be scope for individuals who were either consciously or unconsciously out of step with current royal thinking to raise issues and opinions far removed from those which the Crown was seeking to encourage. Hence the extraordinary ferment of ideas which surfaced in England in the final years of the 1520s.

That it was through courtly drama that some of these ideas were expressed is also of interest of itself. It adds further credence to the suggestion that drama was seen as an effective medium for the transmission of even the most controversial of opinions. Further reinforcement of this suggestion and an investigation of its wider implications will be found in the remaining chapters of this study.

---

[66] M. Dowling, *Humanism in the Age of Henry VIII* (Beckenham, 1986); 'Humanist Support for Katherine of Aragon', *B.I.H.R.*, lvii (1984), pp. 46–55.

Chapter 6

RADICAL DRAMA? JOHN BALE'S
KING JOHAN

THE AUTHOR

The turbulent career of John Bale touched upon many spheres of activity. As a cleric, polemicist, playwright and controversialist he has attracted much scholarly attention.[1] He thus needs little introduction for students of the period. Yet some brief details of his life will illustrate the context in which our present subject, his play *King Johan*, came to be written.

Bale was born in Suffolk in 1495, and from the age of twelve he was educated in the Carmelite house at Norwich. By 1514 he was studying at Cambridge University, and he was to spend periods at both Louvain and Toulouse before he obtained his Bachelor's degree in 1529. Whilst at Cambridge he exhibited none of that incendiary brand of evangelism which was to mark his later career. There is no evidence to link him with the White Horse Group of *avant garde* scholars who met to discuss the latest religious ideas. Indeed his energies seem rather to have been channelled at this time into the strictly orthodox activity of compiling saints' lives, intercessionary prayers and an antiphon in praise of the Virgin. A promising career within his order seemed to lie before him. And indeed by 1530 he was made prior of the house at Doncaster. Yet signs of his future heterodoxy began to emerge from this point onwards. In 1531 he was alleged to have taught one William Borman that Christ was not really present in the sacrament of the altar. By late 1533 he had abandoned the regular life and entered the secular priesthood, having, he claimed, been persuaded to renounce his vows by Thomas, Lord Wentworth.

Hereafter his views began to alter radically. He was examined by Archbishop Lee of York after being accused of heresy by Thomas Kirby, Warden of the Friars Minor, who claimed that he had criticized the

---

[1] See, for example, L. P. Fairfield, *John Bale: Mythmaker for the English Reformation* (West Lafayette, Indiana, 1976); J. W. Harris, *John Bale: A Study in the Minor Literature of the Reformation* (Urbana, Illinois, 1940); T. B. Blatt, *The Plays of John Bale* (Copenhagen, 1968); J. N. King, *English Reformation Literature* (Princeton, 1982); R. Pineas, 'Polemical Use of the Scriptures in the Plays of John Bale', *Nederlands Archief voor Kerkgeschiedenis*, 66 (1986), pp. 180–9.

honouring of saints. An intervention by Thomas Cromwell, the King's Principal Secretary and future Vicegerent-in-Spirituals, himself a reformer, secured his release. Thereafter he seems to have entered the service of John de Vere, fifteenth Earl of Oxford, for whom he began to write plays of a progressive stamp in favour of the Royal Supremacy. These texts do not survive, but the titles of two of them, *Of the King's Two Marriages* and *The Impostures of Thomas à Becket*, indicate their nature.

Bale's first secular cure, the vicarage of Thorndon, Suffolk, again brought him into controversy, this time with his more conservative parishioners. When their accusations of heresy levelled against him reached the ears of Charles Brandon, Duke of Suffolk, he was imprisoned at Greenwich. Only a second intervention by Cromwell, this time prompted by a petition from the scholar and antiquarian John Leland, gained him his freedom.[2] By 1538–9 he was apparently leading a troupe of actors who performed before Cromwell, and he may have entered the Vicegerent's service more formally at this point. Certainly the latter's fall in 1540 led to Bale's flight into exile in Germany, from where he bombarded the realm with polemical pamphlets. He returned during the reign of Edward VI to secure a number of livings. But his refusal to brook at any price what he saw as popery led to his flight from Ireland, where he had been despatched as Bishop of Ossory, within nine months of his arrival. During the reign of Mary Tudor he again fled to the Continent, this time maintaining his controversial literary output from Basle. But at the accession of Elizabeth I he returned once more to find preferment again, dying in 1563 as a prebendary of Canterbury.

A prolific writer, Bale was tireless in his advocacy of the protestant cause. Yet he was also an enthusiastic bibliophile and antiquarian, who compiled bibliographies and biographical accounts of contemporary writers without which much of their now lost work would be unknown. For all the heat of his controversial output, the meticulous care exhibited in these bibliographies stands as a tribute to his scholarship.

Both sides of his career, the scholarly and the controversial come together in *King Johan*, a play based upon carefully researched historical detail, yet forged in the fire of a polemical imagination.

TEXT AND PERFORMANCE

King Johan provides the student of Henrician drama with both unique potential for close political analysis and unique problems of textual

---

[2] *L. P.* XII, 112. Leland's lengthy description of Bale suggests that he thought him unknown to Cromwell at this time. Perhaps it was the scholar's suggestion that he was 'worthy a better fortune than to be a poor parish priest' which prompted the Vicegerent to grant him some measure of patronage (see pp. 172–3, below).

integrity. It is the only extant play-text of the reign for which a precise date of performance can be determined. Yet, paradoxically, it is also a play for which no definitive text exists. The only contemporary version of the play to survive consists of two imperfectly dovetailed sections of text written in different hands at different times and a discarded (and subsequently partially recovered) fragment excised from the first part during compilation.

The first and larger section constitutes some eighteen folio sheets of material, written in a single hand (conventionally termed 'Hand A') and corrected and amended both by Hand A and a second hand (Hand B, evidently Bale's own).[3] From this, four sheets have evidently been removed, of which two have subsequently been recovered. The latter have been corrected in both hands and partially cancelled. The second section of text, written and corrected solely in Bale's hand, takes up the play at the point at which Section A was cancelled and continues it to the conclusion. How can so idiosyncratic a document be accounted for?

Although there remains cause for some doubt, what seems to have happened is this.[4] The A text, which originally constituted a complete (although shorter) version of the play, was compiled by a scribe from an existing manuscript (datable on internal evidence to 1538).[5] This text was then corrected by the scribe, probably soon after its completion. At some point after 1558, probably after 1560,[6] Bale himself returned to the play and began to revise it to fit the altered circumstances of the first years of the reign of Elizabeth I. He removed some passages which no longer suited his purposes, corrected and expanded others and added whole new sections on interfoliated sheets. Then, upon reaching the twenty-first sheet, he decided to abandon the messy intercollations and began a fresh draft. He cancelled the remaining sheets and discarded them, expanding the material contained in them into eleven new sheets.[7]

The curious state of the text creates obvious difficulties for any analysis of the sort undertaken in the previous chapters. How can the circumstances of a play's creation be brought to bear upon it when that play is so obviously a product of more than one moment? Fortunately it is possible to be more specific about the genesis of the play than the summary

---

[3] For the painstaking reconstruction of the text, and arguments for its provenance, see J. H. Pafford, ed., *King Johan by John Bale*, Malone Society (Oxford, 1931), pp. vi–xxix. All line references to the play in this chapter refer to this edition.

[4] Ibid.

[5] Ibid., p. xiii. See below, pp. 173–7.

[6] Ibid., pp. xiv–xv. The paper upon which the B text was written contains the watermark '1558'. At line 2643 there seems to be a reference to Elizabeth I's proclamation against Anabaptists of 22 September 1560.

[7] Two of the discarded sheets were later rediscovered in the Ipswich Corporation records, and found their way into the hands of John Payne Collier, ibid., pp. v–vi.

provided above would suggest, owing in large part to the chance survival of a reference to *King Johan* in performance.

On 11 January 1539, the Archbishop of Canterbury, Thomas Cranmer, wrote to Cromwell, in part concerning the inquisition of one Henry Totehill, a shipman of St Katherine's, Tower Hill, who was brought before him accused of 'naughty communication ... concerning the bishop of Rome and Thomas Becket'.[8] In order that Cromwell might better judge the nature of the alleged offence, Cranmer enclosed a transcript of the testimonies of the three witnesses involved. From these it is evident that Totehill's 'naughty communication' arose during arguments provoked by a performance of an interlude at Cranmer's house (probably that at Ford in Kent). As the first witness, John Alforde, aged eighteen, deposed

he had ben in Christmas tyme at my Lorde of Canterbury's, and ther had harde an enterlude concernyng King John, aboute viii or ix of the cloke at night; and Thursdaye, the seconde daye of Januarye last paste, spake theis wourdes following in the house of Thomas Brown: That it ys petie that the Bisshop of Rome should reigne any lenger, for if he should, the said Bisshop wold do with our King as he did with King John. Wherunto (this deponent saith) that Henry Totehill answered and said, That it was petie and nawghtely don, to put down the Pope and Saincte Thomas; for the Pope was a good man, and Saincte Thomas savid many suche as this deponent was from hangyng: which wourdes were spoken in the presence of Thomas Browne and one William, servaunte unto the said Totehill.

This account is confirmed and elaborated upon by the second witness, the above-mentioned Thomas Browne, of 'Shawlteclyfe', Kent. He explained

that about viii of the clocke on Fridaye the iii daye of Januarye last paste, as he remembreth, one Henry Totehill beyn in this deponente's house at Shawlteclyf, this deponent tolde that he hadde bene at my Lorde of Canterbury's, and there hadd harde one of the beste matiers that ever he saw, towching King John; and than sayd that he had harde divers tymes prelates and clerkes say, that King John did loke like one that hadd run frome brynnyng of a house, butt this deponent knewe now that yt was nothing treu; for as far as he perceyved, King John was as noble a prince as ever was in England; and therby we myght perceyve that he was the begynner of the puttyng down of the Bisshop of Rome, and thereof we myght be all gladd. Then answerd the said Totehill, that the Bisshope of Rome was made Pope by the clergie and by the consent of all the Kinges Christen. Then said this deponent, Holde your peace, for this communication ys nawght. Then said Totehill, I am sorye if I have said amyss, for I thought no harme to no man.

Doubts have been raised whether this performance and Bale's play can have been one and the same.[9] But the circumstantial evidence for the

[8] J. E. Cox, ed., *The Miscellaneous Writings and Letters of Thomas Cranmer*, Parker Society (Cambridge, 1846), pp. 387–8.

[9] See, for example, S. Anglo, *Spectacle, Pageantry and Early Tudor Policy* (Oxford, 1969), p. 269n.

identification seems compelling. A man named Bale, it is known, led an acting troupe patronized by Cromwell. It is even possible that the troupe was Cromwell's own (that referred to elsewhere as The Lord Privy Seal's, the Secretary's, or simply Master Cromwell's players[10]). Certainly on two occasions in 1538–9 this company performed plays at Cromwell's expense, on at least one of these occasions at Canterbury. Cromwell's accounts contain the following payments.[11]

Balle and his fellowes: The same daye [8 September 1538] gyven to them by my lordes commaundement at Saynt Stephens besydes Caunterbury for playing before my lorde – xls.

Bale and his ffelowes: The last of January [1539] gyven to him and his ffelowes for playing before my lorde – xxxs.

Thus we have a performance before Cranmer of a play of King John at Christmas-time 1538–9, a performance in January of a play performed by Bale's company for Cromwell, and a play called *King Johan* written by John Bale, containing, as what follows will demonstrate, material directly relevant to the current interests of both Cromwell and Cranmer. It would surely be reasonable to assume that Bale's play and that performed at Cranmer's house were one and the same. For there to have been two anti-papal plays of King John circulating simultaneously would seem too unlikely a coincidence. It may also have been that the performance before Cranmer that Christmas was that paid for, after the event, by Cromwell on 31 January. But this last is a less safe conjecture. Whether true or not, however, the connection between Cromwell, Bale and Cranmer is still evident, and this, as will be suggested below, is of considerable significance for any study of the play.

It is, then, possible to identify the play with a definite performance during the Christmas period 1538–9, and with a definite location, the Archbishop of Canterbury's residence. But how much of that original performance can be recovered from the existing play-text? Clearly the complete play as we have it cannot have been produced at that time, for material in it was added after 1558. It is more likely that the A text was closely related to the 1538–9 performance.[12] But only a portion of that text survives. And, crucially, its conclusion is now lost with the missing two sheets of the scribal copy.

[10] I. Lancashire, *Dramatic Texts and Records of Britain: A Chronological Topography to 1558* (Cambridge, 1984), p. 380

[11] *L.P.* XIV (ii) 337, 339.

[12] The 1538–9 performance provides the most likely occasion for the transcription of the play by the scribe from what was probably Bale's original holograph text. Perhaps the copy was prepared as a more legible prompt copy or acting text with the performance in mind. Or perhaps it was copied in fair hand at Bale's behest as a presentation copy after the event, with the intention of offering it to Cromwell, Cranmer or Henry VIII.

There survives, then, only a truncated copy of the original play. But it is nonetheless possible to infer something concerning the lost portion. As J. H. Pafford has observed, because it may be deduced that the A text was originally written on twenty-two sheets, the lost lines can only have filled a further two sheets. For the surviving A text and the recovered sheets constitute between them twenty sheets. If the text filled those sheets it would have run to about 1975 lines. Thus a maximum of around 180 lines must have been lost.[13]

But what could have been contained in those missing lines? As B. B. Adams has noted, the surviving A text concludes in the midst of John's dying speech. Thus in theory the play might have concluded very quickly on the penultimate sheet. But in the A text there is also an acting direction indicating (after line *79) that the actor playing Pandolphus should 'go owt and dresse for nobelyte'.[14] As Nobility does not reappear in the remaining lines of the surviving A text, it must be concluded that he was intended to do so in the missing lines, either at, or immediately after, John's death.[15] This would suggest that a shorter version of the scene involving Nobility which concludes the B text also brought the A text to a close.

It has also been suggested that there must have been an attack upon Thomas Becket in the missing section, as Henry Totehill was said to have complained that the play 'was petie and nawghtely don, to put down the Pope *and Saincte Thomas*'.[16] But this does not seem convincing. It assumes that Totehill's reference to Becket concerns the interlude rather than the general political and religious changes around which the alleged conversations with Alforde and Browne revolved. And such an assumption is unwarranted. In the evidence presented to Cromwell there is no suggestion that Totehill himself actually saw *King Johan* performed. The men who definitely did witness the interlude were his accusers Alforde and Browne. Both raised the subject of the play at the latter's house on 2 and 3 January, Alforde using it as the occasion to bemoan the power of the Pope, and Brown to register his satisfaction at the break with Rome. It is difficult to escape the conclusion that they did so in order to bait a man with known conservative sympathies. And Totehill rose to the occasion. But he did not take issue with them over the interlude itself. He raised general points of religious principle. He told Alforde that 'it was petie and nawghtely done, to put down the pope and Saincte Thomas, for the pope was a good man', and he told Browne that the papal supremacy was created and endorsed by

---

13 Pafford, p. x.
14 I adopt Pafford's lineation, in which an asterixed line number refers to those two sheets of cancelled A text discarded by Bale but subsequently recovered.
15 B. B. Adams, *John Bale's 'King Johan'* (San Marino, 1969), p. 5.
16 My italics, see ibid., p. 6.

both the clergy and all Christian Kings. His reference to 'it' in the first statement quoted seems to refer, not to the play, but to government policy in general. He said that it was a pity that the Pope was put down and that it was naughtily done, not that 'it', the play, was naughtily done, as it intended to put down the Pope. Such statements seem entirely in keeping with what Totehill was reported to have said in discussions unrelated to the interlude.[17] Thus the remark is more likely to have referred to recent steps taken by the Crown to enforce the repudiation of papal authority and the vilification of Becket rather than to the specific content of *King Johan*.[18]

But if those passages concerning Becket which occur in the B text (notably at lines 2539–55) need not necessarily have also occurred in the A text, what else might the lost conclusion have contained? As was suggested, the general form of the last scene seems likely to have followed that of the B text. But a number of the actual lines of verse must have been written at different times. The concluding prayer for Queen Elizabeth I and the reference to her action against the Anabaptists (line 2634), must surely have been added after 1560. Other passages, however, amounting to the majority of the existing text, look like survivals from the earlier draft.

At points in Imperial Majesty's speeches to the estates figures, for example, and during his interrogation of Sedition, there are references to events in the late 1530s treated as recent occurrences. Sedition's reference to the assistance that he has offered to the conservative clergy, for example, contains a clear allusion to the Pilgrimage of Grace of 1536 in the mention of the disorder

> I attempted, in the Northe but now of late
> And sens that same tyme, in other places besyde
> (lines 2468–9)

Does 'now of late' suggest a recent event? Or does the mention of other disturbances 'sens that same tyme' imply a longer perspective? The latter might refer specifically to Bigod's rising in the North in early 1537, which provided an almost immediate epilogue to the Pilgrimage, or it might refer to the whole range of more or less religiously motivated risings and disturbances throughout the reigns of Edward and Mary. The dating of this passage thus remains provisional.

More obviously, the use of the conditional case and the future tense in Imperial Majesty's references to the realization of the Royal Supremacy

[17] Cox, *Misc. Writings*, p. 338.
[18] For the attack upon the cult of Becket during 1538, see ibid., p. 378. The shrine was taken into royal hands and despoiled in September 1538, and in November of that year a royal proclamation condemned him as no saint 'but a rebel and a traitor to his prince', ordered the removal of all images of him from churches and elsewhere and the suppression of his festival days. Hughes and Larkin, I, pp. 270–6.

suggest the early years of the Reformation rather than the later (lines 2333–5). It is also noticeable that Clergy refers to monks and monasteries in these passages as if they still existed in considerable numbers. This was the case in 1538–9, but not in 1560. 'If ye wyll make [the Realm] sure', he tells Imperial Majesty,

> ye must exyle sedicyon
> False dyssymulacyon, with all vayne superstycyon
> And put private welthe, out of the monasteryes
> Than usurped power, maye goo a birdynge for flyes
> (lines 2393–6)

Again, when Sedition confesses that the prelates have been deliberately lax in enforcing the reforming Injunctions issued by the Crown, it is difficult not to detect a direct reference to the Royal Injunctions issued by Cromwell in 1536 and 1538. As Sedition admits,

> Ye gave injunctyons, that Gods wurde myghte be taught
> But who observe them [?], full manye a tyme have I laught
> To see the conveyaunce that prelates and priestes can fynde
> (lines 2461–3)

> In your parlement, commaunde yow what ye wyll
> The popes ceremonyes, shall drowne the Gospell styll
> Some of the byshoppes at your injunctions slepe
> Some laugh and go bye, and some can playe boo pepe
> Some of them do nought, but searche for heretyckes
> Whyls their prestes abroade, do playe the scysmatykes
> (lines 2475–80)

> the prelates do not preache
> But persecute those, that the holye scriptures teache
> And marke me thys wele, they never ponnysh for popery
> But the Gospell readers, they [examyne very strayghtly]
> (lines 2493–6)

> In some byshoppes howse, ye shall not fynde a testament
> But yche man readye, to devoure the innocent
> We lynger a tyme, and loke but for a daye
> To sette upp the Pope, if the Gospel woulde decay
> (lines 2501–4)

This account of a godly prince imposing reform upon crypto-papist episcopates who persecute reforming preachers and do not even keep copies of the Bible in their own houses seems far more plausible as a reference to the situation in 1538 than to that of 1560. In the latter period the bench of bishops had a clearly reformist look to it, the Marian catholics having been deprived, many in favour of returned exiles such as

Edmund Grindal (appointed first to the see of London), John Parkhurst (Norwich), John Jewel (Salisbury), Edwin Sandys (Worcester) and William Barlow (Chichester). It is extremely unlikely that Bale would have accused such men, his fellow exiles, of hunting out reforming preachers and failing to read the Scriptures. Such passages read far more convincingly as attacks upon the Henrician bishops of the late 1530s, men such as John Stokesley (London), Stephen Gardiner (Winchester), Richard Sampson (Chichester) and Richard Nix (Norwich), whose sympathies with even the cautious innovations of the Henrician era were suspect, and who faced just such accusations of covert popery from their reformist critics.[19] Bale's contempt for such men and his anxiety at their continued favour would explain their introduction into the A text. Their retention in the B text may well have been intended as both a warning and an encouragement to the new breed of godly bishops who filled the episcopal bench in Queen Elizabeth's early years.

If the suggestions advanced above are correct, the final pages of the A text must have resembled a condensed version of the final scenes of the B text, with little of substance having been added in the final revision save the references to the new Queen. If this was so, and the re-education of Nobility, Clergy and Civil Order and the confession of Sedition completed the earlier draft, then the *King Johan* of 1539 was both structurally coherent and politically acute. The religious crisis of John's reign had begun with the defection of the estates. The Reformation and the settling of religion was subsequently achieved by their reconciliation with his eventual successor, Imperial Majesty. Yet, as befits a play which was the product of a continuing and only partially complete reformation, the final mood is not one of complacency in a job well done, but of caution and warning.

By having Sedition reveal the scope of his activities and the extent of the episcopal collusion in them in the final scene, Bale leaves his audience with a sense of the magnitude of the task still to be achieved and of the obstacles in their path. The reform of the abuses which brought about John's destruction, the play suggests, has yet to be fully accomplished. The threat still remains that all that has been achieved hitherto may be reversed by those still in positions of power who

> ... lynger a tyme, and loke but for a daye
> To sette upp the Pope, if the Gospel woulde decay
> (lines 2503–4)

The aptness of this warning was to be demonstrated, as we shall see, within

---

19 B.L. MS Cleopatra E IV, f. 9 (R. B. Merriman, *The Life and Letters of Thomas Cromwell* (2 vols., Oxford, 1902), II, pp. 144–5). See below, pp. 205–6.

four months of the play's performance, when the Act of Six Articles affected an apparent reversal in policy towards the Church and re-established a number of conservative interpretations of key points of doctrine.[20]

POLITICAL THEMES AND ACTION

The play ostensibly concerns King John of England (1199–1216) and his struggles with the Papacy and the domestic Church. Mixing historical and pseudo-historical characters, such as John himself, Archbishop Steven Langton and 'Simon of Swineshead', with allegorical abstractions; and mixing historical details (drawn predominantly from the English *Brut*[21]) with protestant polemic, Bale produces a drama which makes overt the parallels between his conception of John and the current religious crisis in Henrician England. What follows will provide a necessarily much abbreviated summary of the play.

Having entered the place alone and established in soliloquy his right to rule, John is approached by a poor widow, England, who appeals to him against her spoliation at the hands of the clergy, and the exile of her spouse, God.[22] John is astonished at her condition and, despite the interjections of a third character, the vice, Sedition, he resolves to summon the equivalent of a parliament to discuss the redress of her grievances.[23] Left alone with John, Sedition confesses his allegiance to Rome and his alliance with the regular clergy, and proudly declares that he has seduced all the great estates of England to his cause. But he escapes to adopt a clerical disguise before the King can confront him with Nobility and so test his claim.

Once the three estate figures, Nobility, Clergy and Civil Order (the lawyers), have gathered, John announces his intention to reform the Church. The three are eventually persuaded to assist him, but Clergy proves equivocal in his loyalty and subsequently reveals to Nobility his intention to resist the King's demands and 'sewe unto Rome, for the churches lyberte' (line 619).

20 See below, pp. 220–1.
21 For the account which formed the basis of Bale's narrative, see F. W. Brie, ed., *The Brut or the Chronicles of England*, E.E.T.S. (London, 1906), pp. 154–70. For his other borrowings, see Adams, *King Johan*, pp. 25–37.
22 Taking his cue from John 1:1, 'In the beginning was the Word . . . and the Word was God', Bale equates the vernacular Scriptures, the Word of God, with God himself. Thus the ban upon vernacular Bibles was, he claims, a ban upon God.
23 John announces (lines 142–6) that he will summon 'my nobylyte . . . Next them the clargy, or fathers spirituall . . . Than the great Juges, and lawers everychon', the conventional description of the parliamentary classes. Does the fact that Bale's reforming hero looks to Parliament as the natural vehicle for reform support Professor Elton's contention that the men of Cromwell's circle saw Statute as the central instrument of reform? G. R. Elton, *Reform and Renewal* (Cambridge, 1973), p. 68.

The action then shifts to the Continent (possibly to Rome itself, although the text is unclear), where Sedition meets with Clergy's messenger to the Pope, Dissimulation. These two, in the time-honoured manner of dramatic vices, exchange confidences concerning the tricks of their respective trades. They then encounter two new characters, Usurped Power (who proves to be the Pope in his holiday clothes) and Private Wealth, a monk. After much elaborate business, in which the characters 'bring in' each other and Sedition is borne aloft by them all, both Dissimulation and Private Wealth appeal to Usurped Power on behalf of the Church in England. A plan is then devised to defeat John's reforming intentions and restore Clergy to his former wealth and influence. Usurped Power will summon a General Council at which, under the cover of a call to unite against the Turks, he will advance the influence of the religious orders and of superstitious ceremonies, and attack preachers of the Gospels as heretics.[24] Meanwhile, Sedition and Private Wealth will travel to England to place the Realm under interdict and excommunicate John, unless the latter abandons his intention to reform the Church. Private Wealth will travel as 'the Cardinal Pandolphus', Dissimulation as 'Raymundus', a legate who will unite other Christian princes in a crusade against the 'heretic' John, and Sedition as Steven Langton, the Archbishopelect of Canterbury, whose controversial election John had refused to acknowledge, thus provoking the schism.[25] All the vices then depart to go about their business.[26]

Upon the entry of Nobility and Sedition it becomes apparent that the locus of the drama has shifted back to England again. Equally evidently time has elapsed. For Nobility begins by bemoaning the increasingly

[24] The Fourth Lateran Council of 1215 is the historical analogue here. But the allusion is also to the Council proposed by Pope Paul III in 1538, which Henry and the German Lutherans were attempting to prevent. *L.P.* XIII (ii), 1148.

[25] Of the three aliases, both Pandolphus and Langton are historical figures drawn from the *Brut* and elsewhere. The former, although not a cardinal, was the Legate sent from Rome by Innocent III to declare the Interdict. The latter was the centre of John's dispute with the monks of Canterbury. For the history of these events in the sources available to Bale, see *The Brut*, pp. 155–63; E. Zettl, ed., *An Anonymous Short English Metrical Chronicle*, E.E.T.S. (London, 1935), pp. 40–1; A. H. Thomas and I. D. Thornley, eds., *The Great Chronicle of London* (London, 1938), pp. 3–5; H. O. Coxe, ed., *Wendover's 'Flores Historiarum'*, English Historical Society (London, 1841–4), 241–2. For a brief protestant reassessment, see W. Tyndale, *The Obedience of a Christian Man* in H. Walter, ed., *Doctrinal Treatises and Introductions to Portions of the Holy Scriptures by William Tyndale*, Parker Society (Cambridge, 1848), pp. 338–9. For modern studies, see S. Painter, *The Reign of King John* (Baltimore, 1949); J. C. Holt, *Magna Carta* (Cambridge, 1965); W. L. Warren, *The Governance of Norman and Angevin England, 1086–1272* (London, 1987), pp. 125–71.

[26] At this point Hand B inserts an interval heralded by a brief speech by 'The Interpreter'. There appears to have been no such break in the A text, where the play continued immediately with the entry of Nobility and Sedition.

heated disputes between the King and the Church. Playing upon Nobility's simplicity of mind and his loyalty to the Church, Sedition then persuades him, under cover of the confessional, to take the Church's side against John, a feat which he subsequently achieves with greater ease with Civil Order, who sees the financial profits to be gained from co-operation with Clergy. Once the lay estates have been won over, 'Pandolphus' enters and excommunicates John, placing England under interdict when the King refuses to concede to papal demands.

Once excommunicated, John is shunned by his subjects. Only England and her son Commonalty remain loyal. But the latter is too poor and weak to be of assistance, having been milked of his wealth by the avaricious Church. He is also blind, as England points out, having been deprived of his sight 'for want of knowlage in Christes owne veryte' (line 1542), and so without guidance is as likely to side with the Pope as with John. Thus the King is unable to defend England when she is threatened with invasion by the catholic powers (France, Spain, Scotland and, rather more implausibly, Scandinavia), and is forced, in order to prevent a massacre, to surrender his Crown to Pandolphus and swear loyalty to the Pope. In the wake of this surrender, Clergy is restored, Steven Langton installed as Primate and further humiliating concessions are imposed by the triumphant vices. Yet this is still not enough for the latter. To complete the Church's victory Dissimulation contrives to poison John, killing himself in the process, thus claiming a martyr's death. John is left to contemplate the full extent of clerical treachery in his last moments.

With John's dying speech the A text ends. But in the continuation in Bale's hand, two new characters, Veritas and Imperial Majesty, enter for the final scenes. The former lectures the estates on their folly in supporting the Pope against their anointed sovereign. The latter completes their re-education with a recapitulation of the divine origins of kingship. He then lures Sedition into giving a full confession of his collusion with Clergy and of the popish conspiracy to conceal the truth of the Gospels. With the iniquities of Roman Catholicism revealed, the play, in its final form, concludes with a prayer for Queen Elizabeth and her Council, 'To the prayse of God, and the glorye of the Gospell' (line 2645).

That Bale fashioned his historical and moral material to provide a piece of thorough-going reformist propaganda is widely recognized and is readily apparent from even the bald summary of the plot provided above. He takes as his subject what was a legal and jurisdictional dispute within the catholic Church and treats it as a doctrinally motivated schism. And he moulds from the unpromising material of the essentially catholic King John a protestant hero and martyr, a precursor of the ideas which were to motivate Henrician caesaropapism.

The twin principles which govern the actions of Bale's John are the certainty of his own divine ordination, with the responsibilities attendant upon it, and a resolve to base all spiritual life upon the text of the Scriptures. In order to establish the divine nature of kingship and the universal nature of royal jurisdiction in the minds of his audience, Bale has each of the virtuous characters assert John's right to rule and stress his responsibility to reform the Church in the opening scenes. As England, echoing Tyndale, informs Sedition, like any Christian King,[27]

> ... be he good or bade, he [John] is of godes apoyntyng
> The good for the good, the badde ys for ylle doyng.
>
> (lines 103–4)

In her appeals to John to redress her grievances, the point is frequently repeated. She has come to him, she says, 'knowyng yowr grace to have here the governance / By the gyft of god' (lines 123–4) and as 'ye are a ryghtfulle Kyng / Apoyntyd of god' (lines 127–8). In accepting her petition, John makes the same point.

> ... owr powr ys of god
> And therfor we wylle, so execute the rod
> That no lewde pryst shalle, be able to mayntayne the.
>
> (lines 225–7)

Caesaropapism and reforming zeal are united in John's declarations to his erring estates. As Dissimulation was to warn Usurped Power, John is determined to establish his own supremacy in England against papal interference.

> he [John] contemmythe yowre autoryte and seale
> And sayethe in his lond, he wylle be lord and kyng
>
> (lines 924–5)

And the inevitable consequence of this supremacy will be a reformation in the Church, for, as John states,

> Ffor non other cawse, god hathe kynges constytute
> And gevyn them the sword, but forto correct alle vyce
>
> (lines 1277–8)

> The powr of princys, ys gevyn fro god above
> And as saythe Salomon, ther hartes the lord dothe move
> God spekyth in ther lyppes, whan they geve jugement
> The lawys that they make, are by the lordes appoyntment
> Christ wylled not his [disciples] the [ir] princes to correct
> But to ther prescepttes, rether to be subjecte
>
> (lines 1343–8)[28]

---

27 Tyndale, *Obedience*, Walter, *Doctrinal Treatises*, p. 194.
28 For similar statements, see lines 1401–14.

> The chyrches abusyons, as holy seynt powle do saye
> By the princes powr, owght for to be takyn awaye
> He barythe not the sword, with owt a cawse (sayth he)
> In this neyther bysshope nore spiritualle man is free
> Offendyng the lawe, they are under the poweres alle
>   (lines 1500–4)

The King John whom Bale presents is not simply a reforming autocrat, but a thorough zealot in the protestant mould, a figuration of the writer's own opinions and passion. He stands unequivocally behind the demand for the Scriptures in English and the protestant attack upon the ceremonial aspects of catholic worship. 'Yt was never welle', he declares,

> syns the clargy wrowght by practyse
> And left the scriptur, for menns ymagynacyons
>   (lines 336–7)

Taking to heart the Second Psalm, he enjoins his hearers to 'Seke to the Scripture, late that be yowr refuge' (line 1466) and he defies Pandolphus to prove the validity of his powers by the only acceptable authority.

> That sentence or curse, that scriptur dothe not dyrect
> In myn opynyon, shalle be of non effecte
>   (lines 1429–30)

> Prove yt by Scriptur, and than wyll I yt alowe
>   (line 1432)

Hence he rejects those ceremonies which he and the reformers alike considered to be merely man-made observances deliberately contrived to conceal the pure unmediated word of God.

> Take to ye yowr trayshe, yowr ryngyng, syngyng and pypyng
> So that we may have, the scryptures openyng
> But that we can not have, yt standyth not with yowr avantage
>   (lines 1389–91)

In articulating his desire to purge the Church of its abuses, John's language becomes Bale's own, the vitriolic haranguing tones of the reformist preacher. 'I rew yt in hart', he laments, evoking Luther,

> that yow nobelyte
> Shuld thus bynd yowr selfe to the grette captyvyte
> Of blody babulon, the grownd and mother of whordom
> The Romyche churche I meane, more vyler than ever was Sodom
> And to say the trewth, a met spowse for the fynd [fiend]
>   (lines 369–73)

In its current state, he claims, the Church is

> no holye chyrche, nor feythfulle congregacyon
> But an hepe of adders, of antecristes generacyon.
> (lines 482–3)

Its priests are correspondingly 'becum belles prystes / Lyvyng by ydolles, yea, the very antychrystes' (lines 1353–6), seeking their own lucre before the salvation of their charges.

Both John's language and his deeds, then, mark him out as a passionate reformer. In so portraying him Bale seeks to reclaim John's reputation, and the past in general, from the clutches of those monastic chroniclers whose accounts provided the version of history available to most Tudor readers. He is rewriting the history of England from a protestant perspective.

In a society that valued tradition and abhorred the concept of innovation, the reformers needed, if they were to establish their beliefs, to prove themselves the heirs of a venerable tradition stretching back as far into the past, if not further, than the Church of Rome. It was this attempt to discover, or fabricate, a protestant, oppositional, church tradition which prompted William Tyndale to call for a revision of history which would show the Pope and the established Church to be the innovators and the reformers as a hidden and persecuted remnant of the pure Church of the Apostles. This process was to reach its apotheosis in John Foxe's *Acts and Monuments*, a six-volume chronicle of the hidden Church from the time of Wycliff to its triumphal re-emergence in the Reformation. And the search found in Bale a writer anxious to reproduce in dramatic form this newly discovered protestant version of history. He creates in John an imperfect prefiguration of Henry VIII, the true godly prince who would restore the integrity of the Church and cast off its idolatrous, popish accretions. John provides a vital link between the hidden Church and the Henrician Reformation. As both godly prince and martyr he partakes of both the validating qualities of the protestant hero. Hence every opportunity is taken to demonstrate both his efforts to initiate reform and his suffering for his beliefs at the hands of an ungodly Church. As he apostrophizes towards the close of the play (lines 1395–400):

> Oh lord, how wycked, ys that same generacyon
> That never wylle cum, to a godly reformacyon
> The prystes report me, to be a wyckyd tyrant
> Be cause I correct, their actes and lyfe unpleasaunt

If the protestantization of John provides what might be seen as the positive aspect of Bale's polemical purpose, the demonization of the

catholic Church forms its darker side. In order to establish the thesis that
the reformers – symbolized by a king of Old Testament purity in John –
form the earlier and truer tradition, the play constantly presents the
papacy and the priesthood in the role of innovators and as the disrupters of
established norms. As John informs the audience after his surrender of his
Crown to Pandolphus, the authority which he has been forced to recognize
is entirely false.

> my crowne I gave up lately
> To the pope of Rome, whyche hathe no tyttle good
> Of jurysdyccon, but usurpacyon onlye
>
> (lines *123–5)

Taking up the language of reforming legislation and official pronouncements on religion,[29] Bale symbolizes the papal usurpation of authority by
actually naming his papal character Usurped Power and giving to his
minions the names of those iniquitous qualities supposedly represented by
the established Church, Dissimulation, Sedition, Private Wealth and Treason. Through this naming device and the constant reference to the alien
and unnatural nature of the priesthood and its observances, Bale dramatizes the reformers' polemical contention. He has England reject the entire
clergy as no sons of hers ('Nay, bastardes they are, unnaturalle by the
Rood' (line 69)). And has Sedition confess both his alien origins and his
treasonable intentions simultaneously.

> I am not her [England's] chyld, I defye hyr by the messe
> I her sonne, quoth he, I had rather she wer hedlesse
> Thowgh I sumtyme be, in England for my pastaunce
> Yet was I neyther borne here, in Spayne nor in Fraunce,
> But under the pope, in the holy cyte of Rome
> And there wylle I dwelle, un to the day of dome.
>
> (lines 181–6)

But the process of degradation does not stop there. Bale not only appeals
to native xenophobia by fraudulently portraying the English clergy as
foreign interlopers, he goes further and attempts entirely to dehumanize
the catholic priesthood. The religious are described throughout the play

---

[29] See, for example, the 'Act Extinguishing the Auctoryte of the Busshop of Rome', of 1536,
which spoke of 'the pretended Power and usurped auctoryte of the Bishopp of Rome' (A.
Luders *et al.*, eds., *Statutes of the Realm* (11 vols., London, 1810–28) III, p. 663) or the Act
for the cancellation of licences and dispensations from Rome, which referred to the 'dyvers
and many usurped powers, jurisdictions and auctorities of the pope' (ibid., p. 672). See
also ibid., p. 464. The Royal Proclamation of 16 November 1538 talked of the Pope's
'usurped authority' (Hughes and Larkin, I, p. 267).

as less than human, specifically as swine, whose bestial behaviour ought to revolt Bale's civilized audience. The clergy, England claims,

> The wyld bore of Rome, god let hym never to thee
> Lyke pygges they folow, in fantysyes dreames and lyes
> And ever are fed, with his vile ceremonyes
> (lines 71–3)

By describing the clergy as pigs Bale is able to anathematize the practices of the Roman Church as inhuman and foul. When England is asked to justify her description of the Pope, she does so with vigour.

> For that he and his to suche bestlynes inclyne
> They forsake godes word, whyche is most puer and cleane
> And unto the lawys, of synfulle men they leane
> Lyke as the vyle swyne, the most vyle metes dessyer
> And hathe gret pleasure, to walowe them selvys in myre
> So hathe this wyld bore, with his church unyversalle
> His sowe with hyr pygys and monstres bestyalle
> Dylyght in mennys draffe, and covytus lucre alle
> Ye *aper de sylva*,[30] the prophet dyd hym call
> (lines 78–86)[31]

And later she resurrects the image, conjuring a vision of an almost troglo-dytic sect, driven to suppress the Scriptures in order to conceal its own sub-human shortcomings.

> The popys pyggys may not, abyd this word to be hard
> Nor knowyn of pepylle, or had in anye regard
> Ther eyes are so sore, they maye not abyde the lyght
> (lines 119–21)

The vilification of the Catholic clergy is further achieved by Bale's continued stress upon the extent of their malign influence. It is not simply that he has his clerical characters display the abuses which anti-clerical writings had lampooned since Langland and beyond.[32] Bale's clerics are resolute and defiant in their corruption. And their demonic malice against anyone who, like John, seeks to reform them is the motor which drives the action of the play.

Sedition, the first cleric to appear, exemplifies this trait. Unlike the traditional flattering, fawning, vices of morality drama, who contrive

---

[30] 'The boar from the wood', Psalm 80: 13.

[31] Note also the allusion to 'This vyle popyche swyne' at line 107, and Sedition's remark upon hearing Dissimulation singing the Litany. 'I trow her cummeth sum hoggherd/ Callyng for his pygges' (lines 630–1).

[32] In having Sedition recite a litany of fraudulent relics at lines 1219–30, Bale borrows from this earlier tradition, but his major strategy is markedly more protestant in both tone and object.

behind a façade of friendly concern to engineer the protagonist's ruin, he is open in his defiance. When asked his name by John he boldly replies 'I am Sedycyon, that with the pope wyll hold' (lines 89–90). He is also candid about both his malice and his power. When ordered by the King to leave the place, he defies him,

> I wyll not away ...
> ... I shall abyde, in England, magry yowr harte.
> Tushe, the pope ableth me, to subdewe bothe Kyng and Keyser
> > (lines 95, 98–9)

> I am Sedycyon playne
> In every Relygyon, and munkysh secte I rayne
> Havyng yow prynces in scorne, hate and dysdayne
> > (lines 188–90)

> By the holye masse, I must lawghe to here yowr grace
> Ye suppose and thynke, that ye cowd me subdewe
> Ye shalle never fynd, yowr supposycyon trewe
> Thowghe ye wer as strong, as hector and diomedes
> Or as valyent, as ever was achylles
> > (lines 233–7)

Then, when ordered to remain, so that he might be confronted with Nobility, Sedition leaves, slipping past John's attempt to detain him, in a further demonstration of his independence.

Sedition, Usurped Power and Private Wealth are not conventional anarchic vices in the tradition of Skelton's Fansy or Freewill and Imagination in *Hick Scorner*, occupying an ambivalent social position somewhere between sturdy beggar and upstart courtier, they are powerful and influential men, the leaders of an alternative hierarchy. In them Bale symbolizes an oppressive, persecuting, papal establishment, endowed with great wealth and confident in its own ability to overawe and neutralize any opposition.[33] John, for all his royal authority, takes on almost insuperable odds when he opposes them. Thus his stand appears all the more heroic. But Bale does not stress the power of the clergy simply to give his hero the appearance of greater courage. He does so, as was suggested above, to set John's struggle, and by implication that of Henry VIII also, in the tradition of martyrdom and oppression which the reformers were fashioning for themselves. Moreover, by exemplifying the Roman Church as tyrannous and cruel he also performs a more immediate political function by tacitly justifying the fierce repression of those loyal to the Pope which was being carried out in England in the wake of the Act of Supremacy of 1534. By

[33] Note Sedition's claim to 'holde upp the pope, as in other places many', 'For his holy cawse, I mayntayne traytors and Rebelles / That no prince can have, his peples obedyence / Except yt dothe stand, with the pope's prehemynence' (lines 214, 220–2).

executing such internationally respected individuals as Thomas More and John Fisher, repressing the stricter religious orders and dissolving monastic houses in large numbers, the Henrician regime laid itself open to just such charges of tyranny as Bale levelled at the papacy.[34] By dramatizing the adherents of the Pope and the upholders of the old religion as seditious insurrectionaries, an all-pervasive fifth column of the alleged catholic conspiracy, Bale offered powerful and emotive justification for their destruction.[35] With the propagandist's gift for playing upon the baser instincts, he attempts entirely to reverse his audience's perception of contemporary English Catholicism. He replaces the pathetic figures of Fisher, More and the Carthusian monks, whose executions had shocked European society, with the arrogant, overbearing, figures of Sedition, Treason and Private Wealth, whose abuses cried out for punishment.

POLEMIC AS DRAMA

On one level, then, Bale is doing no more than converting the polemical prose of the reformist writers and Crown propagandists into dramatic action. Where the statute releasing individuals from papal licences and dispensations spoke of the Pope's 'many usurped powers', Bale actually names his Pope Usurped Power. Where the polemicists asserted the universal competence of royal authority and the independence of the Church in England, Bale has those assertions advanced by his virtuous characters in set-piece speeches, to the discomfiture of his straw-man apologists for Catholicism. But in presenting this material as drama, Bale brought to bear upon it the potential of a new medium. And his response to that potential reveals both the possibilities and the limitations of polemical drama in the period.

As the briefest of glances at the Corpus Christi cycles show, the use of drama for didactic purposes has a long history. But, as those plays themselves suggest, dramatic writers seem to have been far from certain that drama was a suitable medium for unproblematic didacticism. As we have

---

34 For accounts of Henry VIII's campaign against the Church, see J. J. Scarisbrick, *Henry VIII* (London, 1968), pp. 241–354, 384–423; G. R. Elton, *Reform and Reformation* (London, 1977), pp. 174–200, 230–72. For accusations of tyranny laid against Henry and his Government, see B.L. Add. MS 28590, f. 302 (*L.P.* XIII (ii) 1053); *L.P.* XIII (ii) 1088, 1110, 1148, 1162; XIV (i) 98.

35 Note, for example, Sedition's taunt 'Serche and ye shalle fynd [me], in every congregacyon / That long to the pope, for they are to me fulle swer / And wylle be so long, as they last and endwer' (lines 192–4). His claim to live in monasteries provokes John to promise to suppress the corrupt religious houses. 'Loke wher I fynd the, that place wylle I put downe.' But, in what is a clear statement of encouragement for the Henrician suppressions, Sedition slyly asks 'What yf ye do chance, to fynd me in every towne / Where as is fownded, any sect monastycalle [?]'. John's reply is uncompromising, 'I pray god I synke, yf I dystroye them not alle' (lines 257–60).

seen, when closely directed, drama might effectively marshal audience responses to its own ends. But when performed with less authorial control, by its very nature drama creates ambiguity and the possibility for contradictory responses. One reaction to the difficulties created by the latter situation which was explored by the early dramatists was to tone down the drama, to reduce the audience's perception of fictive personae, at moments of didactic import, thus focusing attention upon the message rather than the medium. Hence at times the Corpus Christi plays become little more than versified theological tracts divided between multiple speakers.[36] But, despite individual successes, this was hardly a satisfactory response to the problem. And Bale's attempt to reconcile polemic purpose with dramatic form faced similar difficulties.

The lengthy scene in which the various vices debate how best to accompany each other into the place is a fine example of Bale's didacticism at odds with the requirements of effective drama. Clearly the scene was devised to provide a memorable visual representation of the history of papal usurpation. It presents each element in the protestant conception of the papal conspiracy to subvert the true faith in England, and seeks to demonstrate how each relates to the other. Thus Dissimulation 'brings in' Private Wealth, who in turn brings in Usurped Power and all three bring in Sedition. And indeed polemic and dramatic purposes combine in a splendid iconographic moment as the three clerics Private Wealth, Dissimulation and Usurped Power (the first two in regular habits) carry Sedition upon their shoulders. But Bale's repeated and insistent glosses upon the action, inserted into the lines of all the characters in order that the polemical point is not lost, serve only to interrupt the progression of events and reduce the scene almost to the level of poorly realized dumb-show. The political message is first elucidated by Dissimulation.

> fyrst pryvat welthe, shalle bryng in usurpyd powr
> With his autoryte, and than the gam ys ower
>   (lines 780–1)

But despite his confidence in the brevity of the plot, a further seventy lines of explication are devoted to it before Bale is convinced that the message has been conveyed. First Sedition addresses the audience.

> Surs marke welle this gere, for now yt begynnyth to worke
> False dyssymulacon, dothe bryng in privat welth
> And usurpyd power, whiche is more ferce than a turcke
> Cummeth in by hym, to decayve all spyrytualle helthe
> Than I by them bothe, as clere experyence telthe

<hr />

[36] See, for example, the Parliament of Heaven section of the N. Town cycle, P. Meredith, ed., *The Mary Play from the N. Town Manuscript* (London, 1987).

> We iiij by owr craftes, kyng Johan wylle sone subdwe
> That iij C yers alle Englond shalle yt rewe
>
> (lines 764–71)

Then Dissimulation reminds them

> Of the clargy fryndes, reporte lyke as ye se
> That ther privat welthe, cummythe ever in by me
>
> (lines 772–3)

Private Wealth then declares that

> Of me privat welthe, cam fyrst usurpyd power
> Ye may perseyve yt, in pagent here this howr
>
> (lines 779–81)

Finally they all leave the place in order to return bearing Sedition, who speaks the lesson again. They are carrying him, he declares,

> That yt maye be sayde, that fyrst dyssymulacon
> Browght in privat welthe, to every cristen nacyon
> And that privat welthe, browght in usurpid power,
> And he Sedycyon, in cytye towne and tower
> That sum man may know the feche of alle owur sorte
>
> (lines 788–92)

Even then Bale gives Sedition a further five lines to itemize once more the characters' provenance and anarchic qualities for the audience's benefit, should anyone have missed the already laboured point. Here at least it seems that the need for clear polemical statement stands in the way of the dramatic effectiveness of the scene.

Yet this is not always the case. Elsewhere the possibilities inherent in dramatic exposition are utilized by Bale to create action which advances beyond the limits of prose polemic. In the latter genre the author can provide only argument and assertion. He must persuade his readers through logic and rhetoric. The object of the attack is always beyond the document and capable of responding with counter arguments and counter-polemic. In drama, however, the author controls an entire system of his own creation. By manipulating the contending figures he can determine both sides of the argument and so produce a conclusive victory for the side of his choosing. Not only can he give the reformers all the best arguments, he can also produce representatives of the catholic Church who will falter before these arguments and, better still, confess their own guilt and iniquity. He need not simply assert that the clergy are duplicitous sinners, he can produce clergymen who will admit as much. Thus Dissimulation admits to being a knave, to blinding the people with his tricks, and to failing to keep his rule, Clergy confesses his ignorance of the Scriptures, and the Pope himself, in the form of Usurped Power, reveals that all his powers are fraudulent.[37] The latter admits that indulgences and pardons are 'not worthe a rottyn warden' (line 989), and goes on candidly to list the deceptions which he intends to institute at the General Council in order to further his dominion.

> I shalle soche gere a vaunce
> As wylle be to us, a perpetualle furderaunce
> First eare confessyon, than pardons, than purgatory
> Sayntes worchyppyng than, sekyng of ymagery
> Then laten servyce, with the ceremonyes many
> Wherby owr bysshoppes, and abbottes shalle get mony
>   (lines 1112–17)

> I wylle alle so reyse up, the fower beggyng orderes
> That they may preche lyes, in alle the cristen borderes
>   (lines 1120–1)

Bale is thus able not only to launch attacks upon the Catholic clergy but to prove those attacks valid, seemingly by his enemies' own testimony. The approach is far from subtle. But its effectiveness, at least with those broadly in sympathy with its message, may be judged from the favourable accounts offered by John Alforde and Thomas Browne. As we have seen, the latter thought that the play was 'one of the beste matiers that ever he sawe' and Alforde took the warnings contained within it seriously enough to fear for the safety of the King.[38]

More subtle, perhaps, is Bale's use of the dramatic medium itself to imply criticisms of catholic worship. For a major theme of the play is the portrayal of Catholicism as an externalized, theatrical form of worship rather than a sincere internal devotion. In Bale's conception, the Church maintained its ascendancy through its manipulation of costume and spectacle, which concealed the fraudulent nature of its doctrine. The clergy are described as 'such lubbers as hathe, dysgysed heades in their hoodes' (line 36), 'in syde cotys wandryng, lyke most dysgysed players' (line 66). Their services are merely empty shows, 'popetly playes' (lines 416–17) performed by 'a Rabylle of latyne mummers' (lines 428–9). Such analogies

---

[37] Lines 305–6, 682, 718–19, 721, 1435–6.

[38] Cox, *Misc. Writings*, pp. 387–8, see above, pp. 172–3. That placing self-condemnatory statements in the mouths of catholics was seen by the reformers as an effective propaganda device may be judged from the articles of surrender drawn up by the commissioners for a number of the religious houses suppressed in 1538. The Grey Friars of Aylesbury, for example, were made to subscribe to the acknowledgement that 'the perfection of a christian living, doth not consist in dumb ceremonies, wearing of a grey coat, disguising ourself after strange fashions, ducking and becking, in girding ourselves with a girdle full of knots, and other like papistical ceremonies, wherein we have been most principally practiced and misled in times past' (*L.P.* XIII (ii) 501). A similar confession was extracted upon the surrender of the White Friars of Stamford (ibid., 565).

between acting, playing and the Catholic liturgy are made throughout the text. But the very performance of such practices in a play makes the comparison more obvious. Bale takes pains to show his clerical characters both in and out of their costumes. Sedition appears in his own garb before John, but refuses to meet Nobility until he has changed into a religious habit.

> I wold not be sene, as I am for fortye pence
> Whan I am Relygyouse, I wylle returne agayne
> (lines 302–3)

Similarly Dissimulation does not recognize Usurped Power as the Pope when he is out of his robes (line 834), and the latter has to convince him that he retains his authority in lay attire ('Dowght not of my powr, thowghe my aparelle be lyght' (line 860)). The implication is clearly that any spiritual authority which relies upon costumes, and thus disguise, is in fact worthless, and worse, fraudulent. The contrast with what Bale saw as the pure, undisguised, faith of the reformers is put most strikingly by John, who demands,

> a churche, not of dysgysyd shavelynges
> But of faythfulle hartes, and charytable doynges
> (lines 431–2)

Thus by presenting the catholic clergy as players within the context of a play, Bale makes doubly obvious the reforming criticisms of the ritualistic aspects of Catholicism. As, for him, Catholicism was a religion of performance rather than belief, he presents his clergy forever doing things. They escort each other into the place, and enact the ritual gestures of the confessional, of supplication, absolution and excommunication. Similarly the liturgical acts themselves, the ceremonies and language of excommunication, absolution and confession are performed in the play, sometimes in burlesque form, sometimes faithfully.[39] By taking them out of the validating context of divine service and presenting them as the substance of his drama Bale removes their mystery and foregrounds their theatricality.

Yet this conscious use of theatricality to parody what Bale saw as the abuses of catholic observance masks a deeper anxiety about the use of drama for theological ends. As his work for the Earl of Oxford and his subsequent prolific dramatic output suggest, Bale did not share the implacable opposition to religious drama seemingly practised by some of the early Lollards and exemplified in the fifteenth-century polemical tract *A*

[39] E. S. Miller, 'The Roman Rite in Bale's *King Johan*', *P.M.L.A.* LXIV (1949), pp. 802–22.

Tretise of Miraclis Playinge.[40] Yet his work was, nonetheless, caught in the classical reformist dilemma over what constituted an acceptable use of representative art for spiritual ends and what was merely idolatry. Like a number of his fellow reformers, he had attacked the Corpus Christi cycles, not only for their promulgation of an inherently catholic vision of sacred history, but also for their alleged cheapening of the divine message. In mixing moments of high, transcendent, seriousness with comedy (one thinks of the comic scenes in the Chester and Wakefield Shepherds' plays or the black humour of the soldier's 'business' in the York *Crucifixion* play[41]) the cycles were, in the view of their critics, dissolving the crucial distinction between message and medium, between the 'earnest' subject matter and the artistic, playful, form, and so reducing the redemptive sacrifice of Christ to a mockery. More fundamentally, in impersonating Christ or God the Father at all, in assuming human motives for their actions and showing them acting much as ordinary human beings might, the 'mystery' plays were actually demystifying and so misrepresenting the nature and promises of God. If one of the central aspects of the unseen nature of the Divine was simply that, that it was unseen, then representing it visually necessarily perverted its substance.

Part of the problem, as Bale saw it, is revealed in his remarks to Bishop Stokesley during his examination for heresy of 1536. Bale was accused, *inter alia*, of having denied the veracity of Christ's harrowing of Hell. This he strongly denied. He had, he claimed, told his parishioners, not to reject the notion of Christ's descent into Hell itself, but to,[42]

be very cyrcumspect in receyvyng the seyd artycle. And not to beleve yt as thei se yt set forth in peynted clothes or in glasse wyndowes, or lyke as my self had before tyme set yt forth in ye cuntre yer in a serten playe. For thowgh the sowle of Christ soch tyme as hyse corse lay in the grave, ded vysytt hell, yet can we not justly suppose that he fawgt vyolentlye with the devyls for the sowles of the faythfull sort and so toke them owte of ther possessyon.

In order to contemplate the true nature and import of Christ's actions, parishioner and playgoer alike needed, in Bale's view, to transcend their appreciation of the physical representation and comprehend the invisible

---

40 For the *Tretise*, see C. Davidson, *A Middle English Treatise on the Playing of Miracles* (Washington, 1981). For a wider historical analysis of evangelical criticism of mimetic art, see P. Collinson, *The Birthpangs of Protestant England: Religious and Cultural Change in the Sixteenth and Seventeenth Centuries* (London, 1988), pp. 94–126.

41 R. M. Lumiansky and David Mills, eds., *The Chester Mystery Cycle*, E.E.T.S. (2 vols., 1974); A. C. Cawley, ed., *The Wakefield Pageants in the Towneley Cycle* (London, 1958); R. Beadle, ed., *The York Plays* (London, 1982).

42 PRO SP 1/111, f. 182. For a stimulating discussion of this remark and of Bale's attitude to drama in general, see R. D. Kendall, *The Drama of Dissent: The Radical Poetics of Nonconformity, 1380–1590* (Chapel Hill, 1985), pp. 90–130.

truth beyond it. But this was easier to say than to achieve in practice, as the reformer's increasing frustration with 'popish' iconography suggests.

It was not that Bale and those that thought like him held the commonalty incapable of looking beyond the material image to the spiritual truth. Their unease lay in their realization that all such worldly vehicles for conveying higher wisdom were inherently flawed. By its very nature successful drama, like successful ecclesiastical sculpture or successful religious portraiture, attracted attention to itself. The latter through its use of lustrous colour and its depiction of heightened expression and gesture proclaimed its own seductive attractions. It pointed towards rather than beyond itself, celebrating its own composition. Similarly drama concentrated attention upon the visual spectacle which it offered and stressed its audience's role as witnesses to an unfolding truth. Thus in a number of the Corpus Christi cycles the distinction between a pious commemoration of biblical history and a mass-like reenactment of it became blurred.[43]

Apologists for the Cycle plays might argue that by depicting theological truths in terms familiar to their audiences (by subjecting the souls in Hell to physical rather than spiritual torment, or depicting Satan's fatal pride as a very human sartorial vanity) the plays were presenting important lessons in the most effective and emotive terms available, and were only following the examples of generations of preachers. But, for the reformers, this reduction of the universal and the mysterious to the human and the familiar was anathema. Moreover it diverted attention from the one reliable vehicle for divine revelation, the Gospels. Thus the 'quick pictures' of religious drama came to exemplify the seductive idolatry of the old faith.

But if any attempt to represent the Divine in dramatic form ran the double risk of either blasphemously belittling its subject in an attempt to be comprehensible or, in the manner of images, of stressing the metaphor rather than the message, how could the convinced reformer make use of the dramatic medium? Bale seems to have approached the problem from a number of angles.

In *The Three Laws*, for example, he confronted the difficulties directly by including God the Father among his cast of characters. But he did so

---

[43] Kendall, *Drama of Dissent*, p. 62. The author of the *Treatise* cited the miracle playwright's concern for form rather than content as one of the chief evils of the genre. 'These miraclis playeris and the fautors of hem ... as they maken the miraclis of God onely a mene to ther play, and the pley the ende of the miraclis of God, han at more pris ther pley than the mirclaclis of God. [Thus they] ... ben verre apostaas, bothe for their puttun God bihinde and ther owne lustis biforn, as they han minde of God onely for sake of ther play and also for they deliten hem more in the play than in the miraclis self', Davidson, *A Middle English Treatise*, p. 50.

only after carefully providing his actor with lines which stressed the inadequacy of any such representation.[44]

> I am Deus Pater, a substance invisible,
> All one with the Son, and Holy Ghost in essence.
> To angel and man I am incomprehensible,
> A strength infinite, a righteousness, a prudence,
> A mercy, a goodness, a truth, a life, a sapience.

By proclaiming the incorporeal nature of the entity impersonated before them, Bale sought to dispel from the minds of his audience any notion of verisimilitude. In the last line quoted, the actor seeks almost to define himself out of existence. But such a solution to the problem could only be partially successful. A human actor representing God remains a human actor and the danger that the audience will respond to him in human terms is not dispelled.

In *King Johan* that danger is partially avoided, in that Bale presents us with no divine figures, preferring instead to portray the Catholic Church in all its worldliness, persecuting human victims, and in turn being corrected by a semi-human figure in Imperial Majesty. By concentrating upon the vices and villainies of a fallen and all-too-human Church, the danger of belittling the subject does not arise. But in seeking to portray the other abstractions necessary for the plot, most notably the character Veritas, Bale nonetheless compromises his objections of principle in the interests of good drama. The play thus only partially reconciles the tensions which drive it. Like Bale himself it is as much a creature of the catholic world it rejects as of the reformed one which it heralds. And the problems of methodology which it exposes may partially explain Bale's eventual rejection of the dramatic form in later years in favour of less 'idolatrous' prose.

'KING JOHAN' IN CONTEXT: THE CROWN, POLITICS AND RELIGION IN LATE HENRICIAN ENGLAND

The above has illustrated a number of ways in which the play is a product of Reformation criticism of the Church in general. What follows will demonstrate how it is a product, more specifically, first of the moment of its production, during the twelve days of Christmas 1538–9, and second of its place of performance, the residence of Archbishop Cranmer.

That *King Johan* draws analogies between its central protagonist and Henry VIII has been remarked upon above and noticed by most commentators. But the precise nature of these analogies has rarely been pursued. It is important to remedy this deficiency, for the play makes use of these

---

[44] J. S. Farmer, *The Dramatic Writings of John Bale* (New York, 1966), pp. 4–5. See Kendall, *Drama of Dissent*, p. 101.

correspondences in a number of ways. And here the circumstances of the 1538–9 performance, by a company financed by one of the chief architects of the English Reformation, in the residence of another, is of crucial import.[45] For at that moment the English Reformation (as far as it was then achieved) was under direct threat, both from without and within, and each threat is reflected in the play.

The papal plot against John, it will be remembered, involved the despatch of two legates from Rome. One, Pandolphus, was sent to England to excommunicate the King and place the realm under interdict. The other, Raymundus, went to the princes of Christendom to raise them for a crusade against the schismatic realm. Meanwhile Sedition and Dissimulation attempted to suborn the great estates of England in order to confound John's plans for reform. In portraying John's plight in this way, Bale's concern seems to have been less to reflect accurately the events of the early thirteenth century as to provide a dramatic representation of the threats facing England in 1538–9. For the possibilities of excommunication and interdict, the threat of internal sedition and the activities of a papal legate were matters of grave concern to the government at this time.

Reginald Pole had, like his kinsman Richard de la Pole, been a thorn in Henry's flesh for a number of years. As a catholic exile who possessed probably the most realistic claim to the throne after Henry and his heirs he had always provoked concern. But his appointments as Cardinal and Papal Legate and his mission to the Netherlands in 1537 in what was a thinly disguised attempt to rally opposition to reform and exploit the crisis prompted by the Pilgrimage of Grace, gave him a novel and singular importance in English eyes. This journey eventually came to nothing, not least because Pole arrived too late to be of any use to Robert Aske and the Pilgrims. But in the following year he was again despatched from Rome under equally fraught circumstances.

Throughout the summer of 1538 Henry and Cromwell had watched anxiously as the two great catholic powers, France and the Empire – hitherto great rivals – had gradually edged towards a rapprochement. First their representatives met under Papal auspices at Nice, with Pole in

---

45 The suggestion that the play formed part of an officially inspired dramatic propaganda campaign has been rightly criticized by Professor G. R. Elton (G. R. Elton, *Policy and Police* (Cambridge, 1972), p. 186, n. 1). But Bale's sympathies with the circle of reformers working around Cromwell, and his knowledge of their objectives and strategies colours the play to such an extent that it seems certain their views are reflected in it. For restatements of the older view, that Bale 'brought into being [a] ... full-scale, government-directed, theatrical attack on papistry' and that such plays as *King Johan* 'were obviously ... systematically planned ... to reflect as accurately as possible the official view of the catholic church and the Reformation programme', see *The Revels History of Drama in English*, II (1980), p. 16 and D. Bevington, *Tudor Drama and Politics, a Critical Approach to Topical Meaning* (Harvard, 1968), p. 97.

attendance, and between 15 May and 20 June negotiated a ten-year truce. Then in July Francis I and Charles V finally met at Aigues Mortes and pledged lifelong friendship. The implications of this alliance for 'heretical' England were fully understood in Rome and Westminster alike, as was Pole's significance in the new diplomatic equation which it created.[46] The prospect of a combined Franco-Imperial invasion aimed at the reimposition of papal authority in England, coupled with catholic insurrection stirred up by Pole and his allies became a prime concern of the Government. Pole became a bogey figure in protestant imaginations, representative of all manner of fears of papal power abroad and reactionary intrigue at home. He was rumoured to be already in England encouraging his supporters,[47] or leading an army of catholic mercenaries towards the realm.[48] When he actually left Rome on a mission to Francis I and the Emperor, designed to coordinate action against England, the Government reacted with a mixture of fear and anger, commissioning vicious invectives which condemned him as a detestable traitor and a monster.[49] This fear of Pole's mission is reflected in Bale's treatment of the Papal Legates in *King Johan*, particularly in his creation of the ahistorical figure Raymundus, whose role, like Pole's, was to stir the catholic princes into action against England. In his two legates, Bale dramatically presents both halves of the strategy which Pole was perceived to be pursuing, first raising Europe for an invasion, second bringing the bulls which would excommunicate the King, lay England under interdict and turn that invasion into a crusade.

That Bale chose during Christmas 1538–9 to present a play about the occasion on which England was placed under Papal interdict and its King excommunicated had, then, a precise political significance. Throughout the autumn of 1538 threats of excommunication and interdict were emanating from Rome.[50] These were partially realized on 17 December when the Bull of Excommunication, suspended since 1535, was finally published, formally declaring Henry VIII a schismatic.[51] That the Government feared the further step of interdiction is demonstrated by the fact that someone, almost certainly Cromwell himself, had his secretary Ralph Sadler copy out the text of the constitutions which Henry II had drawn up in Normandy to bind his subjects on oath not to assist the importation of

[46] B.L. MS Nero B VI ff. 148 (*L.P.* XIII (ii) 117); 132 (ibid., 117). See also Hall, p. 828.

[47] *L.P.* XII (ii) 267, 1062.

[48] R. Morison, *An Invective Against the Great and Detestable Vice of Treason* (London, *c.* February, 1539), S.T.C. 18111, sigs. B iii and D iii.

[49] Ibid. See also Morison's *Exhortation to Stir all Englishmen to the Defence of their Country* (London, *c.* March, 1539), S.T.C. 18110, ff. 6 (v), 16(v), and Hall, p. 828. For Pole's mission, begun on 27 December 1538, see *L.P.* XIII (ii) 1110; XIV (i) 28, 46, 126, 200, Scarisbrick, *Henry VIII*, p. 361.

[50] B.L. MS Nero B VI, f. 120 (*L.P.* XIII (ii) 509).

[51] *L.P.* XIII (ii) 1087; XIV (i) 13.

bulls of interdiction.[52] Clearly, although papal authority in England may well have meant little to either Henry or Cromwell, papal influence there was still something to be guarded against.

That the prospect of invasion following upon excommunication was also taken extremely seriously may be judged from the near frantic countermeasures which Henry instigated, and which provide a subtext to all governmental activity in late 1538 and early 1539.[53] The simultaneous withdrawal of both the French and Imperial ambassadors from England during February 1539 appeared to mark the prelude to the expected attack. And indeed the appearance of sixty ships lying off the Downs on Easter Day caused the men of Kent to rise up and muster in harness to fight off an invasion, only to stand down again when the ships disappeared.[54]

Meanwhile the Government was attempting to secure munitions on the Continent from those sources not controlled by the enemy. As befits the cautious diplomat, Cromwell made these approaches apparently casually, explaining his interest to the royal agents in Germany in terms of general prudence in troubled times. 'Forasmoch as store is no sore, and that wisdom wold that we shuld be in a redines for to withstand all chaunces.' But the confident façade was shattered and the Crown's true nervousness revealed by a hastily appended postscript to the same despatch.[55]

Syns the lettere was wryten hitherto it hathe been thought notwithstanding anything wrytten herebefor, [?questi]on shalbe made unto the said Bernard de Mella[56] to knowe whether he wuld with a shorte warnyng, furnishe to the Kinges highness twoo hundred Gonners or canonnyers shoters of grete peces and a thowsand or xv C hackebushes yf nede shuld requre ... And upon warnyng by his grace to hym gyven, howe sone he shall thinke he might provyde them, and yf he cannot furnishe the hole, howe many he thinketh he may provyde.

The Government's fears of imminent attack are also evident in the works which Cromwell commissioned from the pamphleteer Richard Morison, most notably in his *Exhortation to Stir all Englishmen to the Defence of Their Country*, probably published during February 1539 and so written at the time that Bale's troupe were performing *King Johan*. In this tract the Reformer sought to raise the nation in defence of King,

[52] Ibid., XIII (ii) 685.
[53] Ibid., 232, 288, 937, 1111, 1162; XIV (i) 144, *C.S.P.Sp.* VI (i) 12; B.L. MS Cotton Vespasian C VII, f. 87 (*L.P.* XIII (ii) 429). See also Scarisbrick, *Henry VIII*, p. 362; Elton, *Policy and Police*, pp. 202–3. For rumours of invasion and expressions of support for the idea from continental sources, see *L.P.* XIII (ii) 660, 896, 996, 1053, 1136, 1148; XIV (i) 158. Clearly Henry's anxiety was not unwarranted.
[54] Hall, p. 827. These may have been the same vessels which had left Flanders in early March, prompting what Cromwell described as 'marveillouse strange ... suspicion and conjecture' in England. B.L. MS Harleian 282, f. 187 (Merriman, II, pp. 185–6).
[55] B.L. MS Vit. B XXI f. 145 (Merriman, II, pp. 186–90).
[56] 'The Kinges trusty friend', Bernhard von Mylen, minister of the Elector of Saxony.

country and reformed religion with a mixture of rabble-rousing rhetoric and messianic zeal. God would protect his own, he declared, 'thowe that the tyrant of Rome, accompanied with a M. legions of dyvels, bestowe all their strengthe and malyce' against them.[57]

Let this yelling Egle approche ... let her come with all her byrdes about her, let a traytour cary her standard: doth not god say, her wynges shall be cut, her kyngedome wax feble, the Lyon [Henry VIII] waxe stronge and save the residue of goddes people, filling them full of joye and comfort, even while the worlde endureth. Let us, let us therefore worke lustely nowe, we shall play for ever hereafter. Let us fight this one fielde with englysse handes, and englysshe hartes, perpetuall quitnes, rest, peace, victorie, honour welthe, all is owers.

Behind the rhetoric, however, lies the fear of a smaller, unprepared, nation facing potentially insuperable odds. And it is this fear which motivates the work. As with most propaganda it is anxiety which it articulates, not confidence. Moreover it speaks for a minority, even within the political elite, which lacked confidence in the resolve of the majority, rather than for a united realm. Hence Morison's need to stress, in the wake of the Pilgrimage of Grace, in which much of the north of England had risen against the religious changes instigated at Westminster, the supposed unanimity of support for the Reformation. 'I truste as we be one realme', he suggests, 'so our enemies shall fynde us of one harte, one fydeletie, one allegiaunce'.[58] But the reality of a divided nation, upon which the reformers in the Government felt they could not rely in a crisis, is tacitly acknowledged elsewhere in the text.[59]

The Crown's fears of internal disaffection found more concrete expression in the violent suppression of the, so-called, Exeter Conspiracy. The possibly deluded ramblings of Sir Geoffrey Pole, Reginald's brother, seemed to provide evidence of treasonable plottings, or at best dangerous disloyalty, among the Pole family and its circle in England. And with the inexorability usually associated with self-fulfilling prophecies the more the Government searched for the plots they feared among men and women suspect on both dynastic and religious grounds, the more evidence of plotting they found. Finally sixteen noble and gentle suspects were executed, including the Marquis of Exeter, Lord Montagu, Sir Edward Neville and George Croftes, Chancellor of Chichester Cathedral. In a postscript to the affair Sir Nicholas Carew, Henry's Master of the Horse, followed them three months later for allegedly concealing their plans.[60] In

---

[57] Morison, *Exhortation*, ff. 16 and 31.
[58] Ibid., f. 20(v).
[59] See, for example, ff. 5(v) and 26(v).
[60] *L.P.* XIII (ii) 703, 753, 772, 796, 804, 821, 829; XIV (i) 979. For an account of these events, see M. H. and R. Dodds, *The Pilgrimage of Grace, 1536–1537, and the Exeter Conspiracy* (2 vols., Cambridge, 1915) II, pp. 297–328.

lashing out at the culpable and the innocent alike the Government only confirmed its worst fears of widespread intrigue and disaffection. Both the highest reaches of the nobility and the innermost parts of the Court seemed to be tainted with sedition. If ever the sixteenth century saw an 'age of paranoia' it was in these last years of the 1530s, when the reforming circle within the Government saw itself hedged around by enemies.[61]

In Bale's play we see a careful articulation of the grounds for this paranoia. In portraying John as a reforming monarch betrayed by his clergy and abandoned by his nobility, Bale provides a dramatic analogue for the position in which Cromwell and the reformers perceived themselves. Yet it is not simply the case that, reacting to the Exeter Conspiracy, Bale used the play to accuse the entire nobility of treason. The play embodies a more sensitive response to political realities.

As a number of critics have noted, Bale's portrayal of Nobility is equivocal and, in part, not unsympathetic.[62] Sedition is swift to claim Nobility as one of his own and as a scourge of the Gospel (lines 276–84). But it is only through deception that Nobility is converted to the papal cause. It is his sense of honour, his concern for the 'great othe' which he took when he was dubbed a knight 'ever to defined, the holy churches Ryght' (lines 363–5) upon which the vices play, not any inherent wickedness in his character. As he is permitted to say when questioned by John, 'that I have don, was of a good intent' (line 479). Yet, as John chastises him, his actions do, despite his good intentions, bring about the downfall of his prince. He is, nonetheless 'a mayntener of sedycyon' (line 1519).

This equivocal attitude towards the character is surely, in part at least, grounded on Bale's knowledge of the political context in which the struggle for religious reform took place. The Tudor nobility was not monolithic. Exeter and Montagu were not typical. Nor was it simply the case that there were conservatives and radicals, the one opposed to the Crown's initiatives, the other supportive. There were noblemen sympathetic to the Old Religion, but not all of these were hostile to the Royal Supremacy. The Henrician Reformation was by and large enforced in the shires by men who were at best ambivalent concerning doctrinal and liturgical innovation and who, like the Duke of Norfolk or the fourth Earl of Shrewsbury, acted out of a mixture of loyalty to the Crown and careful

---

61 For the assertion that the entire Tudor period was dominated by a sense of paranoia, see L. B. Smith, *Treason in Tudor England: Politics and Paranoia* (London, 1986).

62 Note, for example, T. B. Blatt's summary of the character as 'an easy going, thick-headed gentleman with little learning, and a love of tradition, who seldom thinks for himself, and is quickly swayed by the last persuasive speaker. Essentially he is a good but feeble character'. Blatt, *The Plays of John Bale*, pp. 109–10. Contrast Bale's treatment with Tyndale's bald description of the same event, 'how was our King John forsaken of his own lords, when he would have put a good and godly reformation in his own land'. Walter, *Doctrinal Treatises*, p. 17.

political calculation.[63] To succeed in their aims the reformers needed the acquiescence of such men just as much as they needed the positive support of sympathizers like the Earl of Oxford. Hence Bale's rather indulgent attitude towards Nobility in the play. The links between Catholicism and sedition are forcefully put, but the context of the play as a whole offers the nobility the prospect of recovery if, and only if, they adopt the Reformed faith. They are encouraged to reform themselves rather than condemned out of hand. Hence John seeks, adapting traditional arguments for a nobility based upon virtue, to redefine nobility in reformist terms.

> Sum thynkyth nobelyte, in natur to consyst
> Or in parentage, ther thowght is but amyst
> Where habundance is, of vertu, fayth and grace
> With knowlage of the lord, nobelyte is ther in place
> And not wher as is, the wylfulle contempte of thynges
> Pertaynyng to god, in the obedyence of kynges
>
> (lines 1520–5)

Unlike Dissimulation and Private Wealth (the regular clergy for whom no place is granted in Bale's idealized reformed England), Nobility is not banished but re-educated. He forms a pillar of the new society, along with the reformed (secular) Clergy and Civil Order. Thus Bale prevents the play from alienating entirely those powerful men upon whom his vision depended.

The play is, then, carefully constructed to reflect contemporary circumstances. The reformed King's struggle with papal legates and catholic armies abroad and with Sedition at home reflect accurately Henry VIII's diplomatic and political situation in 1538–9. But *King Johan* should not be read merely as a dramatic representation of current events. It is not simply a work of popular propaganda, written to improve domestic morale in the face of external threat. It is also a piece of political and religious special pleading. In this context its intended audience was, not popular, but elite. It sought to make its points to the closed circle of men, chief among whom was the King himself, upon whose actions the future course of the Reformation depended. And here the writer's connections with Cromwell and Cranmer are crucial.

---

[63] Norfolk, who with the Earl of Shrewsbury and the Duke of Suffolk, led the suppression of the Pilgrimage of Grace, claimed never to have read the Bible in English, and swore that he never would, for 'it was merry in England before the New Learning came up' (*L.P.* XVI, 101). See also George Joye's disparaging remarks concerning the Duke's ignorance of the Scriptures in *The Defence of the Marriage of Priestes, Agenst Steven Gardner* (Antwerp, 1541), sig. CII.

CONTINUED REFORMATION?
THE REFORMERS AND HENRY VIII

To this point, the Reformation in England, although limited in extent, had proceeded at a pace satisfactory to the more convinced reformers in the Government, among whom were numbered both Cromwell and Cranmer. A number of what they saw as the grosser abuses of catholic practice had been officially condemned and steps towards the reform of the Liturgy were already in train. The Ten Articles of 1536 had begun the dismantling of the system of works and observances upon which the catholic faith was based by formally distinguishing between those divinely instituted practices which were essential for Salvation and those which were merely convenient, designed by man to keep 'a decent order and honest policy' in religion.[64] In the latter category were placed many of the central pillars of catholic observance, prayers to saints, the veneration of images and the whole panoply of rites and ceremonies which punctuated and characterized the liturgical year. In the former category were placed only three of the traditional sacraments, Baptism, Penance and the Sacrament of the Altar. Over and above these the sole sufficiency of Christ as a channel of Salvation was continually stressed.

The attempt to erode popular allegiance to catholic ceremonies was continued in the Injunctions issued by Cromwell in his capacity as Henry's Vicegerent-in-Spirituals in the same year. These enjoined the clergy to demonstrate to their parishioners the protestant implications of the Articles.[65] Further progress towards a reformed Church was made with the publication of the, so-called, *Bishops' Book (The Godly and Pious Institution of a Christian Man)* in September 1537, which attempted to provide the parish clergy with a thorough exposition of the central articles of faith contained in the Creed, the Pater Noster and the Ten Commandments, all interpreted in a protestant vein. Moreover, in the year preceding the performance of *King Johan* at Cranmer's residence, the pace of reform had increased with the *ad hoc* dissolution of a number of the larger monasteries, the suppression of the mendicant orders and the issue, in October 1538, of a second set of Injunctions which, *inter alia*, enjoined the clergy to provide a copy of the Bible in English for popular reading, and ordered the destruction of 'idolatrous' images and the suppression of pilgrimages and saint worship.[66]

Despite the optimism of some reformers, however, those men who were closest to Henry VIII knew that the course of reform had not been smooth,

---

[64] *E.H.D.* V, p. 795.   [65] Ibid., p. 805.
[66] Ibid., pp. 811–14. All of these measures are alluded to in the play.

and its continuation along current lines could not be guaranteed.[67] Hitherto the King had supported the initiatives of his more radical ministers, and had introduced reforming measures himself. But, as became increasingly clear, his conception of the reformed Church towards which they aimed differed markedly from the vision cherished by Cromwell, Cranmer and the more radical bishops.

Henry's failure – or his refusal – to sanction the single-minded pursuit of godly reformation prompted John Foxe, writing from the perspective of the 1560s, to portray him as the prisoner of his own advisers. In a view which has found a number of modern advocates, the martyrologist suggested that,[68]

even as the King was ruled and gave ear sometimes to one, sometimes to another, so one while it [reform] went forward, at another season as much backward again, and sometimes clean altered and changed for a season, according as they could prevail, who were about the king.

But this account should not be accepted at face value. Foxe's polemical purpose rather than any desire for straightforward factual reporting determined his approach here. He needed to reconcile two seemingly contradictory impulses behind his work. First there was the desire to eulogize Henry, the founder of the English Reformation (in order both to justify the religious changes of his reign and – more particularly – to give an attractive royal pedigree to the sort of further reforms which he wished Henry's daughter, Elizabeth I, to sanction). Second, Foxe clearly needed to explain why the lionized Henry did not always unequivocally support reform, and even at times seemed to speak against it. He could not admit that the King's commitment to Protestantism was less than enthusiastic, or his entire thesis would be compromised. Hence his recourse to the familiar medieval device of attributing unattractive royal decisions to bad advice. Henry was, Foxe concluded, prevented from pursuing a thorough-going reformation by the malign influence of popish councillors.

A more plausible explanation for the hesitant progress of reform in the reign, however, would identify the King himself as the dominant restraining influence. Henry was a man who believed in keeping his options open. Hence his refusal to side definitively with the advocates of either reform or conservatism. Whilst he was happy to initiate radical changes in Church government, and to reform the institutions of the established Church along what might be loosely termed 'Erasmian' lines, he was far

[67] For an optimistic reformist account of the state of religion in England, see Nicholas Partridge's letter to Bullinger of 17 September 1538, which stated that 'Religion is making good progress among us. The King has sent persons to preach the truth in all parts of England ... The flames of Purgatory are extinguished' (*L.P.* XIII (ii) 373).
[68] Foxe, V, p. 260.

less willing to tamper with doctrine, except in those areas in which his passionate, but idiosyncratic, theological study left him convinced that it was essential. He saw the benefits for the Crown in the repudiation of papal authority and the subjugation of the Church to royal control, and subsequently in a closer alliance with the protestant princes of Germany, if that offered the prospect of diplomatic assistance against the papacy and support for the Royal Supremacy at home. But he did not share Cromwell's sympathies with the Lutheran Princes's theological position. Thus he would not buy their assistance at the expense of his own beliefs, or if its acquisition involved the loss of his room to manoeuvre in the diplomatic arena. Hence his refusal, despite the entreaties of his ministers, to commit England to the Confession of Augsburg, and his insistence upon the retention of what the Germans saw as the three great abuses in English religious practice, private masses, communion in one kind only and the prohibition of clerical marriage.[69]

Both theology and political calculation distanced Henry from his reforming ministers. It is clear from his will, for example, with its conventional requests for masses and intercessions for his soul, that he persisted in a belief in the concept of Purgatory, even if he did not acknowledge the legitimacy of the name itself.[70] He also differed from them in believing firmly in the doctrine of Transubstantiation, and in being unwilling entirely to abandon the catholic doctrine of works.[71] These differences had largely been concealed and marginalized in the early years of the break with Rome by a coincidence of interest between a King anxious to achieve his 'divorce' and consolidate the Royal Supremacy, and ministers wishing to dismantle the institutional and liturgical superstructure of the catholic Church. But the unanimity was not immutable.

As was suggested above, Henry was quite prepared to undertake the reform of abuses, where he was convinced that they existed. But governing his willingness to act was an unformulated, but nonetheless practical, working conception of *adiaphora*, 'things indifferent'. Beyond the core of beliefs to which he held tenaciously throughout the last years of his life, there existed a wide band of ideas and practices about which he was

---

[69] For the negotiations between the Crown and the German Princes during 1538, see J. Ridley, *Thomas Cranmer* (Oxford, 1962), pp. 163–4.

[70] Note also his hostile annotations to Hugh Latimer's arguments against the existence of Purgatory (B.L. Cotton MS Cleo. E V, f. 130), and the careful justification of prayers for the dead in the Ten Articles, although 'the place where they be, the name thereof, and the kind of pains there ... be to us uncertain by Scripture' (*E.H.D.* V, p. 805). Cranmer had preached against Purgatory at Paul's Cross as early as February 1536 (B.L. Cotton MS Cleo. E IV, ff. 131(v)–132 (*L.P.* X 462)).

[71] The King's running argument with Cranmer over the respective merits of Works and Faith in the quest for salvation may be followed in their annotations to the draft of the *Bishops' Book*. See, for example, Cox, *Misc. Writings*, pp. 84, 92–3, 94, 95, 96.

prepared, under propitious circumstances, to entertain a degree of discussion and debate. As the key distinction in the Ten Articles suggested, there were things which were not necessary for salvation, but which might be more or less conducive to stable government and the good of the commonweal. Such things might be examined on an individual basis as circumstances dictated and, where necessary, reform undertaken. Thus when presented with evidence of widespread corruption and inefficiency among the religious houses, coupled with sound economic, political and social reasons for their dissolution, Henry could decide upon, first a limited, then a more general spoliation. But that he did so without the reformer's conviction that monasticism *per se* was unacceptable, or the assumption that the dissolution implied an official rejection of the existence of Purgatory, is evident from his subsequent refoundation of houses at Stixwold and Bisham, and his arguments over Purgatory with Latimer.[72] Moreover, he remained convinced that reform of such *adiaphora*, however worthy, must give way to more pressing political and diplomatic concerns.[73]

It was this fundamental contingency to Henry's interest in reform which posed the gravest threat to Cromwell and his allies. For it meant that at virtually any moment both they and their cause might be abandoned if the political situation suggested it. And with the crisis prompted by the threat of invasion in late 1538 such a moment seemed to have arrived.

Alarmingly for the reformers, they and Henry saw the solution to English problems in late 1538 lying in diametrically opposed directions.[74] Both Cromwell and Cranmer felt that the opposition of the two great catholic powers, backed by Rome, could only be met effectively by an even stronger commitment to reform, a further purification of religion and a closer alliance with the protestant princes of Germany. The King, conversely, saw a need to disarm the opposition with apparent concessions, to search for a reconciliation with the European catholic princes through a restatement of the essential conservatism of English doctrine, and a distancing of the Crown from the extremes of reformed opinion. Thus the

---

72 B.L. Cotton MS Cleo. E V, f. 130.

73 Note, for example, Henry's actions in 1545 during negotiations with the Emperor over joint action against the French. Earlier in the year he had responded enthusiastically to suggestions for further reform of the Liturgy forwarded by Cranmer, adding 'creeping to the Cross' to the list of practices to be abolished. Yet immediately it became clear that prospects of agreement with Charles V were improving, he abandoned all such potentially contentious reforms, informing his bishops that these and 'any other innovation, change or alteration, either in Religion or ceremony' must cease. Cox, *Misc. Writings*, p. 414; Scarisbrick, *Henry VIII*, p. 472.

74 For accounts of the differing positions of Henry, Cromwell and Cranmer at this time, see Elton, *Reform and Reformation*, pp. 274–83; A. G. Dickens, *The English Reformation*, p. 246; G. Redworth, 'A Study in the Foundation of Policy: The Genesis and Evolution of the Act of Six Articles', *J.E.H.* 37 (1986), pp. 42–67.

distinct possibility arose that Henry might desert the reformers and align himself more closely with his more conservative bishops who, with the Duke of Norfolk and other conservative noblemen, formed the makings of a reactionary administration in waiting.

Chief among the opponents of reform whom Henry had never entirely removed from his confidence (perhaps with just such purposes as now suggested themselves in mind) were the bishops of Winchester, Durham and London, Stephen Gardiner, Cuthbert Tunstal and John Stokesley. These men, and the last named in particular, had already signalled their determination to resist changes in doctrine and practice in a number of ways.

As early as 1535 Stokesley had demonstrated his opposition to one of the central objectives of the reformers, the provision of a vernacular Bible, by refusing to scrutinize that portion of the translated text submitted to him by Cranmer. Alone among the bishops he declared that he would not co-operate in a project which would inevitably lead to the spread of heresy.[75] Again in 1537 Stokesley opposed Cranmer openly, this time on the committee convened to draft the *Bishops' Book*. When the question of defining the Sacraments arose, Stokesley spoke up for those, including Bishops Longland, Clerk and Sampson and Archbishop Lee, who insisted that all seven of those sacraments conventionally recognized should be endorsed in the document. The reformers, Cranmer, Goodrich, Foxe and Latimer among them, argued for the recognition of only three.[76] And when the negotiations with the envoys of the German Princes broke down over the issue of the 'three great abuses', it was again Stokesley who was said to have obstructed matters and encouraged the English bishops to refuse to negotiate further until the King's views were known.[77]

Whilst these men were on the peripheries of government and lacked Henry's ear, they had been tolerated by the reformers. Indeed, the presence of Stokesley, as a token conservative, on the panel which met the German envoys had been welcomed by Cranmer, as it prevented allegations that the negotiations were being conducted by an evangelical caucus eager to conclude a protestant pact at any cost.[78] But once the prospect of their obtaining Henry's full confidence arose, Cromwell and his allies began to

---

[75] Ridley, *Cranmer*, p. 126. [76] Ibid., pp. 118–19.
[77] B.L. Cotton MS Cleo. E V, f. 212. Ridley, *Cranmer*, pp. 162–3. *L.P.* XIII (i) 1095, 1519 (3); Elton, *Policy and Police*, p. 161. On 29 May 1538 Stokesley was indicted in King's Bench on a charge of Praemunire, for allegedly taking the profession of a number of monks of Sion Abbey and performing 'papistical rites and ceremonies'. Only his complete surrender to the King and Henry's subsequent pardon saved him from ruin. According to Foxe, Stokesley was 'the most earnest champion and defender of the Romish decrees', Foxe, V, p. 379.
[78] *L.P.* XIII (ii) 1296; Ridley, *Cranmer*, pp. 162–3.

treat them as a serious threat. His attempts to implicate them in a plot involving the catholic Friar Dove, Prior of the White Friars at Calais, indicate the lengths to which he was prepared to go to seek out evidence against them.

When it was discovered that Dove had visited a number of the conservative bishops, his interrogators, who included Cromwell's secretary Thomas Wriothesley, began to bombard him with questions aimed at securing evidence of another catholic conspiracy. Who had directed him to take his complaints about sacramentarian preaching in Calais to the bishops of London, Chichester and Durham in particular? What communication had he had with these bishops, and who had witnessed their conversations? What letters had he written to these or other bishops in the past four years? What had he written to my Lord Chamberlain (William, Lord Sandys, one of the noblemen initially suspected of involvement in the Exeter Conspiracy)? Who had directed him to my Lord of Durham (Tunstal)? Why had he visited him, and what communication had he had with him? Was he privy to the letters sent by Stokesley to the Lord Deputy of Calais? And, if so, what did he think the Bishop meant by the words at the end of one of his letters 'wherein he prayed that all should not perish there [Calais] as it is lost here [England]'?[79]

Nothing came of this investigation, but Cromwell continued to keep a weather eye upon the conservatives in the hope of unearthing evidence of conspiracy or secret popery amongst them which might discredit them with the King.[80] Whilst with hindsight this manoeuvring may look like precisely the sort of factional struggle which Foxe described, both Cromwell and the conservatives knew that their positions relied entirely upon their utility to Henry VIII. Their attempts to sway him to their cause involved pursuasion more than manipulation.

In the attempt to convince Henry of the need for continued reform (and thus for reforming ministers) and to deflect the cautious counsel of the conservatives, Cromwell began what must be seen as a concerted bombardment of the King with more or less subtle arguments for and encouragement of reform. Whilst always working within the limits prescribed for him, he nonetheless argued for the stricter enforcement of those advances already achieved. His twin strategies seem to have been, first to convince Henry that he had already committed himself too far to draw back from a policy which was only half finished and required further action, and

---

[79] *L.P.* XIII (ii) 248.

[80] The effectiveness of this pressure may perhaps be judged from Bishop Sampson of Chichester's humble letters to Cromwell, seemingly provoked by rumours that he had aroused the Vicegerent's suspicions, in which he attempted to refute allegations that he had been lax in enforcing the Royal Injunctions. B.L. Cotton MS Cleo. E V, f. 298 (*L.P.* XIII (ii) 278); ibid., XIII (ii) 339.

second to demonstrate that the religious caution of the conservatives amounted to wilful disobedience of royal commands.

In Cromwell's Injunctions of October 1538, for example, much was made of the interim nature of the current state of Church practice. The reforming process was described as a continuing one, and one to which the Crown had already committed itself. The fact that certain ceremonies and uses were permitted to continue, Cromwell stressed, should not be taken as official approval of them. Further reforms were intended and the clergy should prepare the people for them. A sound knowledge of the Pater Noster and the articles of Faith would, for example, soon be required of intending communicants. 'Ye shall declare unto them', the Injunctions instructed,[81]

that ye look for other injunctions from the King's highness by that time, to stay and repel all such from God's board as shall be found ignorant in the premises.

Similarly, although the use of images in churches was not yet made illegal, it was stated that royal directives to that effect would soon be forthcoming.[82]

The King hath in past already, and more will hereafter, travail for the abolishing of such images as might be an occasion of so great an offence to God.

Again, changing the order of service, prayers or fasting days was prohibited, but only 'until such time as the same shall be so ordered and transposed by the King's Highness's authority'.[83] The inference that Cromwell was using the Injunctions to offer hostages to fortune on Henry's behalf in the event of his deciding to renege on further reform cannot be avoided.

The latent tension between a minister anxious to push ahead with further reform (and himself under pressure from his more radical allies) and a King who was unwilling to commit himself in so unsettled a diplomatic climate is also evident in the royal proclamation of 16 November 1538.[84] As Professor Elton has argued, this document seems to represent an uneasy compromise reached between the reforming and conservative views. The first eight articles suggest a retreat from reform and an attack upon Sacramentarianism and other radical reforming preaching, whilst the last two assert the doctrine of Justification by Faith and attack the erastian protestants' hate-figure, Becket.[85] But there is also evidence in the drafting of the proclamation of Henry's own resistance to reform where it might conflict with the wider interests of government.

---

[81] *E.H.D.* V, p. 811.   [82] Ibid., p. 812.   [83] Ibid., p. 814.
[84] Hughes and Larkin, I, pp. 270–6.   [85] Elton, *Policy and Police*, pp. 255–7.

Cromwell's anxiety that the November proclamation should indicate the Crown's continuing commitment to reform may be detected in the repeated assertion that the ceremonies defended within it were not endorsed for all time. They were 'laudable' only in that they were 'not yet abrogated by the King's Highness' authority' and 'as yet . . . not abolished nor taken away by the King's highness'. Thus they should be observed by the people, 'so as they shall use the same without superstition', only,[86]

until such time as his majesty doth change or abrogate any of them, as his highness upon reasonable considerations and respects, therefore both may and intendeth to do.

Not wishing to see himself so strongly committed on the issue, however, Henry added the crucial qualification 'if he considers it expedient for good order'.

In accepting and advancing the Royal Supremacy, the reformers had thrown off papal authority, and had thus gained a degree of liberation. But they had done so at the cost of shackling their hopes of reform to a sovereign whose concerns were inevitably not limited to religion alone. The realization of this crucial limit upon their freedom of action seems to have come only gradually. Thus whilst Cromwell sought to commit Henry to carrying through the implications of earlier reforms, Henry, just as purposefully, ensured that his hands remained free. Cromwell was not opposing directly stated royal wishes, he was merely stating the case for a radical approach to those remaining *adiaphora* which Henry might be prepared to discuss. Where the two men differed was that, at heart, however keen he was to fulfil his master's wishes, Cromwell would have liked to limit Henry's religious options to one – the furtherance of godly reformation – whilst the King was unprepared to undertake such a commitment wholeheartedly.

Perhaps the best examples of Cromwell's attempts to persuade Henry of the merits of the reformers' case, and of the subtle pressure which they exerted to commit him to so doing, are to be found in the propaganda pamphlets which Cromwell commissioned from Richard Morison. Both the reformers' hopes for, and their frustrations with, Henry are evident in the treatment of the King in Morison's *Exhortation*. There, in the spirit of the truly effective political eulogy which seeks to encourage improvement even as it praises perfection, Morison described Henry as just the sort of zealous, resolute, reformer which both the author and his master wished that he was.[87]

---

[86] Hughes and Larkin, I, p. 274.

[87] *An Exhortation*, f. 25(v). It is unclear whether Cromwell's guiding hand ultimately lay behind these passages, or whether a more radical Morison was trying to push both Henry and the Vicegerent towards further reform.

God be praysed, we have a prynce of invincible courage, whose hart god hath so environed with his graces, so furnished with his giftes, so strengthened with the assured affyance of his promyses, that he wol venture al thynge rather than the losse of his subjectes sowles. He woll rather be at utter enmitee with all prynces, then suffer the knowledge of goddes word, to be taken out of his realme.

In reality, of course, it was precisely his unwillingness to venture everything and to be at enmity with all princes for the sake of religion which made Henry so problematic for the reformers. And behind Morison's eulogy, both here and in the *Invective*, is a sense of their impatience with his conservatism and his refusal to be pushed into extirpating what they saw as the dangerous vestiges of popish religion in England. Hence the pointed suggestion in the *Invective* that royal proclamations needed to be followed up if they were to prove effective in the localities. 'I truste', Morison asserts,[88]

as our moste prudente Kynge ceasseth not to send his holsome and godly proclamations abrode, that so one day men shall be sent after them, to se what affecte they take ... where they worke, and where they be ydle, where they have fre passage, and where they be stopped.

That it is Henry's failure to act which prevents further progress and allows the treason which is the subject of the tract to fester, is nowhere openly stated. But it is implicit nonetheless in much of Morison's prose. Most obviously it lies behind the author's remarkable claim that God himself has signalled, through a visitation of the plague, his dissatisfaction with the King's failure to eradicate popery in the North in the aftermath of the Pilgrimage of Grace.[89]

Where as it plesed the Kyng of his clemency and tender love, that his grace beareth to the lyfe of his subjectes, to satisfye the rigor of the lawes, with a few of their dethes, god hath this last sommer by strange kind of sycknes, welle declared unto the commons of the northe, that he was nat contented so fewe were punished, where so many offended.

For the author of a polemical tract commissioned by Cromwell to imply that God was displeased with the King's policies would seem unthinkable, were the context of the assertion not understood. But it seems clear that, just as in the Proclamation and Injunctions, Cromwell was using the semi-official pronouncements of Morison's propaganda as a vehicle for more subtle political persuasion. Behind the polemic designed for public consumption was a message designed for Henry's eyes, which sought to implicate him in the reformers' cause, and to convince him of the need to pursue it to its logical conclusion.

[88] *An Invective*, sig. Dvii.   [89] Ibid., sig. Dviii.

Clearly the call for further godly reformation, usually seen as the issue which divided radicals from moderates in the reign of Elizabeth I, had its origins and antecedents in that of her father. For even within the Government itself there were those who were dissatisfied with the progress of reform by 1538–9 and sought to encourage Henry VIII to carry it further, not least in order to prevent him from abandoning it altogether in the fraught diplomatic circumstances of those months. And it is in the context of this insistent call for further reform, amounting almost to a campaign, that Bale's *King Johan* (in its original incarnation) must be located.[90]

MIRROR FOR A GODLY PRINCE?
'KING JOHAN' AND KING HENRY

It is no coincidence that Bale's play places such stress upon the need for fortitude in godly resolve in the face of external pressures for capitulation. And it is equally significant that the author had Imperial Majesty, the figuration of Henry VIII as Godly Prince, speak the protestant moral of the play and take up the reforming challenge which John was ultimately unable to meet. As with Morison's eulogy of the King, Bale presents Henry dramatically as the ardent reformer in an attempt to persuade him to adopt the role in reality. Hence also the fact that the advice offered to both kings is precisely that which the reformers were giving to Henry.

As England counsels John, the realm will never be safe whilst conservative ministers and the religious remain entrenched as bulwarks against reform.

> Yf yowr grace wold cawse, godes word to be tawght syncerly
> And subdew those pristes, that wylle not preche yt trewly
> The peple shuld know, to ther prynce the lawfulle dewty
> But yf ye permytt, contynuance of ypocresye
> In monke chanons and pristes, and mynysters of the clargy
> Yowr realme shalle never be, with owt moche traytery.
>
> (lines 1576–80)

Clergy reiterates the point, assuring Imperial Majesty that the loyalty of the realm cannot be guaranteed unless all relics of popery are expelled.

---

[90] Other elements in this campaign include the Bill 'drawn and not put up for the Parliament House' in the form of an address to Henry concerning further reform. There the current unfinished state of religious reform is compared to the work of a painter who cannot state that 'he hath painted a man when he hath made all the parts of the body in due proportion, leaving the head, the most noble part thereof, undrawn or unshapen'. SP 1/152, f. 12 (*L.P.* XIV (i) 1064); Elton, *Reform and Renewal*, p. 69 n.9.

> If ye wyll make sure, ye must exyle sedicyon
> False dyssymulacyon, with all vayne superstycyon
> And put private welthe, out of the monasteryes
> Than usurped power, maye goo a birdynge for flyes.
> (lines 2393–5)[91]

The anxiety provoked by the possibility that Henry would turn to his conservative ministers in an attempt to achieve a rapprochement with the Catholic Princes seems evident in the allegations of treachery laid against popish bishops in Sedition's confession.[92]

> Ye gave Injunctyons, that Gods wurde myghte be taught
> But who observe them [?], full manye a tyme have I laught
> To see the conveyaunce that prelates and prestes can fynde
> (lines 2461–3)
>
> In your parlement, commaunde yow what ye wyll
> The popes ceremonyes, shall drowne the Gospell styll
> Some of the byshoppes at your injunctions slepe
> Some laugh and go bye, and some can playe boo pepe
> Some of them do nought, but searche for heretyckes
> Whyls their prestes abroade, do playe the scysmatykes
> (lines 2475–80)

In its general encouragement of further reform at a moment in which the King was reappraising his commitment to reformation in the Church, and in its attack upon conservative churchmen, then, the play proves itself a product not simply of the 1530s in general, but of the specific moment of its performance at Cranmer's house at Christmas 1538–9. Similarly the treatment of specific liturgical issues in the text must be set in the context of this attempt to sway Henry VIII in the direction of continued reform.

Perhaps the most obviously controversial matter in the play is Bale's treatment of the practice of auricular confession. The precise nature of the priesthood and their role as the mediators of grace was a vexed issue for the reformers. And auricular confession provided one of the points at which the general debate had specific relevance. How far was it necessary for layfolk to confess their sins to a priest in order to obtain absolution, and how far was it possible for them, provided that both their contrition and their determination to amend their lives were genuine, to confess privately to God? The answer to this question had fundamental implications for the role of the clergy in society. Thus it is perhaps initially surprising that Bale, the scourge of the catholic priesthood, seems to duck the theological issue in *King Johan* and treats confession rather as a purely

---

[91] These lines are taken from the B text. But, as was argued above, similar scenes are likely to have occurred in the lost conclusion to the A text.
[92] As above.

political matter. Yet that decision is again explicable, given the political context in which the play was written.

In keeping with other early reformers, Bale attacks auricular confession as an instrument of the alleged papal conspiracy to subjugate princes to Roman authority. The confessional is a symbol both of clerical power over the laity and of the secrecy of Roman religion. At confession the layman, whether commoner or prince, must confess his most private sins and weaknesses to the priest. The latter consequently obtains potentially valuable information about, and therefore power over, the penitent. Only a small further logical step was necessary for the reformers to see each priest and each act of confession as part of a vast communication network, relaying information concerning the lords and princes of Christendom back to Rome. There, it was alleged, it was collated and stored, ready for use should the individual concerned attempt to defy papal authority, or should it prove useful in the Pope's attempt to manipulate European affairs to his own ends. Thus the papal primacy was supposedly maintained by what was, in essence, blackmail on an international scale. The point was made succinctly by William Tyndale, who declared in the *Obedience of a Christian Man*, that[93]

The Bishops with the Pope, have a certain conspiration and secret treason against the whole world: and by confession they know what Kings and Emperors think.

In *King Johan* Bale takes up these suggestions and advances them further, making formal confession, with its ritualistic gestures and stylized language, both one of the major motifs in the play and the chief device by which his clerical characters suborn the lay estates. It is under the seal of the confessional, as he admits to John, that Sedition maintains his hold upon layman and priest alike. Confession acts as a double cloak for treason. When a traitor confesses his intentions to a priest, the latter cannot bring the matter into the open, for 'when I [Sedition] am ther [undernethe *benedicite*], the pryst may not bewray me' (line 269). And when it is the priest who is the traitor, he may use the secrets confessed to him to further his cause. It is after sealing Nobility to silence at confession that Sedition tells him of Usurped Power's plan to depose John (lines 1171–2). And it is through the mythical network of confessional spies that the Pope intends to gain the information he needs to thwart the King. As Sedition claims,

---

[93] Walter, *Doctrinal Treatises*, pp. 281–2. Note also Tyndale's suggestion that 'through confessions know they [the Roman clergy] all secrets, so that no man may open his mouth to rebuke whatsoever they do, but that he shall be shortly made a heretic'. Ibid., p. 191. For Hugh Latimer's restatement of this assertion, see G. E. Corrie, ed., *The Sermons and Remains of Hugh Latimer*, Parker Society (Cambridge, 1845), pp. 179–80.

Whan alle other fayle, he [ere confession] is so swre as stele
Offend holy churche, and I warant ye shalle yt fele
For by confessyon, the holy father knowethe
Throw owt alle Christendom, what to his holynes groweth
(lines 271–4)

That Bale follows Tyndale in describing confession as one of the central props of papal hegemony is clear from events later in the play. When Usurped Power outlines his preferred strategy in advance of the proposed General Council, he gives prime position among the practices which he intends to establish there to priestly confession. 'In the meane season', he announces, as Pandolphus and Sedition leave for England,

I shalle soche gere a vaunce
As wylle be to us, a perpetualle furderaunce
Fyrst eare confessyon, than pardons, than purgatory...
(lines 1112–14)

Dissimulation, describing the future council, confirms the Roman intention.

he [the Pope] shalle grownd ther many thynges
Whyche wylle at the last, be cristen mennys undoynges
The popys powr shalle, be abowve the powrs alle
And eare confessyon, a matere necessary.
(lines 1017–20)

In taking up the reformers' assertion and expanding it in his drama, however, Bale was not simply reflecting one of the themes of official propaganda, in the way that he had when naming the Pope Usurped Power, or when stressing the supreme authority of Christian kings in matters spiritual. He was here advancing the views of the more progressive reformers, and going further than royal proclamations and directives would permit.

The Ten Articles of 1536 had stressed the need for auricular confession, and offered a clear rebuke to its critics. The Article concerning Penance declared that, for a Christian to obtain the justifying faith in God's mercy, it was essential to confess to a priest 'if it may be had', and 'the words of absolution pronounced by the priest be spoken by authority given to him by Christ in the Gospel'.[94] Thus the clergy were instructed that 'in no wise they [should] ... contem this auricular confession which is made unto the ministers of the church'.

Henry VIII's own views on the subject may be ascertained from his annotations to the *Bishops' Book* of 1537. From these it is evident that, although he did not believe that auricular confession was actually commanded in the Scriptures, he felt it nonetheless to be a necessary part

[94] *E.H.D.* V, p. 799.

of religious observance.[95] Thus he can be found editing out phrases which seemed to suggest that private confession before God only might be an acceptable alternative.[96]

In criticizing the institution of auricular confession, then, Bale was arguing from a position considerably more radical than that held by the King and promulgated by the official pronouncements of his Government.[97] Hence the caution evident in the wording of his criticisms, which addressed the practice, not as doctrinally unsound, but as politically unacceptable. By associating confession so closely with the maintenance of papal authority, Bale, like Tyndale, sought to blacken the practice without having to make open assertions on matters of principle which would lay him open to allegations of heresy. The failure of his attempt may be judged from the text of the Six Articles of June 1539, which declared definitively that 'auricular confession is expedient and necessary to be retained and continued'.[98]

A second area in which Bale was cautiously advancing radical views in *King Johan* was the much debated issue of Church ceremony and the whole panoply of formal observances attendant thereon. Throughout the play Bale condemns the ceremonial aspects of the catholic liturgy, comparing them, as we have seen, with plays and games. He had John dismiss the entire clergy as 'a Rabylle/Of latyne mummers' (lines 428–9), and call instead for the reformers' ideal of an invisible Church of true believers who would turn 'from ceremonyes dead, to the lyvynge wurde of the lorde' (line 1109).[99] As E. S. Miller has shown, the play parodies and mocks the services and rites of the Catholic Church.[100] But in so doing Bale was treading dangerously close to the limits of orthodoxy. The Ten Articles had, as we have seen, distinguished such ceremonies as Bale ridicules from those observances 'commanded expressly by God and . . . necessary to our

---

[95] Scarisbrick, *Henry VIII*, p. 410.

[96] Cox, *Misc. Writings*, p. 95.

[97] That the reformers, and Cromwell in particular, might have entertained genuine fears concerning the subversive potential of auricular confession when conducted by disaffected priests is entirely likely. The Vicegerent had received a number of reports in the previous two years of individual clerics using the confessional to exhort their parishioners to resist liturgical and doctrinal innovation. In March 1538 he had himself examined one Richard Crouker (or Cronkerne), who was accused of declaring that priests were bound to conceal any treason revealed to them during Confession. (SP 1/130, f. 215 (*L.P.* XIII (i) 633); Elton, *Policy and Police*, p. 346. See also B.L. Cotton MS Cleo E, f. 127 (*L.P.* XI 355) and SP 1/99, f. 97(v) for similar cases. S. E. Brigden, 'The Early Reformation in London, 1520–1547: the Conflict in the Parishes', Cambridge University D. Phil. Thesis, 1978, pp. 152, 171–2; Elton, *Policy and Police*, pp. 121–2, 346.

[98] *E.H.D.* V, p. 815.

[99] The ceremonies of the catholic Church were also among those 'abuses' which Usurped Power intended to introduce at the General Council (see lines 1115–16). Note also Sedition's mock catechising of Nobility in his beliefs (lines 1167–8).

[100] Miller, 'Roman Rite'.

salvation'. Yet they were nonetheless enjoined upon the population as 'such things as have been of long continuance for a decent order and honest policy, prudently instituted and used in the churches of our realm'.[101] The sprinkling of holy water, giving of holy bread, bearing of candles, creeping to the cross and 'kissing of it in memory of our redemption by Christ', all practices mocked in *King Johan*, were specifically described in the Articles as 'laudable customs, rites and ceremonies ... not to be contemned and cast away, but to be used and continued as things good and laudable, to put us in remembrance of those spiritual things that they do signify'.[102]

The *Bishops' Book* confirmed episcopal support for such observances with the careful statement that 'although the said ceremonies have no power to remit sin, yet they be very expedient things to stir and cause us to lift our minds unto God'.[103] But Henry's annotations to that text go further, and again suggest that he took a conservative view of such *adiaphora*. He clearly was not happy with a formulation which left good works and religious observances as merely symbolic gestures. Where the Bishops stressed that 'to have God is not to have him as we have other outward things ... or to worship him with kneeling, or other such gestures', Henry emasculated the statement by the addition of a final word, 'only'. Similarly, where the Book strove to subordinate formal religious observance to the needs of worldly labour, Henry reversed the process. Whereas the text originally stated that 'in time of necessity we may upon the holy day give ourselves to labour, as for saving of our corn and cattle, when it is in danger', Henry added the rider that one might do so, only if it did not mean missing Mass or Evensong, a qualification which prompted a lengthy lecture from Cranmer in response.[104]

Henry's personal commitment to the ceremonial aspects of the faith may be judged from his practice, continued until as late as Good Friday 1539, of creeping to the Cross in the Chapel Royal.[105] Conversely, Cromwell's unease with such practices may be judged from the text of the 1538 Injunctions which, although they did not contradict the defence of ceremonies contained in the Ten Articles and the *Bishops' Book*, strove to give as critical account of them as shifts of tone and emphasis would allow.

All those with cure of souls, the Injunctions announced, were to exhort their parishioners in sermons to be preached at least once in every quarter, to perform,[106]

the works of charity, mercy and faith, specially prescribed and commanded in Scripture, and not to repose their trust or affiaunce in any other works devised by men's phantasies ... as in wandering to pilgrimages, offering of money, candles or

[101] *E.H.D.* V, p. 796.   [102] Ibid., p. 804.   [103] Cox, *Misc. Writings*, p. 103.
[104] As above.   [105] *L.P.* XIV (i) 967.   [106] *E.H.D.* V, p. 812.

tapers to images or relics, or kissing or licking the same, saying over a number of beads, not understood or minded on, or in such-like superstition; for the doing whereof, ye not only have no promise of reward in Scripture, but contrariwise, great threats and maledictions of God, as things tending to idolatry and superstition.

In both his treatment of auricular confession and his ridicule of catholic ceremonies, then, Bale was arguing for reforms more radical than Henry VIII was currently prepared to embrace, and in so doing he was reflecting the views advanced more cautiously still elsewhere by Cromwell, Cranmer and their allies. Perhaps the most obvious example of this trend, however, is to be found in his call for the Bible in English.

As we have seen, Bale's King John is an unequivocal champion of the vernacular Scriptures. 'Yt was never welle', he declares, 'syns the clargy . . . left the scriptur, for menns ymagynacyons' (lines 336–7). He would abandon all the ceremonies of the Church 'so that we may have the scryptures openyng' (line 1390). And he argues for the provision of the Bible in English as the only cure for Commonalty's blindness.[107] Unfortunately for the reformers' cause, however, John's analogue, Henry VIII, was rather less enthusiastic on the subject.

The provision of a vernacular Bible had been a goal of English reformers from Wyclif onwards. Humanist catholics like More had subsequently toyed with the idea. But it only became a fiercely contested issue again with the publication of William Tyndale's strongly Lutheran translation at Worms in 1526. Both Cromwell and Cranmer shared the radicals' enthusiasm for an English text. But if it was to be acceptable to Henry and the conservative bishops, it had to be clearly distinct from Tyndale's version with its heretical associations. Hence the project, begun at Cromwell's insistence, for the printing of a new translation, borrowing much from Tyndale but avoiding his more contentious glosses, conducted throughout the Autumn and Winter of 1538 in Paris by Richard Grafton, Edward Whitchurch and Miles Coverdale. Although this scheme had Henry's support in principle, it was very much Cromwell's initiative, and the organization and the problems were entirely his affair.[108] As the work was conducted in Paris, the centre of the quality book-production industry, it was also subject to the influence of the French catholics and the agents of the Pope. As early as 7 October, the English agent in Paris, Edmund Bonner, reported to Cromwell that attempts had been made by unnamed

---

107 Conversely Usurped Power and his minions are resolute in their determination to prevent the publication of the Scriptures. The General Council will act, we are told, 'for to suppresse the gospelle' (line 1614), whilst Dissimulation will not preach the Gospel but instead defies it 'to the devylle of helle' (line 852).

108 He also informed the French ambassador, Castillon, that it was conducted at his own expense, *L.P.* XIII (ii) 1163.

critics to halt the printing. But it was not until 17 December that a citation before the Inquisitor General in France, Henri Garvais, prevented the Parisian printer, Francis Regnault, from carrying it out. Only Cromwell's influence with the French ambassador, Castillon, eventually rescued the blocks and materials from destruction and secured their shipment to London, where work was finally completed in April 1539.[109]

At the precise time that Bale must have been preparing *King Johan*, then, the provision of an English Bible was a matter close to the heart of his patron Thomas Cromwell. And the fears of the Vicegerent, and of reformers generally, concerning the future of the project, no doubt influenced the play's portrayal of a catholic plot to suppress the Gospels. As Cromwell knew, however, the main obstacle in the way of a biblical text freely available to all Englishmen in their mother tongue was not catholic agents in France but, once again, the innate conservatism of Henry VIII.[110] The King's objections were, it is true, to the political and social implications of releasing a translation, rather than to the principle involved, but they were equally troublesome nonetheless.

The idea of a generally available biblical translation was aired on a number of occasions in the 1530s, not least of which was the abortive attempt to have the bishops collectively prepare an acceptable text. The *Bishops' Book* also leant its support for the prospect. But Henry's unease with the possibility of uncontrolled access to the text, and his distance from Cranmer over the matter, can be detected in their respective annotations to the Book. The Bishops had declared that,[111]

> they that can read may be well occupied upon the holy day, if they read unto other such good works which may be unto them instead of a sermon. For all things that edify man's soul in our Lord God be good and wholesome sermons.

Henry, however, was anxious at the democratic overtones in the idea that any individual might read 'unto other' without restriction. For he added the phrase 'such as they have cure of' after 'other'. Cranmer took exception to this, complaining that

> he that can read may be well occupied, if he read some part of the scripture unto them which cannot read; not as taking the office of a priest or bishop upon him,

---

[109] Ibid., XIII (ii) 557, 1085, 1163. See also ibid., 972, 1043, 1086 and 1136.

[110] That Henry did not share either the reformers' veneration of the Word, or the humanists' desire to establish an authentic text is suggested by his attempt, in annotating the *Bishops' Book*, to rewrite sections of both the Pater Noster and the Creed, inserting material of his own in the process, acts of presumption which drew down upon him one of Cranmer's sternest lectures. 'We should not alter any word in the Scripture, which wholly is ministered unto us by the Ghost of God', wrote the Archbishop, 'but the Scripture must be set out in God's own words, and if there be an ambiguity ... after it be declared, according to the true sense thereof'. Cox, *Misc. Writings*, p. 106.

[111] Ibid., p. 102.

except he be called thereunto, but of charity moved, as he shall see necessity time and opportunity.

He thus pointed out, somewhat naively, that Henry's addition would set perhaps unforeseen limits upon that liberal ideal.

if these words be added ... it might seem that no man were well occupied to read good works, but the father to the children, the master to his servants, the parson to his own parishioners and such like.

Far from being unforeseen, however, this consequence had been Henry's motive for adding the phrase. To limit the reading of the Bible and other 'good works' to figures of social responsibility and to contexts in which their responsibility was emphasized, made access to the Scriptures far more readily controllable, and removed the spectre of anarchic squabbles over points of doctrine which seemed to haunt Henry's mind.

Unsurprisingly the experiment introduced with the Injunctions of 1538, whereby a Bible was to be provided for public use in each church,[112] was soon qualified in answer to Henry's anxieties. Citing a 'great murmer, malice and malignity' among his subjects, the Proclamation of April 1539 hedged the reading of the biblical text around with new restrictions. The cause was said to be the disputes and contentions arising among those who were 'taking and gathering divers Holy scriptures to contrary senses and understanding'. Henry's own hand in the drafting is evident from his lengthy annotations and amendments. These contentious preachers, the text stated, had used 'the Scripture permitted to them by the King's goodness in the English tongue' as the source of their erroneous arguments.[113] This, Henry added, was

much contrary to his highness' expectation: for his Majesty's intent and hope was that they that would read the Scripture, would with meekness and wish to accomplish the effect of, read it, and not to maintain erroneous opinions and preach.

As the proclamation tersely observed, these were 'such fashions and feats as it is not convenient to be suffered'. Thus it announced Henry's intention to quell division 'by terrible *good and just* laws' (here and below the italics indicate Henry's additions). In the interim it was forbidden for anyone to read the Gospels 'with any loud or high voices'. 'Such as can *and will*' read the Scriptures may instead 'quietly and reverently read the Bible and New testament *quietly and with silence* by themselves *secretly* at all times and places convenient for their own instruction and edification'.

The illiterate were thus effectively barred from access to the biblical texts except on occasions when they were expounded by a licensed

---

[112] *E.H.D.* V, p. 811.
[113] B.L. Cotton MS Cleo. E V, fo. 311 (Hughes and Larkin, I, pp. 284–6).

preacher. All religious debate in the Church over interpretations of the text was to cease. Henry's social conservatism had triumphed over his ministers' religious idealism. Once more the Scriptures would be, in practice if not in theory, the possession of that privileged section of society which might be trusted to use them sensibly. The reaction was consolidated in the *King's Book* of 1543, Henry's belated official response to the *Bishops' Book* of 1537, which gave the distinction between the Scriptural haves and have-nots formal expression in the statement that 'God ... hath ordered some sort of men to teach other, and some to be taught'. The former needed access to the biblical text, the latter did not.[114]

Despite Bale's attempt to fashion in John a figure which Henry might emulate, then, time and the King's inclinations were again to disappoint the author's expectations of reform. The vernacular Scriptures were subjected to restriction and censorship almost as soon as they were issued.

In his treatment of all three issues, then, the attack upon auricular confession, the ridicule of good works and liturgical observances, and the call for a freely available English Bible, Bale was arguing for changes in religious policy which had not yet been, and in most cases were never to be, sanctioned by Henry VIII. The dramatist had found himself checked by the dilemma experienced by all the reformers who had invested their expectations in the erastian Reformation which Henry had set in motion in England. Whilst the only realistic hope for sustainable reform lay with the Crown, Bale had to support the King and vaunt the Royal Supremacy. Yet whilst Henry remained only equivocally committed to the reforms they desired, they found themselves, not carried along in the wake of a zealous prince in full sail, but forced to encourage and goad as best they could the dead weight of royal scepticism overland, ever aware that at any point it might turn about and crush them. The reforming language of Bale and the other reformers linked to Cromwell's circle, however lurid it at times became, thus needed to be circumscribed by caution. Always the need for further reform had to be articulated in terms thought likely to appeal to Henry (hence auricular confession was attacked as a seditious papal device and the vernacular Bible described as an instrument of national liberation from Roman ignorance). And those questions upon which Henry was known to be sensitive had to be treated with particular care. Hence Bale's failure to mention anywhere in the play the violent controversy concerning the Sacrament of the Altar, perhaps the most vexed point of debate between reformers and their conservative critics.

Although Bale and Cranmer, and probably Cromwell too, had, by 1538, abandoned belief in Transubstantiation, John and Imperial Majesty

---

[114] *E.H.D.* V, p. 817.

remain silent on the point.[115] For Henry himself was known to accept the miracle of the Mass, and had demonstrated through his personal interrogation of the sacramentarian heretic John Lambert in November 1538, his unwillingness to tolerate dissent on this point. The reformers close to the Crown had, therefore, decided to keep silent on the issue for a time, for fear of drawing down Henry's anti-Sacramentarian prejudices upon themselves.[116]

Indeed, despite both Cromwell and Bale's general sympathies with the sacramentaries' reforming motives, the author actually uses *King Johan* to attack them in order publicly to distance Cromwell's circle from their unacceptable views and avoid guilt by association.[117] Bale gives to Imperial Majesty an unequivocal condemnation of Sacramentarianism.

> The Anabaptystes, a secte now rysen of late
> The scryptures poyseneth, with their subtle allegoryes
> The heades to subdue, after a sedicyouse rate
> The cyte of Mynster, was lost through their debate
> They have her[e] begonne, their pestilent sedes to sowe
> But we trust in God, to increace they shall no growe.
>
> (lines 2579–84)

Yet, for all their vigilance in the matter, and despite their attempts to interest Henry in the call for further Reformation, the damage had already been done by the end of 1538. Both the rise of Sacramentarianism, with its anarchic overtones, and the threat of a Catholic crusade against the realm, had pursuaded Henry that he could no longer countenance what he saw as unbridled reform. Hence the clear reaction evident in early 1539 which was to lead to the Act of Six Articles.[118] Although royal backing for

---

115 SP 1/133, f. 174 (*L.P.* XIII (ii) 1237).   116 *L.P.* XIII (ii) 991.

117 Note in this context Cromwell's anxiety that the outbreak of sacramentarian preaching in Calais be suppressed quickly and quietly, and his concern when Prior Dove took complaints about it to the conservative bishops Stokesley, Sampson and Tunstal. His fear that the Prior was providing his enemies with evidence which might implicate the reformers is evident from the close questioning to which Dove was put on the subject, Merriman, II, pp. 139–40, 148–9; *L.P.* XIII (ii) 248 and above, p. 206. The allegation that conservative bishops used charges of Sacramentarianism and Anabaptism to blacken reformers' names and secure their conviction for heresy is also to be found in *King Johan*. 'if your true subjectes, impugne their [the bishops'] trecheryes / They can fatche them in, anon for sacramentaryes / Or Anabaptystes, thus fynde they a subtyle shyfte' (lines 2483–5).

118 Redworth, 'Six Articles'. The new emphasis upon the essential conservatism of the English Church was also reflected in less obvious ways. In early 1539 the dominance of reformers among those chosen to preach at Paul's Cross was broken, and Stokesley and the conservatives were offered the opportunity to nominate preachers. Similarly in the City's mayoral election of that year, the religious conservative Sir William Hollys was finally elected, having been barred from the office for the previous three years by royal letters of support for rival candidates. This time Henry offered no objections. Brigden, 'Early Reformation', pp. 121–3. Closer to Bale's own case, the Keeper of the Carpenters' Hall in London was arraigned during 1539 'for procuring an interlude to be openly played, wherein priests were railed at and called knaves', Foxe, V, p. 446.

individual reformers continued beyond 1539, it is clear that Henry's publicly stated preference was now for more conservative policies. Temporal concerns had deflected the march towards the New Jerusalem.

Although the central role played by Henry VIII in the progress and retardation of reform in these years is again attracting the attention of historians.[119] The remarkable extent to which his will and personality dominated the religious expressions of those advocates of reform within the government still requires further statement. Bale's *King Johan* provides one measure of that domination. That Bale, an ardent reformer and elsewhere an outspoken critic of all that he saw as papist or ungodly, should have tempered his play to the preferences and prejudices of the King reveals how far those associated with Cromwell's circle were aware of both Henry's central importance and his maddening ambivalence. Such men knew that, if reform was to succeed, the crucial battle was not that against popular ignorance and superstition, but against royal scepticism. Bale's uncharacteristic moderation over Transubstantiation is just one illustration of his desire to present the reformers' case in terms likely to appeal to the King.

It may have been that Bale intended that his troupe should take the play to Court after the performance at Cranmer's residence. Thus he might have the opportunity to place his arguments before Henry directly. He may, conversely, have intended to present the scribal copy of the text to the King. Alternatively, the courtiers who would have been present among Cranmer's guests may have been his target. Or he might simply have intended the play to demonstrate to Cromwell, whose patronage he clearly sought, that he was not simply a religious firebrand, but a writer who might provide subtle and persuasive dramatic propaganda for the reformist cause. Whichever is the case, it is clear that, for all its passages of unmediated polemic, *King Johan* merits inclusion among the other, ostensibly more sophisticated, plays of persuasion considered here. It is a text firmly embedded in the struggle for religious reform within the governing circle during 1538–9. As with all the plays examined above, it not only reflects political activity, but strives to influence that activity in the interests of its author. To study such a play, far from involving a retreat from the mainstream of political history, takes one to the heart of religious and political controversy in this period.

---

[119] Redworth, 'Six Articles'.

Chapter 7

COURT DRAMA AND POLITICS: FURTHER QUESTIONS AND SOME CONCLUSIONS

The preceding chapters have, through the study of examples of one specific dramatic form, the Interlude, raised a number of important questions, some particular, others with a more general significance. Not all of these questions have proved capable of definite answer. Indeed it has often been the simplest yet most fundamental questions which have proved the most intractable. What, for example, did it actually mean to be a Court playwright in Henrician England? We have looked at a number of examples of the playwright's craft, but how was playwrighting in general organized? Clearly there was no playwrighting profession as such. As Richard F. Green has argued of poets generally, writing had to be conducted as a 'spare-time', or at best part-time, occupation, supported by rewards from other sources.[1] But, more generally, what did the process of play-commissioning and playwrighting itself entail, particularly in the specialized context of the Court or a baronial household?

Much work has been done recently on the literature of earlier and later periods, concerning elite literary patronage, its extent and implications.[2] But, although we now know rather more than we did about the mechanics of patronage (who wrote what for whom and with what consequences for the nature of literary production) in the reigns of Elizabeth I, James I and Charles I, or in the age of Chaucer, we are still lamentably ignorant concerning the situation in the early sixteenth century. Much work clearly needs to be done, not least in the area of dramatic patronage, to establish more precisely what such patronage actually involved.

In the previous chapters a number of specific case studies have revealed a close relationship between the plays performed in or around the Court and the specific social, political or religious concerns of the King at that

---

[1] R. F. Green, *Poets and Princepleasers: Literature and the English Court in the Late Middle Ages* (Toronto, 1980), pp. 4, 11–12, 203–11.

[2] See, for example, G. F. Lytle and S. Orgel, eds., *Patronage in the Renaissance* (Princeton, 1981); H. Dubrow, 'The Sun in Water: Donne's Somerset Epithalamium and the Poetics of Patronage', in H. Dubrow and R. Strier, eds., *The Historical Renaissance: New Essays on Tudor and Stuart Literature and Culture* (Chicago, 1988), pp. 197–219; M. G. Brennan, *Literary Patronage in the English Renaissance: The Pembroke Family* (London, 1988).

moment. Indeed, all the plays studied above seem to have been in this sense occasional works, written for a particular audience at a particular time and with equally particular persuasive ends in mind. Only subsequently did they, in some cases, become part of the general repertoire of the touring companies, at which point much of their specific political significance would have been lost. But the lack of detailed external evidence prevents our answering a number of further questions central to any deeper understanding of the playwrighting process in its courtly context.

How, exactly, did plays come to be performed at Court or in a baronial hall, for example? Was the author or the patron the driving force behind the process? And can we speak in any meaningful way of plays being 'commissioned' and, if so, what might such a commission have involved? Did Henry VIII or the Duke of Suffolk make specific demands about the nature and content of the plays which they wished to see performed? Or were things done rather more subtly, based upon tacit understandings and unspoken assumptions? When he 'brought a play to Court', or wrote for the Royal Household, could a man like John Heywood, already attuned to the general political climate there, anticipate what sort of play would find favour? Or, as the needs and interests of the Crown were forever shifting, often in response to political decisions taken in some secrecy, did he have to be told what would be acceptable? And, if the latter, by whom and how subtly? Must we envisage a Cromwell or a Lord Chamberlain summoning Heywood to his rooms to outline precisely what sort of play His Majesty would appreciate, or would a quiet word in the corridor have sufficed?[3] And how far were such guidelines subsequently enforced? Were the playbooks scrutinized before the performance in an attempt to eliminate any

---

[3] As R. F. Green notes (*Poets and Princepleasers*, pp. 203–4) the history of royal and aristocratic patronage of other literary genres provides examples of both the general and the specific commission. In commissioning what was to become the *Confessio Amantis* from John Gower, for example, Richard II is said to have requested only that the poet write 'som newe thing', whereas Philip the Bold, Duke of Burgundy, was rather more specific in his request for a life of his brother Charles V from the pen of Christine de Pisan. In the latter's account of her commission, it was 'Monterbaut, the treasurer of the said lord [Philip]' who informed her that

it would please him [Philip] if I [Christine] would compile a treatise on a certain subject (which he [Monterbaut] would not completely reveal to me until I might be able to hear the exact intentions of the said prince); I, therefore, moved with desire to fulfil his wishes as far as my modest abilities allowed, travelled with my household to Paris, where he was at the time, at the Louvre ... Having arrived in his presence ... I told him the reason I had come and the wish I had to serve his highness and to please him ... provided that I might be informed by him of the nature of the treatise on which it pleased him I should work. Then he ... graciously ... declared to me the approach and the subject it pleased him I should adopt; and, after many fine proposals received from his grace, I took my leave with this pleasant commission'

(Christine de Pisan, *Livres des fain et bonnes meurs du sage roy Charles V*, ed., S. Solente (2 vols., Paris, 1936–40), I, pp. 7–9; cited and translated, Green, *Poets and Princepleasers*, p. 204.

obviously offensive or unhelpful material? Or was self-censorship, based upon a desire to attract future commissions (or to win royal favour more generally) assumed to be enough? The description of those overtly political plays performed at Court during the ascendancy of Wolsey in the 1520s would suggest that, in these cases at least, close supervision and direction from above was practised, in order that those plays performed before the French or Imperial ambassadors matched the particular nuances of the English diplomatic position at that time.[4] But in other cases matters may have been handled entirely differently. The available evidence again allows for no certainty.

Whichever was the case, what emerges most obviously from this study is that, far from being either apolitical aesthetes concerned only with time-less verities or professional entertainers intent solely upon reaching a wide, paying, audience, playwrights were actually closely involved in the political process, aware of its informal rules and prevailing currents, and prepared to use their particular talents for political ends. But, again, to say as much is to raise questions rather than answer them. Were these writers actively involved in politics as a matter of personal conviction, for example, or were they simply used as mouthpieces by others who were? To couch the problem in modern terms, did a patron or an interest group (whether religious, political or both) with a case to put before the Sovereign approach a playwright already engaged upon a play for the Court and persuade him to use it as a vehicle for their opinions? Or were these playwrights already so far immersed in political and religious contro-versies that they acted on their own initiatives? The specific studies con-ducted above raise both possibilities, with the balance of probabilities tilting only slightly in favour of the latter case.

The sort of ideas advanced in Skelton's *Magnyfycence*, for example, when added to what is known of the author's wider career and circum-stances, would suggest that he at least was working relatively indepen-dently, attempting to advance his own fortunes by reproducing in dramatic form what he took to be the wishes of the King. But what of John Heywood? Do his evident intellect, his known religious beliefs and his position at Court suggest that his too might have been a well-informed independent voice? Or does his association with the More circle suggest that he was writing, however informally, for a wider interest group? And might that group have also been involved in the production of the *Enterlude of Godly Queene Hester*? Although there are suggestive co-incidences of theme and approach between Heywood's *Weather* and *Hester* which might arouse our suspicions, the lack of any external

[4] See pp. 16–20, above.

evidence conclusively connecting the two prevents the drawing of any firm conclusions.

As for John Bale, we know both that he had links with Cromwell and Cranmer and hence with a group of religious radicals in and around the Court, and that he was more than capable of pursuing vociferously his own opinionated line. We might, therefore, picture him as either a head-strong independent or a responsible party man. How far Cromwell and Cranmer were involved in the creation of *King Johan* consequently remains a moot point. Did Bale perhaps design the play to force the issue of continued reformation despite their advice? Or was he perhaps guided by them to make the tactical concessions to Henry VIII's religious sensibilities contained in the text, with a view towards increasing its persuasive poten-tial? Or were both the boldness and the political sophistication evident in the play Bale's own? Again the lack of evidence precludes the drawing of any definite conclusions. Even where, as in the case of *King Johan*, we possess what appears to have been a working copy of the text, written partly in the author's own hand, we cannot tell what determined a particu-lar deletion or interlineation. Bale's hand on the pen has left its trace: the hand on his shoulder, if it existed, has not.

As we have seen, the plays considered above prove on close examination to be relatively complex political devices. They are not simply pieces of dramatized propaganda or didactic exhortations in dialogue form. They frequently contain more than one rhetorical current, and these do not always work to the same end. Indeed, at times the subcurrents of a given play actively oppose the surface flow, giving the finished work impli-cations quite at odds with its apparent purpose. What broader conclusions should be drawn from these rhetorical and political undercurrents? Do they imply that these plays were actually beyond the control of their patrons and sponsors? When, for example, Henry VIII watched *Hester* (if indeed he did), would he have been surprised or even shocked by what he saw? As we have noticed, the author adopted the prevailing courtly rhetoric declaring both a new royal indpendence after the fall of Wolsey and a desire for reform of the Church, and reflected it in his play. But he used it to argue against royal interference in Church affairs rather than for it. Similarly, Heywood's *Weather* employed much the same sort of language and many of the same ideas to appeal to the inherently unsympa-thetic King for protection for the Church. In each case Henry, or his advisers, would have been confronted, in part at least, with arguments largely contrary to those which the King privately cherished. How are we to imagine the latter responding in such cases? Was he necessarily the dupe of ingenious, subversive, playwrights who clearly manipulated him into

allowing them the opportunity to deliver lengthy expositions of disagree-
able political themes? Or was there perhaps more to it than that? Was the
Crown perhaps one further step ahead of the game?

Did the King or his advisers perhaps select a playwright like Heywood to
write for the Court in full knowledge of his political and religious
opinions; aware that the resulting play was likely to be conservative rather
than radical in its implications? Knowing that the type of plays performed
at Court might act as a semi-public barometer of royal feeling on an issue
(rather as the choice of Court preachers would act as an indicator of
prevailing religious sympathies in later years) might the Crown have
selected a conservative playwright at a given moment as an act of policy?
Might such a commission have acted as a tacit warning to religious
radicals, whether at Court or in Parliament, enabling the King to signal his
displeasure and so check their enthusiasm without his having to distance
himself from them in any more formal or public way? Was the selection of
playwrights another of the means by which those in authority might either
judge or subtly influence the prevailing political climate?

For want of the all-important external evidence we are again unable to
do more than raise such questions. It is quite possible that the general tenor
of the previous paragraph is correct and that the selection of Court
playwrights, like that of Court and Paul's Cross preachers, was a complex
process fraught with political implications. But it may equally well not
have been. It is possible that Henry VIII never exercised his prerogative to
select such entertainments, beyond registering his approval or disapproval
of those which he had seen. Thus the responsibility for commissioning
such plays, and the opportunities attendant upon it, may have devolved
upon his ministers. Yet again, it is possible that what might be termed the
Court's 'dramatic establishment' was so few in number in this period that
virtually anyone who could offer an entertaining play would eventually be
employed. Too little is known about the informal processes which
governed artistic patronage and recommendation at Court for definite
statements to be made, even on such fundamental issues as these.

And what of those plays performed beyond the immediate confines of
the Court? Did their production also involve royal consent, or was it
independent of central interference? The fact that even those plays which
seem to have been performed, initially at least, outside the royal household, such as Skelton's *Magnyfycence* and Bale's *King Johan*, still closely
mirrored and sought to influence royal opinions suggests that such performances were expected to have an impact at Court. But how might this
have been realized? Perhaps reports would have filtered back to the royal
household. Perhaps courtly audiences were more mobile than we might

assume. Either way such plays suggest that the major centres of elite drama, both in London and beyond, were to some extent part of a single extended forum for intellectual and political debate.

Support for this last assertion may perhaps be found in a striking account provided by the Spanish ambassador, Chapuys, of how Henry VIII travelled some thirty miles, ten of them on foot, at two o'clock in the morning, in order to see a dramatic performance based upon the Book of Revelations.[5] The production, which Chapuys terms a 'pageant' (*'triomphe'*) but which was probably more akin to the Corpus Christi cycle productions on their pageant wagons than to civic ceremonial, evidently took place outdoors, as Henry is said to have found a vantage point in a nearby house from which to overlook the performance. And what he saw clearly delighted the King. 'So much pleasure did he receive', Chapuys noted,

at seeing the heads of . . . ecclesiastics cut off, that in order to laugh more at his ease, also to encourage his people to persevere in such amusements, he sat bareheaded [and so recognisable]. Indeed, the thing seemed so good to him that the next day he sent his lady [Queen Anne Boleyn] a message that she would do well to come and assist in the representation of the same mystery, which was to be acted on the Eve of St Peter.

Although this is an isolated and probably atypical occurrence it suggests a number of things. Evidently Henry was kept informed about dramatic performances, even those some distance beyond the current location of his household, and was given some idea of their likely content and appeal. It may not have been his regular habit to appear incognito at such performances, but the fact that he knew of the play at all, and moreover, knew sufficient about it to prompt so inconvenient a journey,[6] suggests that Skelton and Bale were not unrealistically optimistic in expecting their plays to have some influence with the King. 'The Court circle', where drama was concerned, may well have been surprisingly widely drawn.

In addition to what they suggest about the nature of dramatic activity in and around the Henrician Court, the preceding chapters also carry

[5] *C.S.P. Sp.* V (i), 179 (*L.P.* VIII, 949). Chapuys' letter is dated 30 June 1535, yet he refers to a performance on 'St. John's Eve' (26 December 1534?). Thus, if this dating is correct, his 'news' is rather old. But his account of the play would seem in keeping with the general tenor of the festival of St John. The prescribed biblical texts for 27 December included *Revelations* 1 and 22 which, with their concentration upon Judgement Day, would seem to fit the theme of this 'pageant'. See R. C. Hassel, Jr., *Renaissance Drama and the English Church Year* (Lincoln, Nebraska, 1979), pp. 30–7, for an account of St John's Day drama later in the sixteenth century.

[6] It is hardly likely that Henry would have travelled ten miles on foot (carrying, Chapuys tells us, a two-handed sword!) without good reason to think he would enjoy the play.

implications for our view of court politics and its procedures; and particularly for our view of the role of the Sovereign in the political process. That these playwrights took so much care to couch their arguments in terms likely to find favour with the King, suggests that they thought both that he was generally worth persuading and that it was possible to sway him on a given issue. A King who was the plaything of faction, or who habitually delegated decision-making to others, would hardly have warranted the attention afforded him in these plays. A King who was an inflexible autocrat would be equally unlikely to inspire attempts at persuasion, particularly if the advice being offered was likely to prove unwelcome. What a study of the courtly drama of the reign suggests is rather a King who was personally in control of events, yet who was thought to be sufficiently pragmatic to encourage counsel on a variety of issues.

But how was such counsel offered and, more generally, by what mechanisms did political debate operate within the Henrician Court? A number of stimulating studies covering the formal evolution of the King's Council as an institution have recently been published.[7] But we still lack, and are unlikely to find, the detailed evidence which would tell us precisely what went on within the Council Chamber on any given day. We have the headings of debates and resolutions but, apart from a few isolated accounts of heated arguments, and more frequent mention of carefully stage-managed formal orations arranged for the benefit of foreign ambassadors, we know little about who said what and to what effect when the major political issues were discussed by the Council.[8] And, if we know little about the course of discussion in the central institution of government, we know still less about the informal processes which governed debate beyond it. Thus any new material which can be brought to bear upon the subject is surely welcome.

Although this study has considered only one very specialized form of political exchange, it does, then, have a wider significance. Again, the subtleties to which these playwrights went in order to dress their views in a language and a discourse acceptable to the King hardly suggests a political climate in which the frank and open discussion of important issues was always possible. Yet neither does it suggest an atmosphere in which the cowed acceptance of every royal whim was the norm. But within the

---

[7] See, for example, J. A. Guy, 'The King's Council and Political Participation', in A. Fox and J. Guy, *Reassessing the Henrician Age: Humanism, Politics and Reform, 1500–1550* (Oxford, 1986), pp. 121–50; 'The Privy Council: Revolution or Evolution?' in C. Coleman and D. Starkey, eds., *Revolution Reassessed: Revisions in the History of Tudor Government and Administration* (Oxford, 1986), pp. 59–86 and *The Cardinal's Court* (Hassocks, 1977); G. R. Elton, 'Tudor Government: The Points of Contact: The Council', in *Transactions of the Royal Historical Society*, 25 (1975), pp. 195–211.

[8] See, for example, *L.P.* II (i) 1959.

continuum between the two, where was the Henrician balance struck? It would be interesting to know, for example, how far the authors of these plays used them as the vehicles for their views because they felt they were particularly conducive to that end, and how far because they had no other outlet. Was sponsorship of political drama the last recourse for a group or individual who was denied a voice at the Council table, or who felt unable to voice such views in so formal a context? Or was it simply part of a broader persuasive campaign which, like the educational programme envisaged by Erasmus,[9] utilized every means of access to the Sovereign in a blanket approach? The answer to such questions is again dependent upon precisely how independent or, conversely, how representative we consider the playwrights to have been. But upon such answers rests our conception of the political atmosphere of the Henrician Court.

Even the briefest study of the major events of the reign suggests that no single model of political activity will apply to all cases. The King's public position, and consequently the atmosphere of the Court, was always contingent upon the particular circumstances of the moment; upon the diplomatic situation; governmental perceptions of the extent of domestic resistance to royal policies; the success or otherwise of the various royal marriages and, not least, Henry's own mercurial temperament which was itself partly a product of all these things. At times the King might encourage a degree of free discussion on an issue, or at least wish to create the appearance of free discussion. At other times and on other issues the kind of draconian censorship associated with the idea of a 'Tudor despotism' might obtain.[10] To take one very obvious example, in the relative political stability of the late 1520s, the need to gain wider support for his case, coupled perhaps with an unduly optimistic view of the likely outcome, encouraged Henry to welcome public discussion, both at home and abroad, on the validity of his marriage to Katherine of Aragon. In the very different circumstances of the early and mid-1530s, legislation was required to suppress any discussion of the legality of the beleagured Boleyn marriage. Depending upon the wider circumstances, then, Henry might adopt diametrically opposed responses to similar circumstances.

Whilst it might always be unwise to voice open opposition to royal wishes on matters of high policy, this did not mean that all independent

---

[9] See above, p. 9.

[10] For a debate over whether or not one can talk of a 'Tudor Despotism' in the 1530s, see, for example, J. Hurstfield, 'Was there a Tudor Despotism after all?', *Transactions of the Royal Historical Society*, 17 (1967), pp. 83–108; G. R. Elton, 'The Rule of Law in Sixteenth Century England', *English Historical Review*, 75 (1960), pp. 208–22 and *Policy and Police: the Enforcement of the Reformation in the Age of Thomas Cromwell* (Cambridge, 1972), pp. 217–425.

thinking and expression were necessarily stifled.[11] Where discussion was circumscribed, the evidence of the previous chapters would suggest, it accommodated itself to the limits imposed upon it by finding subtler forms of expression, by suggesting through nuances of opinion what could not be stated baldly. Behind the appearance of sycophancy such plays, in the spirit of the true *encomium* or the *speculum principis*, adopted a more robust attitude.

The simplicity and directness of some of the public utterances of those in authority under Henry VIII (one thinks perhaps of Suffolk's forceful clapping of his hand on the board at the closure of the Blackfriars' Court and his declaration that 'it was never merry in England whilst we had Cardinals among us' or Wolsey's rather arch display of gratitude for the tokens sent to him by the King after his initial disgrace[12]) might mislead us into thinking of the Henrician Court as a place of little sophistication or subtlety. But we should be wary of using the behaviour of courtiers and ministers on formal and public occasions as evidence of how they might

---

[11] Even this statement requires qualification, however, for the reign affords a number of examples of individuals speaking directly to Henry with startling boldness and frankness on issues of high political importance apparently without suffering dire consequences. We might consider, for example, the occasion on which Elizabeth Barton, the Nun of Kent, upbraided Henry in his garden at Hanworth during the Christmas period 1529–30, accusing him of wishing to divorce Queen Katherine only in order that he might satisfy his 'voluptuousness and carnal appetite' by marrying another, and threatening dire consequences for him if he should do so. The Nun, it appears was simply sent home with a 'quiet' answer (A. Neame, *The Holy Maid of Kent: The Life of Elizabeth Barton, 1506–1534* (London, 1971), pp. 126–7). Note also the account of an interview between Henry and Sir George Throckmorton a member of the Reformation Parliament contained in the latter's confession, written in October 1537. According to Throckmorton he had been summoned before the King to explain his temerity in speaking out in the Commons against the Act in Restraint of Appeals. Instead of meekly accepting a royal rebuke, however, Throckmorton evidently felt sufficiently emboldened to try his hand at some marital advice, suggesting to Henry that he, Throckmorton, 'feared if ye [Henry] did marry Queen Anne, your conscience would be more troubled at length, for it is thought ye have meddled with the mother and the sister'. Faced with so direct a criticism of his personal conduct, Henry could only splutter 'never with the mother', leaving the dependable Cromwell to clear up the legal and moral niceties with the coda 'nor never with the sister neither, and therefore put that out of your mind'. P.R.O. SP 1/125, fo. 247. Throckmorton too, it seems, walked away from the encounter with nothing more than a reprimand.

[12] For Suffolk, see pp. 158–9, above. For Wolsey, see G. Cavendish, *The Life and Death of Cardinal Wolsey*, E.E.T.S., 243 (Oxford, 1959), pp. 101–4. On receiving a ring, sent by Henry as a token that the Cardinal should 'be of good chere and take no thought for he should not lake', Wolsey knelt in the mud, 'holdyng uppe his handes for joye' and throwing down his cap, having 'rent the laces' after some awkward attempts to undo them with dignity were thwarted by an intractable knot, explaining to the astonished messenger, Sir Henry Norris, that he did so because, having heard his 'comfortable & Joyfull newes I can do no lesse than to rejoyse / ffor the sodden Joy surmounted my heveng no respect nowther to the place or tyme / but thought it my very bounden dewtie to render thankes to god my maker and to the Kyng my soverayn lord and mayster / who hathe sent me suche comfort' (ibid., p. 101).

act in their more relaxed, recreational moments. What might be an appropriate form of expression for a large public gathering, or for a moment of acute political significance, when one wished to make a single, unambiguous point, might not be so appropriate for a more private, informal, occasion, when intentions were more complex. And in a number of the plays considered above we possess texts designed for performance during the Court's more private, recreational, moments, when political interaction might operate on a less overt, almost subliminal, level. Such plays attest to a level of sophistication to political persuasion not always recognized by scholars of the period.

And if these plays indicate something about the forms of political activity in the period and the language in which it was discussed, they also suggest something about its content. In particular they highlight a number of the issues and problems which seem to have preoccupied the King and his ministers throughout the reign. They bear witness most obviously to a continuing governmental anxiety at the prospect of foreign invasion, and especially of invasion accompanied by domestic support for rival claimants to the throne. In this the members of the de la Pole family inevitably loom large. This anxiety manifested itself, not only during the 1530s, when Henry's religious policies provoked such internal disaffection as might predictably give rise to fears of disorder, but from the very start of the reign. *Hick Scorner*, written in 1514 and Bale's *King Johan* and the other propagandist literature written in the period 1538–9 (we might also note John Skelton's poem, *Howe the Douty Duke of Albany*, written in 1523), suggest an underlying sense of insecurity which lasted throughout the period and might surface at any moment of diplomatic uncertainty.[13] Far from enjoying with confidence the secure throne which he is said to have inherited from his father, Henry VIII seems never to have been entirely convinced of the stability of his own regime.

Less specifically, a study of these plays and of the political concerns which they articulate draws attention to the ways in which individuals perceived the responsibilities of government. In particular they suggest a good deal about Henry's own conception of the role of Sovereign, and the element of self-absorbtion, even of self-obsession, which coloured his execution of that role. That drama was used as a political instrument in so conscious a fashion at this time is thus singularly appropriate. For if, as the previous chapters have suggested, the reign of Henry VIII saw early drama at its most political, it also saw royal politics at their most theatrical.

[13] For the plays and protestant literature, see pp. 43–5; 195–201, above. For Skelton's poem, see Walker, *Skelton*, Chapter 6. This evidence, suggestive of a continuous anxiety, qualifies the implication (in S. J. Gunn, 'The French Wars of Henry VIII', in J. Black, ed., *The Origins of War in Early Modern Europe* (London, 1987), pp. 28–51, p. 30) that pretenders to the English Crown were thought of as a threat only during time of war.

Henry's conception of his office was, it seems, intimately bound up with the idea of performance, with what Stephen Greenblatt has termed self-fashioning.[14] At signal moments in his life – most notably at the expulsion of the minions and the fall of Wolsey, but also at his accession to the throne and the collapse of the Amicable Grant, during the various royal divorces and remarriages and after the fall of Cromwell – Henry seems deliberately to have refashioned his own public persona for political effect. Echoing both literary models and conventional wisdom he represented himself publicly in a new and virtuous guise as a means of evading the unwelcome implications of previous miscalculations or reverses. When problems arose, Henry literally acted his way out of a crisis, devising the script, not only for himself, but also for those courtiers and ministers whom he drew after him. Hence, in response to the revelation of the minions' 'excesses', one finds Henry appearing as the responsible statesman, flamboyantly cleansing the Augean stables of his own creation, turning a potentially humiliating situation into an opportunity for self-advertisement and as-sertiveness. Similarly, at the fall of Wolsey, one sees the King, not shame-faced at the extent to which he had allegedly been duped by the Cardinal, but proudly proclaiming his previous naivety to Parliament and foreign ambassadors alike, as it enabled him to pose as the newly recovered sinner, the Sovereign who had, like the heroes of morality drama, learned from his errors and emerged a wiser, better, man.[15] It was not simply that he was adept at letting others take the blame for decisions for which he was ultimately responsible. He seems to have been quite prepared and indeed eager to parade his own past weaknesses, but only in so far as that allowed him simultaneously to parade his present strengths.

Hence time and again one finds Henry employing the same strategy, playing the same role, as the King whose eyes have suddenly been opened to the crimes of those ministers and companions in whom he had placed his trust. Whether that 'crime' was Wolsey's secret instigation of the Amicable Grant, Anne Boleyn's multiple adultery or the treacherous double-loyalty of his clergy, Henry was able to adopt the role of the outraged innocent and so steal the moral high ground. At the very moment that his own supposed ignorance and lack of foresight were being revealed, he was able to turn things to his own advantage, presenting himself as the too trusting, too generous, master, 'bluff King Hal', whose own simple virtue had almost prevented him from realizing the sins of those around him. Thus the King was able through the sometimes subtle, but more often

---

[14] S. Greenblatt, *Renaissance Self-Fashioning from More to Shakespeare* (Chicago, 1980). Cynics might detect a close correlation between the elegant practice of 'self-fashioning' and plain, old-fashioned, 'lying' in the current context.

[15] See pp. 69–74; 163–6, above.

simply audacious, donning and shedding of roles, to stay one step ahead of any political crisis. Through the resolute maintenance of a 'that was then but this is now' mentality, he contrived to avoid all blame for his own actions, yet still remain unshakeably in control of events.

How far this strategy was a calculated response to the exigencies of political leadership and how far an almost sub-conscious mechanism for rationalizing failure, born of the need to reconcile evident miscalculation with the notion that the King should do no wrong, can never be known. No doubt it was in part at least the product of a genuine attempt to live up to the high ideal of Kingship which Henry cherished. But the political usefulness of this method of operating is beyond question. In a system in which the Sovereign was notionally in absolute control, but in practice had to balance the political forces in both the centre and the localities in order to maintain his authority, this capacity to admit mistakes and alter the direction of policies without having to concede responsibility for them was invaluable. It enabled him to adapt the notion of 'evil counsellors', through which critics of royal policies had traditionally voiced their dis-agreement, to his own ends, whether as a means of tacitly acknowledging the strength of criticism on an issue (as with the Amicable Grant or the minions) without losing the political initiative, or of dressing his own desires in the language of the general good (as with the fall of Wolsey or the royal divorces). And it is a measure of Henry VIII's strength of character and of the extent to which he dominated the political history of the reign that those shifts of persona and policy were readily taken up by those around him and were almost immediately reflected in the rhetoric and behaviour of the Court.

Those historians who have identified Henry's mercurial temperament and his apparent inability to follow through his resolutions for any pro-longed period as evidence of his manipulability are thus surely mistaken. For it was his very inconsistency and unpredictability which made him so difficult to manage and manipulate. A King who might at any moment decide that he would not be held responsible for his previous actions was extremely difficult to commit to any given policy, however far that policy had already been pursued. At any moment everything might be aban-doned, leaving the minister(s) involved to take whatever blame Henry wished to alot. In such circumstances, offering unsolicited advice on an issue before Henry had declared his own preferences in the matter might be perilous indeed, particularly if that advice was offered in an open and un-ambiguous manner. In such circumstances it would be better to wait and see the direction of royal thinking, so that one might at least couch one's views, however inimical to royal wishes, in a language that might gain them a hearing. It might be safer still to offer Henry, not direct advice, but rather the materials from which such advice might be extracted, were the King of a mind to do so. Such advice had what would be termed in the parlance of the later Reagan years 'deniability'. And in this notion might lie another reason for the attractiveness of the dramatic form as an instrument of political advice and persuasion in this period. A dramatic performance gave ideas a powerful emotive force, yet expressed them in a subtle, allusive and eminently deniable form. In a world in which the Sovereign was the main-spring of policy-making, yet also a master of political damage limitation, both these virtues of the dramatic form would have appealed to any aspiring counsellor who was less than certain of his own position.

That plays were thought of as effective vehicles for political advice and persuasion at this time is, then, suggestive in a number of specific ways. But it also carries wider implications for our view of Tudor Court culture. Drama is an effective vehicle for the transmission of political ideas in an environment in which values, or at least a discourse about values, are shared. Drama, even of the most strident kind, is a subtle medium when compared with other forms of political exchange. It relies for its effects upon the manipulation of fictional personae and the relationships created between them; upon various shades of irony and displacement of intention; upon saying one thing and meaning another. Thus, although it provides a potent means of presenting political ideas and of investing them with a moral or emotional resonance, it does so only when its author(s), performers and audience share at least a core of values and assumptions. They must share a commitment to a pervading rhetoric, and beyond it to a conceptual frame, which the dramatist can then fine-tune in pursuit of his effects.

Once the political consensus breaks down, however, and even fundamental assumptions are open to reappraisal and argument, then the subtleties of the dramatic form become liabilities in the eyes of those with political messages to disseminate. Then moralists and polemicists alike turn to other less equivocal forms of writing; the prose tract, treatise, sermon, supplication of proclamation. Significantly it was the period immediately prior to the Reformation in which drama in England seems to have become a significant medium for political persuasion at Court, in the same way that it was to be again before the Civil War.[16] These were years in which the Court consensus, the discourse of a common culture and polity, was open to serious scrutiny, but had not yet fragmented in the face of new, more radical, ideas. Thus vital issues were debated, but could be handled with a subtlety and sophistication for which the dramatic form

[16] For the latter, see Sharpe, *Criticism and Compliment*, pp. 1–108, 179–264 and Butler, *Theatre and Crisis*, *passim*.

was eminently suitable. Conversely, once the radical Reformation had begun to grip and (as in the Civil War period) fundamental assumptions about the status of the Church, the relationship of monarch to subject, and the nature of society itself became the subject of heated debate, writers with a need to transmit ideas quickly and effectively largely turned to other forms.[17] The Reformation, like the Civil War and its aftermath, was the great age of the prose tract and the pamphlet, the bold statement of intent. This perhaps explains John Bale's decision, taken after his problematic experiments with a protestant drama-cycle in the 1530s, to turn to polemical prose as the most effective vehicle for his radical views in the 1540s and 1550s.

For those writing in the midst of the Reformation controversy, drama seems to have proved ineffective for their purposes. But writers of the pre-Reformation era were less sceptical, in part at least because they were surer of their audiences. It took a considerable amount of confidence in the capacity of his hearers to understand his intentions for the anonymous author of *Hester* to state his case in dramatic form. When he wished to argue for greater independence for the religious orders, he did so, not by presenting a petition to the King or to Parliament on their behalf, but by producing a dramatized version of the biblical story of Esther, without any authorial comment or prologue to alert the audience to the specific contemporary relevance of the play. He did so with such confidence because he knew that both he and his audience shared certain assumptions about the political functions of biblical parable and the role of religious drama as a vehicle for social commentary. More particularly he was able to manipulate their shared faith in conventional attitudes towards the role of the King in a personal monarchy, the functions of well-regulated religious houses and the universal evils of upstart ministers. Thus he could both appeal to and subtly influence their conventional expectations to evoke sympathy for the case he was advancing without having openly to declare his intentions. In the heat of the doctrinal battles of the Reformation such delicate manipulation was to give way to the sort of simple, unambiguous slogans which litter the prose pamphlets and which are already evident in Bale's later plays; monasticism is morally and spiritually corrupt, image-worship is idolatry, the pope is Antichrist.

[17] For the problems associated with protestant polemical drama in the mid-Tudor period, see R. Pineas, 'Polemical use of the Scriptures in the Plays of John Bale', *Nederlands Archief voor Kerkgeschiedenis*, 66 (1986), pp. 180–9 and 'The English Morality Play as a Weapon of Religious Controversy', *Studies in English Literature*, 2 (1962), pp. 157–80; John N. King, *English Reformation Literature: The Tudor Origins of the Protestant Tradition* (Princeton, 1982), pp. 271–318. The last named offers a more positive view of the vitality and polemical potential of the dramatic form in the mid-Tudor period, but see pp. 278–9 for an acknowledgement of the basic premise advanced above.

In part, of course, this shift marks a change, not only in subject matter, but also in prospective audience. Where the Court playwright broadly speaking knew his audience, the later Reformation polemicist, aiming at a wider 'public' readership, did not. Hence the arguments of the latter had to be pared down to their simplest form, to the lowest common denominators. Between the two forms there had been a clear shift in intention, based upon a different perception of what constitutes the authority to which the writer is appealing and where it is to be found. For the pamphleteer the widest dissemination of his ideas was desired, so that his conception of the truth might reach as many potential converts as possible. For the Court playwright, intent upon political persuasion, the focus was far narrower. For him the important part of his audience might be numbered in single figures and was ultimately an individual, whether a noble patron or the ultimate patron, the King. For playwrights like Skelton and Heywood, the aim was primarily to persuade those who held power at the centre to use that power in certain ways, not to reach a wide audience or readership. The latter aim was only a by-product of the former. And this brought specific priorities and opportunities. In such circumstances, as we have seen, the dramatic form possessed clear advantages over any more explicit form of advice literature. For such men at least, there would have been wisdom in Hamlet's assertion that

> the play's the thing
> Wherein [to] ... catch the conscience of the King.
> (III, ii, lines 600–1)[18]

---

[18] P. Alexander, ed., *William Shakespeare: The Complete Works (the Alexander Text)* (London, 1951), p. 1046. Thomas Scott, writing somewhat later, was to make the same point rather more baldly, 'sometimes Kings are content in playes and maskes to be admonished of divers things' (Thomas Scott, *Vox Regis* (London, 1622), pp. 34–5).

INDEX